CONTINUITIES

By Frank Kermode

Romantic Image
The Living Milton (Ed.)
Wallace Stevens
Puzzles and Epiphanies
The Sense of an Ending
Continuities

CONTINUITIES

by Frank Kermode

RANDOM HOUSE / NEW YORK

FIRST PRINTING

Library of Congress Catalog Card Number: 68-28539

Manufactured in the United States of America by The Haddon Craftsmen, Inc., Scranton, Pennsylvania

CONTENTS

The Modern

I. MODERNISMS:

Types and Times

Poets

Critics

Novelists

Epilogue

PREFACE

This selection of pieces written between 1962 and 1967 is in one sense a sequel to *Puzzles and Epiphanies*, which collected work from the three years before that. But although it occasionally takes up the same subjects it does seem to me a very different kind of collection. Whereas the earlier book was said to have a family resemblance to *Romantic Image*, a more speculative work of 1957, this one will undoubtedly be seen to take after another more solemn cousin, *The Sense of an Ending* (1967). It is called *Continuities* because it often returns to the cultural problem of schism and continuity, words which I picked up from V. W. Turner's *Schism and Continuity in an African Society*. I lacked the nerve or folly to call the book *Schisms and Continuities*, and anyway am more in favour of continuities than of schisms.

Choosing what to include in a volume of this sort is not easy, and friends are usually astonished at what is put in and left out. For example, I wanted to include two pieces on Marshall McLuhan and also a long television conversation I did with him in January 1965 which was never broadcast because the B.B.C. thought it would be unintelligible. Now every schoolboy could understand it, which is why I decided not to have it in. And so with the other pieces, although I am not convinced that their objections to McLuhanism are quite obsolete. Sometimes one leaves in a rather old-fashioned piece out of affection, as here with the Dowson essay, and leaves out perhaps better things. The Dante essays ends the volume because it represents, for me, only, a sort of end, a sort of beginning.

Incidentally, this does not mean that I regard the kind of criticism here reprinted as anything but serious, though the level of seriousness varies a bit; and when I find it subjected to routine academic censure I find myself wondering whether the complainant is not one of those who might himself benefit from its peculiar discipline, and occasionally pass on the benefit to his pupils in graduate school, where it is not always easy to distinguish the solemn from the barbaric. Good literary journalism is valuable and rare. It would be too much to assert that it has only 'genius, wit and taste to recommend' it, but to dismiss it as irremediably ephemeral, and at the same time to promote the preservation of the average doctoral dissertation, is to fall into what could very well be named 'the common cant.'

Here I refer, of course, to this *kind* of work, not to the present book, which is for the reader to judge; I am only saying that the *genre* is more than respectable. The essay on Edmund Wilson tries to use the example of a great critic to state this more explicitly. Wilson can deal justly with other writers without neglecting the meditative movement of his own mind, and he can satisfy, without loss of intellectual integrity, the nonspecialist's urgent and entirely proper demand for amenity of exposition and fine texture. This is the kind of journalism I call valuable and rare. It is rare not because those who could easily do it have better things to do, but because it is more demanding than most of what passes for scholarship. It calls incessantly for mental activity, fresh information, and civility into the bargain. Of course I agree that they do not always come.

The pieces here collected appeared first in the *New Statesman* (I.iii, II, III, VI, VII, X, XVII, XVIII, XIX, XXI, i and ii, XXII, i, XXIII, XXIV, XXV); the *New York Review of Books* (IV, XII, XIV, XVII, ii, XX); *Encounter* (I.i, I.ii, part of IX, XI, i); *Sewanee Review* (VIII, X), *Book Week* (XI, ii) and *Atlantic Monthly* (XXII, ii). To the editors of these periodicals I offer my gratitude for their help, and for their permission to reprint. Parts of the long essay on Lawrence, and parts of the 'Afterthoughts on Wallace Stevens' were included in a series of Alexander Lectures at the University of Toronto in 1967, and, attenuated as they are, must represent my gratitude to Clifford Leech and my other Toronto hosts.

CONTINUITIES

Chapter One

THE MODERN

I. MODERNISMS

(i) *Discrimination of Modernisms*

Recently an advertisement for an 'ardent novel available only by mail' described the work as 'the story of a *modern* American marriage.' A favourable review was then cited, explaining that 'the painfully significant enigma' of modern marriage is the ambition and aggressiveness of woman. The husband in Meredith's sequence, lying there in tragic parody of a knight on a tomb, thought it was her infidelity. To both novelist and poet, 'modern' seems to mean something not altogether agreeable and disturbingly at odds with the way things used to be. If pressed, they might talk about radical changes in sensibility, as they affect love. Pressed harder, they might have to admit that ambition, aggression, infidelity, are no newer in women than refined or perverse sensibility in men.

The fact is that we all use the word in this unexamined way, and nobody notices how nearly meaningless it is until called to order by some pronouncement about The Modern. The context will usually be aesthetic, but even this limitation is not enough to ensure accurate definition. In 1894 John Lane announced that his *Yellow Book* 'would seek always to preserve a delicate, decorous and reticent mien and conduct' but 'at the same time have the courage of its modernness'; that it would be 'charming,' 'daring' and 'distinguished.' The first number included a poem by Gosse, Saintsbury on wine, and a very good story by James, but only Beerbohm's 'Defence of Cosmetics' could be called 'daring' or, in its fashion, courageously modern. Later this might be said of the realism of Crackanthorpe; for modernism was not only the dangerous line of Beardsley, the clever excess of Wilde and Beerbohm; it was also the French cult of things as they now are. These two modernist strains were well distinguished by Arthur Waugh, in his attack on the magazine; he found on the one hand 'a want of restraint which starts from enervated sensations,' and on the other an 'excess which results from a certain brutal virility,' itself the consequence of 'coarse familiarity with indulgence.' Or you might say, exquisite sensibility and realism. The new sensibility required formal experiment, which was therefore associated with 'decadence'; squatness and ugliness of presentation, a prudent lack of enterprise in content, could now confer upon publishers who declined the financial and social risks of modernity a certain adventitious virtue. 'Modernness,' in its Flaubertian alliance of formal experiment and realism, took over the old role of shock and protest, and its practitioners dissociated themselves from many concerns that seemed characteristically bourgeois, such as politics.

Politics returned in a later phase of modernism, and has now gone away again; on the whole one would want to say that politics has no essential part in the Movement. If there is a persistent world-view it is one we should have to call apocalyptic; the modernism of the 'Nineties has a recognisable touch of this, if decadence, hope of renovation, the sense of transition, the sense of an ending or the trembling of the veil, are accepted as its signs. At such times there is a notable urgency in the proclamation of a break with the immediate past, a stimulating sense of crisis, of an historical licence for the New. And there appears to be a genuine continuity here, for all modernist art and literature between the 'Nineties and now is associated with similar assumptions in some form or other. Naturally the contents of *The Yellow Book* have long ceased to look modernist; its cosmetic avant-gardism is archaic, as neurasthenia is archaic; its artists were not only Beardsley and Conder but Puvis de Chavannes and Moreau. The radical changes that were *implied*, somehow, by what they were doing—revolutions in architecture, music, painting and poetry—were of a kind that shocked such a survivor as Beerbohm and forced Yeats to accept the necessity to 'remake' himself. The difference between *The Yellow Book* and, say, *Blast*, indicates that however persistent the apocalyptic background may have been, some pretty radical changes of manner had occurred. The 'Nineties were certainly precursors, but anybody who thinks about what modernism now means will rightly look more closely at the period between 1907 and, say, 1925; this is true despite the fact that the 'aestheticist' element in later modernism is often underplayed, and still accounts for that disregard of politics in relation to literature characteristic of so much modern criticism, so that Conor Cruise O'Brien justly but hopelessly complains that even intelligent critics are 'acute on small matters and absent-minded on very large ones.'[1]

There is at present much interest in this question of the modern. Last year Professors Ellmann and Feidelson published a huge 'casebook' on the subject;[2] it was a work of which Professor O'Brien might well complain in the same terms, but it was also a serious attempt to get into one volume most of the radical documents of modernism, and to explain the parts of Kant and Blake, Nietzsche and Darwin, Wilde and Pater, as well as Apollinaire and Tzara, Werner Heisenberg and Karl Jaspers. Now Mr Cyril Connolly, by way of choosing and describing its '100 Key Books,' has undertaken to characterise what he calls *The Modern Movement*.[3] He limits himself to the years between 1880 and 1950, and to works in English and French. The American book is vast, solemn, and not easy to get on with; Mr Connolly's is light, bright, superficially stylish; but the Americans offer much useful and reliable information, and Mr Connolly's book does not. It is careless as to detail; the date of Spender's *Struggle of the Modern* is wrong, the *Skeleton Key to Finnegans Wake* is put thirteen years too late, the publication dates of *Four Quartets* are not accurate; you will search the *Inferno* in vain for a passage on Arnaut Daniel. Mr Connolly likes Yeats and quotes him, apparently, from memory; but what he actually wrote about the first night of *Ubu Roi* was 'After us the Savage God.' Perhaps one can take the misprint *Little Gitting* as an unconscious tribute to a contemporary poet and biographer of Keats; but whoever suggests that the opening line of *The Winding Stair* is 'The *calm* of evening, Lissadell' may be called upon to prove that he can be trusted with a great poem.

[1] *Writers and Politics* (London, Chatto; New York, Pantheon).
[2] See below.
[3] *The Modern Movement, 100 Key Books from England, France and America, 1880–1950*. (London, Deutsch & Hamish Hamilton; New York, Atheneum).

It seems a pity that Mr Connolly, so well equipped by temperament and experience, should have settled for *sprezzatura* and forsworn accuracy and sometimes thought itself. He sneers at professional students not for their real faults but because they get things right, and at 'theses' because they begin when 'the Titans depart'; yet after all he is a professional student, and this is a thesis, written, on the author's view, when the Titans have departed, arguing a view of a literary period, and complete with a bibliography (admittedly by another professional hand, and not in any case very useful). Whether we call it a thesis or not, it too often lapses into its own kind of nonsense and bad writing: 'As all objectives were gained and the complacent hypocrisy of the nineteenth century punctured, its materialism exposed, the Movement ground to a halt.' It is hard to say whether a good supervisor would be more depressed by the historical generalisation or by the prose.

However, Mr Connolly is not wholly serious. That books are written in German or Russian will not prevent some of them from being 'Key Books,' and he also omits all books he does not like (Claudel, Stein); all books that are not both good and rebellious, as well as historically important; and all books that are simply think-books (Bergson, Freud, Russell, Wittgenstein, etc.). With what is left he is pleasantly dogmatic. The Modernists inherited 'critical intelligence' from the Enlightenment, and 'exploring sensibility' from the Romantics. As near as it can be dated, the union of these qualities occurred around 1880; the Journals of Baudelaire and the *Bouvard et Pécuchet* of Flaubert ('our two fallen fathers') appeared posthumously in the following year. Mr Connolly's comment on Baudelaire can only reinforce the strong sense we may already have of slapdash unexamined history; he claims that this poet, 'after being for many years the private literary property of Arthur Symons . . . has emerged to be re-interpreted by Sartre and magnificently translated by Robert Lowell.' After 1880 modernism came on in waves: the generation of James, Mallarmé, Villiers de l'Isle Adam, Huysmans, is followed by that of Debussy, Yeats, Proust, Jarry, Valéry, and that by the generation of Eliot, Pound, Lawrence and Joyce; and so on. Admittedly such lists don't lend themselves to fine distinctions and discriminations, but this one makes the subject sound unintelligibly weird.

It is true that there was a sort of *translatio studii moderni* from France to England and America, and that the peak period of the Movement must be placed somewhere around 1910–1925, as Connolly says. But it is begging many questions to argue that after the death of Virginia Woolf and Yeats the Movement became 'degenerate.' He avoids some difficulties by saying that Beckett, together with Robbe-Grillet and Butor, 'falls just outside my dateline' (*whoroscope*, 1930, *Proust*, 1931, *More Pricks than Kicks*, 1934, above all *Murphy*, 1938). The 'frustrated 'forties' saw the end of the Movement. Burroughs and the Beats represent a continuing rebelliousness here attributed merely to the prevalence in America of 'unrevised attitudes to drug-addiction and homosexuality.' The best Mr Connolly can say about the future is that the Movement's 'twin features,' described arbitrarily as 'faith in the intellect' and 'belief in the validity of the imagination,' together with 'the enlargement of sensibility,' will again 'inspire a masterpiece.'

It all sounds much too simple, and it is—labels are doing the work, announced as a labour of historical enquiry; words such as 'imagination' and 'sensibility' are being left to get on with it while the author chats brightly. Why did the Movement peter out? Because there were so many defectors from Humanism: 'some followed Huysmans into the religious fold (Eliot, Edith Sitwell, Waugh, Auden), some became fascists (Pound, Lewis) etc.' Subsequently modernism flourishes best in the theatre, where there is more to rebel against (Artaud, Ionesco, Pinter). If anybody would have been more surprised than Wyndham Lewis to be called a humanist or a defector from humanism, it might perhaps have been Artaud. Malraux defected from humanism by becoming a politician. What can 'humanism' mean in this discussion where 'dehumanisation' is more commonly regarded as a symptom of the modern? Well, Gide and Forster perhaps; but when one speaks of their humanism one is simply in a different context from that appropriate to a discussion of modernism. By his abuse of this word, and in an entirely different way, of 'sensibility,' Mr Connolly simply obscures this interesting issue; his book will add confusion where there is enough already.

I have so far said nothing of the books chosen. They are listed in chronological order, each with a chatty paragraph; *Bel Ami*, for example:

Born in 1850, Maupassant died insane from syphilis in 1893. 'Another man for the scrap-heap,' he cried to his valet. . . . Patron saint of best sellers, he has profoundly influenced Maugham. . . .

Number 1 is *Portrait of a Lady*, Number 100 is *Paterson*. Among the books mentioned which seem to be there not for their 'modernness' but because the compiler likes them are *Siren Land* (hard by Apollinaire and Proust), *The Casuarina Tree*, *Sanctuary* ('Critics enthuse on *The Sound and the Fury*. . . . *Sanctuary*, however . . . is Faulkner for the non-Faulknerites'), *Animal Farm*, and the *Selected Poems* of John Betjeman. *Lady Chatterley's Lover* and *Sea and Sardinia* get in, but not *Women in Love*. On the whole, however, the list, within its limits, is not unreasonable; only the comments are deplorable. The 'Twenties, Mr Connolly's favourite decade, are celebrated by comment on *Ulysses* equally jejune in praise and condemnation, on Radiguet mere gossip, without the slightest justification for the choice, and on Wallace Stevens hasty and meaningless patter. *The Great Gatsby* is a 'light-hearted masterpiece of the boom years,' but its contemporary, *The Sun Also Rises*, unites 'post-war disillusion and the post-war liberation . . . in the physical enjoyment of living and the pains of love. Perhaps that is what expatriation was about.' It is hard even to see what this means.

The 'Thirties—the 'disastrous decade'—were devoted to 'lost causes like anti-fascism'; nevertheless, this was 'a good period to be young in' since the world was 'still open for the traveller (Bali, Afghanistan, etc.).' The 'Forties account for twelve books, including *Darkness at Noon*, *Another Time* (though *Poems*, 1930, did not make it), the two Orwells, Betjeman. *Paterson*, however, makes a good modernist noise at the close, and Williams' 'Nothing is good save the new' neatly echoes Baudelaire at the outset: '*Au fond de l'Inconnu pour trouver du nouveau.*'

It should now be clear that if you want to know what Baudelaire and Williams are talking about this poor little book, so unworthy of its author, will not help you to find out. What will? Since there is so much talk about these and related matters at the moment, it might be useful to look about for recent writing that has something to say. With this in mind, and perhaps somewhat naïvely, I turn to a very large new *Encyclopedia of Poetry and Poetics*[1] and look up 'modernism.' This volume is the work of very learned contributors and editors. If you want to look up *meiosis* or *meiurus, payada* or *penthemimer*; if you need a quick run through Albanian, Byelorussian, Danish, Persian, Romansh or Yiddish poetry; if you are disturbed by the problems of belief, meaning, intention, or by the relationship of poetry with science or religion; if more modern critical terms baffle you, and you are interested in *tenor and vehicle, symbol, pseudo-statement, tension, ambiguity, aesthetic distance*; or in the vexed problems associated with *baroque, mannerist, conceit,* then on all this and more you will as a rule be amply supplied. But if you look up 'modernism' you will be told that it was 'the movement in Hispanic letters which began in the 1880s in Sp. America, blending Sp., Fr., and other foreign influences. . . .' Hard by, however, there is a long entry on *Modern Poetics*; it begins at 1750, which is justifiable, and begins to cater for our present interest when it reaches, after much scholarly explanation, our fallen father Baudelaire and his accursed sons the Symbolists. They were in favour of music and against logic (of course; and for all Mr Connolly says anti-intellectualism is a characteristic of the modern)—and they gave rise to a newly orientated poetry, arcane even when colloquial, interested in mental states below consciousness ('extended sensibility') and prolific of very difficult notions, such as Rilke's *Dinge* and Imagism and the vorticised or classicised Symbolism of Hulme, Pound, and Eliot. Hence 'the theoretical banishment from poetry (we might add the visual arts) of much that has been generally thought to give it seriousness'; and hence also a number of baffling ambiguities in the terminology, still troublesome; for it is hard to say what, for example, 'imagist' means, and even harder to be clear about 'abstraction' (good in, say, Worringer and Stevens, bad, generally, in the literary critics)[2] or even 'intellect,' an anti-poetic instrument which poets are always blamed for not using.

There is some use in the *Encyclopedia* article; it ends with a very cautious statement of one of the major issues in later

[1] Edited by Alex Preminger. *Princeton University Press*, New Jersey; *Oxford University Press*, London.
[2] The *Encyclopedia*, I have just confirmed, provides a good brief account, under *Concrete and Abstract*, of the way they use such words.

modernism, warning us that if we think poetry 'the completest mode of utterance' we should not be too anxious to separate it from other forms of discourse. Can 'art' and 'life' really be as discontinuous as the early modernists implied? More of that later, when it will emerge, I think, that poetry is not the best point of departure here. The theory behind very modern poems (like, for example, the enchanting 'Message Clear' of Edwin Morgan, in the *T.L.S.*, 13 January 1966) seems to derive from the thinking of artists and musicians, and finally we shall have to turn to them. The poetry encyclopaedia has, not surprisingly, no entry under *avant-garde* or New, though there are the Neoterici of Cicero to prove how old the New really is, as well as the New Criticism, now worn out, and the New Humanism, another historical description. It does not help us much with the modern Modern, the new New.

Professors Ellmann and Feidelson find the concept of the modern 'intimate and elusive' but are quite sure it does not refer, as some now argue, only to what was happening almost half a century back; according to them, it 'designates a distinctive kind of imagination, themes and forms, conditions and modes of creation, that are interrelated, and comprise an imaginative whole.' This suggests a sort of imaginative mutation, ways of looking and making virtually unrelated to older ones; and that is another frequent claim one should look into. But it also suggests, and rightly, that we will agree to call a great many different things modern—not only the novel I mentioned at the start, or *Who's Afraid of Virginia Woolf?* ('strange love talk, is it not?' as Meredith remarked) but all manner of superficially incompatible things: *Howl* and *The Waste Land*. Cubism and Pop Art, Stravinsky and Stockhausen, Gaudier-Brzeska and Tinguely. Other things we shall most of us agree not to call modern: Meredith, for instance, Verlaine; and some we're not sure about: Freud, for example. We might even agree, at any rate so far as the arts are concerned, to a useful rough distinction between two phases of modernism, and call them palaeo- and neo-modernism; they are equally devoted to the theme of crisis, equally apocalyptic; but although they have this and other things in common, they have differences which might, with some research, be defined, and found not to be of a degree that prevents our calling both 'modernist.'

Before these or any other phenomena are called 'modern' there must, presumably, be a general sense of escaping from an older state of affairs, an *ancient* state of affairs. *Devotio moderna* was not only a movement for a new morality and a new piety, but a movement against pilgrimages and excessive ornament. The Moderns of the 17th century had a programme with a similar double aspect. Their enemies would call it a preference for grubs and darkness over sweetness and light, but in its positive aspect it was a programme calling for new knowledge and assuming such knowledge could be made relevant to human concerns; while in its negative aspect it contested the view that the culture of their time necessarily imitated and must always be a derivative of ancient culture. This was perhaps the decisive confrontation, involving as it did the overthrow of ideologies both ecclesiastical and secular: the revision of the theologian's *curiositas*, which limited the bounds of intellectual enquiry in one way, and of the secular ideologies, imperial or sentimental-republican, which insisted upon classical norms and tended to equate change with decay. This was the Modernism that created a climate in which hypothesis and fiction replace myth, in which the nature of ideologies is to undergo rapid alteration and fragmentation, as ours do. Imperialism, republicanism, and classicism survive, of course, but much fragmented and modified, and usually in a posture of resistance. In short, the great 17th-century Modernism involved getting out from under something, and modernist programmes have the habit of claiming that this is what they always have to undertake.

What we got out from under is one of those questions that set up, it seems, an infinite recession. Certainly it wasn't Victorian complacency, as Mr Connolly is satisfied to say; and the reason why the American scholars find themselves reprinting Goethe and Kant is quite simply that the historical study of modernism will certainly take you back there, and beyond, to the 17th century obviously, and less obviously beyond that. This was long ago recognised, but stated in a distorted way, by those who sought parallels between the two periods as each exhibiting the catastrophes that come from too much brain and too 'abstract' sensibility. It is now much more fashionable to regard our plight as without parallel, and the past as irrelevant—an equally misleading error, and one which is responsible for further ideological muddle, as well as for certain false oppositions between palaeo- and neo-modernisms.

Nothing can so muddle argument as the claim that there exist no standards by which an argument can be judged, or even no language in which it can be opposed; this claim is now supported by several influential epoch-makers, notably Marshall McLuhan, an admirable and fertile enquirer who has brought science fiction to history and sociology. There are other theorists who overdevelop the metaphor of a cultural *mutation* and say that this renders the old 'humanism' powerless to judge or communicate, since the mutants speak an anti-language and aim at anti-art, anti-ethics, anti-sex; and instead of merely revising the concept of form—as the Romantics and the palaeo-modernists did— have abolished it. Indeed, if we want to understand the similarities and differences between the modernisms we shall have to look at this question of form more closely.

(ii) *Objects, Jokes and Art*

Do we have a 'rage for order'? It has long been thought so, and the arts have long been thought ways of appeasing it. But there is a difference between 'order' and 'an order'; and what looked like the first can become simply the second: the conventional literary epic, or pastoral poetry, or the heroic couplet, or history-painting, or sonata form. In the older modernism, order grew mysterious. Following the organicist view of the Romantics, and the sophisticated gloss put on it by the Symbolists, poets treated it as the property of works purged of personality and emotion, new shapes out there and independent, perceptible by an *élite* which had transcended bourgeois literacy and could operate a logic of imagination divinely void of intellect. Thus the highly original forms of Mallarmé and, later, Eliot, have only a tenuous relation to more vulgar notions of form; and in the novel, for instance, the kind of extreme deviation from prevailing norms which had formerly occurred only now and again became a regular feature. The great experimental novels of early modernism—Kafka, Proust, Joyce, Musil, for instance—are all characterised by a kind of formal desperation.

Yet such forms continue to assume that there was an inescapable relationship between art and order. Admittedly when the forms of the past grew 'rigid and a bit absurd' you undertook a new research and produced modern forms. They might indeed be extremely researched, as Wallace Stevens suggests when he says we can't have the old 'romantic tenements' and that what will now suffice may be much less palpable: merely, perhaps

> a woman dancing, a woman
> Combing. The poem of the act of the mind—

but the act of the mind is still a form-creating act, and the form it creates provides satisfactions of the rage for order that cannot be had in life not so organised, so that art is different from life at least in this respect. And this view of the matter is still in many ways standard. Its various implications—'autonomy,' anti-didacticism, everything that attracts, both for the arts and the criticism that attends them, the epithet 'formalist'—are, whether we like it or not, still in the minds of most of us when we consider a work of art. The first thing we think about is that this is a poem or a painting, and if it were not we should find another way of speaking than the one we choose. '*Art is not life and cannot be/A midwife to society*,' as Mr Auden pedagogically explained. It may be somewhat illiberal, even untruthful, and reactionary by its very nature, as Mr Trilling thinks; he is supported in his opinion by the theorist of the formal *nouveau roman*,[1] and also, as we will see, by the Apollinaire of the New York renaissance, Harold Rosenberg.

The fact that we have inherited the set of aesthetic assumptions I have very roughly sketched above makes it all the more

---

[1] Robbe-Grillet's collection of essays, *Pour un nouveau roman*, published in 1963, has now been translated, together with the short pieces called *Instantanes* of the same year, by Barbara Wright (*Snapshots & Towards a New Novel*, Calder).

Robbe-Grillet comes out strongly for the view that art is gratuitous, and from the revolutionary point of view 'useless, if not frankly reactionary'; the fact that it will be on the good side at the barricades must not be allowed to interfere with our freedom to pursue 'art for art's sake.' This book, obviously one of the really important contributions to the theory of the novel, deserves much more discussion than it has yet had in England or the U.S., and the translation is welcome. Incidentally, there is some justice in his claim that it is other people who have *theories* of the novel; his is an anti-theory, so to speak, and for all his 'formalism' that is modern enough.

I should also mention here Anthony Cronin's *A Question of Modernity* (Secker & Warburg) which is somewhat commonplace in the title essay, and often simply bad-tempered, but as to the matter of art and life there are some fine things, including a brilliant long essay on *Ulysses* and one about the novel which is full of original ideas.

difficult for most of us to understand the new men, who claim to
be destroying the barrier between life and art, asserting their
indifference to the question 'Is this a picture?' and professing
contempt for ideas of order, especially when they can be associated with the art of the past. Nevertheless we shall certainly
understand the older modernism better if we come to terms with
the newer.

There seems to be much agreement that the new rejection of
order and the past is not quite the same thing as older rejections
of one's elders and their assumptions. It is also agreed that this
neo-modernist anti-traditionalism and anti-formalism, though
anticipated by Apollinaire, begins with Dada. Whether for the
reason that its programme was literally impossible, or because
their nihilism lacked ruthlessness, it is undoubtedly true, as
Harold Rosenberg has observed, that Dada had many of the
characteristics of a new art movement, and that its devotees
treated it as such, so in some measure defeating its theoretical
anti-art programme. Raoul Haussmann only recently attacked
the 'Neo-Dadaists' because what they were doing was ignorantly
imitative, but also because it wasn't 'art.' If what we want is to
understand anti-art I suppose our best plan is to follow the signs
back to Duchamp, whose importance in this context is that he
expressly and intelligently sought ways of 'no longer thinking the
thing in question is a picture.'

The point is simply this: whereas such a poem as *The Waste
Land* draws upon a tradition which imposes the necessity of
form, though it may have none that can be apprehended without
a disciplined act of faith, a new modernism prefers and professes
to do without the tradition and the illusion. At this point there
begin to proliferate those manifold theoretical difficulties associated with neo-modernist art. They are usually discussed in
terms of the visual arts and music, probably because they are
palpably even greater in the case of literature. Duchamp could
pick something up and sign it, as he did with his 'ready-mades,'
and this raises problems, but at least it does not move from 'the
plane of the feasible.'[1] In poetry one can of course use chunks of

---

[1] The phrase is Beckett's. His 'Three Dialogues with George Duthuit' (on Tal
Coat, Masson, and Bram von Velde) have just been published, together with the
early Proust essay, by John Calder. They are excellent examples of Beckett's
philosophico-farcical manner in the discussion of the arts,

economic history and the collage of allusion, but usually for some formal irony, or to get a special effect by juxtaposition; simply to sign a passage ready-made by somebody else is not to change it but to plagiarise it. It would not matter if the borrowed passage were in most ways as commonplace as a mass-produced artefact; it would only be a more obvious case of plagiarism. A legal argument about a Duchamp ready-made might be interesting, but one would not expect a plausible defence in a case on literary ready-mades. The closest poetry can get is to cultivate impersonality and objectivity—Williams' wheel-barrow and Robbe-Grillet's out-there coffee-pot. The things made are not wheel-barrows and coffee-pots; but similar theoretical assumptions are involved.

Duchamp used to speak of 'Dada blankness'—a way of making or naming things which has no relation to humanity or nature, no 'responsibility'; 'alien objects of the outer world,' as Lawrence D. Steefel puts it, 'are reduced to instruments of the artist's transcendence of them.'[1] Blankness and indifference, like the 'impersonality' of Eliot, become, from one angle, a kind of egoism, indeed dehumanisation has always been, from this angle, the apotheosis of the *culte du moi*. Dada, at its most apocalyptic, had it both ways, and proclaimed that after the present phase of quasi-Oriental 'indifference' there was to follow an era of purged personality, 'the cleanliness of the individual' (according to Tzara). The extreme and, on the face of it, paradoxical individualism of, say, Eliot, Lewis, and Pound, is the parallel case.

There is, in short, a family resemblance between the modernisms. 'Indifference' and the abrogation of 'responsibility' are the wilder cousins of the more literary 'impersonality' and 'objectivity.' The palaeo-modernist conspiracy which made a cult of occult forms is not unrelated to the extremist denial that there are any. These are the self-reconciling opposites of modernism.

Duchamp, like some of the older poets, is a man whose intelligence has been dedicated to anti-intellectualist ends. The paradoxical pursuit of randomness in the arts—a consequence of doctrinaire anti-formalism—is now carried on with every resource of ingenuity by very intelligent men. To early modernists the subjection of personality and the attack on false orders were

[1] 'The Art of Marcel Duchamp,' *Art Journal*, XXII (Winter 1962–3).

one and the same process; the logicians of neo-modernism have not only accepted the position but developed it into an attack on order, perhaps not successfully, but with energy. Viewed in this light, the new theory bristles with paradoxes as, for instance, in Rauschenberg's remark: 'I consider myself successful only when I do something that resembles the lack of order I sense.'

The theoretical situation is in detail puzzling, but it must be admitted that in its practical and personal manifestations it is often pleasing, and indeed funny. For this reason Calvin Tomkins' book, which is not only a set of 'profiles' but an intelligent presentation of ideas, is as amusing as it is informative.[1] His four subjects are Duchamp, Cage, Tinguely, and Rauschenberg. They are all, as he says, very different—Duchamp more detached, Tinguely more destructive, Cage more programmatic, and Rauschenberg more anti-art than the others—but they have many interests in common. For instance, all of them say that *art is much less interesting than life*, and not generically different from it. *All* seek impersonality (though strong personalities are vividly present in their work) and therefore *experiment with chance*. *All accept that art is characteristically impermanent*, being made up of things without transcendence. And *all* rejoice to *work on the borders of farce*. They make random and unpredictable things in a world consisting of random and unpredictable things, an activity that is anyway absurd; the purposeless is pursued with fanatic purpose, and this is farcical in itself. One difference between a Tinguely machine and a Heath Robinson is that Tinguely takes it past the drawing-board stage, but another is that Robinson aimed to amuse, whereas Tinguely, though he doesn't mind amusing, has no affective purpose at all; and there is a somewhat similar distinction to be drawn between a Hoffnung concert and a Cage recital.

These propositions and attitudes are characteristic of neo-modernism, and the literary man should learn what he can from them. The view that art is not distinct from life, to which (in Cage's words) it is 'inferior in complexity and unpredictability,' is of course 'anti-formalist.' In the past we have simply been wrong in supposing that order is a differentia of art; hence the new doctrine, propounded by Cage and given an elaborate

[1] *The Bride and the Bachelors* (London, Weidenfeld; New York, Viking).

philosophical defence in Morse Peckham's recent book, *Man's Rage for Chaos*, that 'a work of art is what the perceiver observes in what has been culturally established as a perceiver's space. This can be anything. . . .' In Cage's *4' 33"* the pianist sits before a closed piano for four minutes and thirty-three seconds, and the only sound is what floats in randomly from outside—bird song, buses—or what the spectators make themselves. So long as there is a concert-situation there is a concert, although the content of the concert is random and minimal. This is a logical step forward from Satie's musical collage, and is perhaps more like Kurt Schwitters simply planting bits of things before the observer in a 'perceiver's space.' It pushes the protest against 'retinal' art, and its musical equivalent, to the point where it is a protest against the seriousness of palaeo-modernist protest, and where the difference between art and joke is as obscure as that between art and non-art. A point to remember, though, is that the development can be seen as following from palaeo-modernist premises without any violent revolutionary stage.

I myself believe that there is a difference between art and joke, while admitting that it has sometimes been a difficult one to establish; and I would want to call *4' 33"* and Tinguely's famous self-destroying machine ('Homage to New York') jokes, if only because however satisfying they may be, they do not seem sufficient in respect of the needs which what is called art has usually sufficed. But this is to use very inadequate criteria; and having supposed vaguely that neo-modernism was heavily dependent on the extension of modernist *theory*, I was glad to find a philosopher, Arthur Danto,[1] saying this very thing in a sharper way. Danto says the difficulties begin when one forsakes the old mimetic assumptions and says, for example, that a painting of a table is as real as a table. If this seems hard to take when the painting is Post-Impressionist, it becomes easier when the objects painted are strictly inimitable—the numeral 3, for example. Any copy of that simply *is* the numeral 3. What kind of mistake would you be making if you tried to sleep in Rauschenberg's famous *Bed*, which is a bed? You cannot mistake reality for reality. Danto suggests that we use *is* in two distinct senses. We say a spot of white paint 'is' Icarus, and also that 'this is a bed.' These two usages are presumably both present when we

[1] 'The Artworld,' *Journal of Philosophy*, LXI, p. 571 (1964).

say that *Bed* is a bed; but if it has paint on it and is in a 'perceiver's space' then the Icarus *is* is dominant.

Actually for Danto the physical location is less important
than a sort of intellectual or theoretical space—call it the
atmosphere of intellectual assumptions breathed alike by the
artist and the game spectator.

To see something as art requires something the eye cannot descry—
an atmosphere of artistic theory, a knowledge of art: an artworld.

But it all comes to the same thing. If Brillo made their boxes out
of plywood they would still not be Warhols, and if Andy Warhol
made his out of cardboard they would not be Brillo boxes.
Provided the 'space' and the aesthetic convention were right he
could simply sign a real Brillo box ready-made. We know what
it is by where it is, and by our being induced to make the necessary theoretical dispositions (or not, as the case may be). As
Jasper Johns puts it, 'What makes an object into art is its introduction into the art context.' Examination question: what is a
signed Warhol Brillo box, found among a stack of Brillo boxes in
a supermarket? Assuming, of course, that the customer knows
the name, and what Mr Warhol does for a living. Another
related question is, 'What makes an object into a joke?'

The theory so far is, then, that art is whatever you provide
when the place in which you provide it is associated with the
idea, and contains people who are prepared to accept this and
perhaps other assumptions. Mr Peckham would argue that our
failure to have noticed this earlier resulted from persistent
brain-washing of the kind that stuck us with the notion that we
have a 'rage for order'—that we seek the consolations of form
amid natural chaos inhospitable to humans. This in his view is
entirely false. We have, on the contrary, a natural rage for
chaos, and that is why, truth prevailing, the concept of form is
dead. With it, of course, dies the notion that the artist has to do
with establishing and controlling a formal order in his work
(what Keats in ignorance called 'information') and, also, the
notion that this order has a high degree of permanence. Of
course these notions have at one time or another been challenged
before, though perhaps not in their totality. Artists have always
known that there was an element of luck in good work ('grace,' if

you like) and that they rarely knew what they meant till they'd
seen what they said; and there are milder traces of a doctrine of
impermanence in palaeo-modernism, even in poetry, where
Stevens articulates it clearly. But once again neo-modernism
presses the point, and gives it practical application.

The most notable instance of this seems to be the neo-
modernist *interest in chance*, a long way on from what Pope
called 'a grace beyond the reach of art.' Although 'indeterminacy' has affected literature, it has had more importance so
far in music and painting, and these are the areas of theoretical
enquiry. There is obviously room for teleological differences
between artists who employ random methods. Duchamp argued
that 'your chance is not the same as my chance,' and when he
wrote random music insisted on regarding it as personal to himself and also funny. His dislike of order (perhaps as betraying
him) emerges in his publishing the notes on *La Mariée mise à nu
par ses célibataires, même* in random order, so anticipating the
cut-up-fold-in Burroughs techniques as he had anticipated the
methods of aleatory music. Duchamp, incidentally, for all that
he anticipated so many innovations, was always aware of a
tradition, which he saw himself at the end of; he is a very sophisticated figure, and his critical superiority over some of his
imitators is demonstrated by his immediate dismissal of the idea
that there could be any relation at all between indeterminacy in
the arts and indeterminacy in physics—this covert bid for
prestige promotes nothing but confusion, of which (*pace* Peckham) there is quite enough already.

The layman who wants to know what Cage is up to has to
confront the whole problem of chance. Without being at all
solemn, Cage employs his considerable intellectual resources on
constantly changing experiments of which the object is to ensure
that his art shall be 'purposeless play.' Not for the first time in
musical history, harmony (ideologically associated with ideas
of order) had to go; it is replaced by 'duration,' as percussion
replaces melody. Music now deals in every kind of natural
sound (the extreme naturalism of Cage is attributed by Tomkins
to the influence of Coomaraswamy) but every other kind of
sound too, except what might be made by conventional instruments. The piano has bolts between the strings to make it
simply percussive. As to indeterminacy, Cage achieves it by

many methods, including the use of the Chinese I Ching, coin-tossing, and yarrow-sticks. In one piece every note required 18 tosses of the coin.[1] He has now found speedier methods, using, like Rossini before him, the imperfections in paper as a suggestion for notes.

On this view of the matter there can be no question of judging a particular work. 'There are no catastrophes,' he says. But audiences can of course be affected in different ways, and Cage has experienced wildly various reactions from his auditors. Certainly he sometimes makes it seem that aleatory art is, in a manner as yet unexplored, close to humour, as in the view of some tragedy is close to farce. Tomkins quotes Virgil Thomson's account of a concert given in New York's Town Hall in 1958, which was

a jolly good row and a good show. What with the same man playing two tubas at once, a trombone player using only his instrument's mouthpiece, a violinist sawing away across his knees, and the soloist David Tudor crawling around on the floor and thumping the piano from below, for all the world like a 1905 motorist, the Town Hall spectacle, as you can imagine, was one of cartoon comedy . . . it is doubtful whether any orchestra ever before had so much fun or gave such joyful hilarity to its listeners.

This is very sympathetic, but Cage believes that 'everything is music,' and if, out of all the possibilities, he often chooses what makes for hilarity, this is evidence that such an assumption tends to confuse art and joke. There is a current of apocalyptism in all neo-modernism, and it is no bad thing that the Last Days should occasionally be good for a giggle, as they are in Beckett and in Tinguely. 'When seeing a Tinguely mechanism for the first time,' says Mr Tomkins, 'most people burst out laughing.' Peter Selz, the Curator of Painting and Sculpture at the Museum of Modern Art, was delighted with the famous *Homage*, which destroyed itself successfully, though not quite in the manner planned by the artist, before a distinguished audience. 'Art hasn't been fun for a long time,' he said. Duchamp congratulated Tinguely on being funny, and said that humour was a thing of great dignity.

It is, no doubt, part of the picture that all this would have

---

[1] The process is described at length in Cage's *Silence* (Wesleyan University Press, 1961) pp. 60–61. This beautiful and very pleasant book contains material of great interest to anybody concerned with avant-gardism.

been less funny had it gone according to plan. The humour is a matter of chance, of 'aleation.' Aleation in the arts, I suggested, pushes into absurdity a theory based on observation, that chance or grace plays a role in composition. In so far as palaeo-modernism pretended to be classical, it played this down; but between it and neo-modernism stands surrealism, and other manifestations of irrationalism. On the new theory, which has a wild logic, you leave everything to chance, and the result will make its mark either as very natural or as providing the material from which the spectators in the right place will make whatever they need for their own satisfaction. Anything random has some kind of an order, for example a bag of marbles emptied on to a table. Or, as Monroe Beardsley puts it in that interesting section of his *Aesthetics* from which I have already borrowed, 'they are in an order but not in order.' The difference between aleatory art and the art which appealed to 'the logic of imagination' (if for a moment we imagine them both as doctrinally pure) is simply this: the first in theory seeks only to produce an order (and in this it cannot fail) whereas the palaeo-modernists had not reduced grace to chance, and sought to make order.

So far as I can see this would be disastrous to aleatory art were it absolutely true, because the reason why we speak of 'an order' as against 'order' is that we drop the article as a sign of our wish to dignify what interests us more. We have discovered, in the process of getting by amid what Cage thinks of as the wonderful complexities of life, that order is more *useful* than an order: for example, the telephone book would be harder to use if the names were printed haphazardly. In a way, the alpha-betical arrangement is perfectly arbitrary, but it happens to be something that the people who compose it and the people who use it agree upon. It might, of course, be said to give a very imperfect impression of the chaos and absurdity of metropolitan life, or life at large, and the consolation of knowing you can find your way about in it is in some ways on some very strict views perhaps somewhat fraudulent. It is not quite 'order,' anyway, though it is not merely *an* order. And this in-between order is what most of us mean when we talk about 'order' in aesthetic contexts. One can avoid a divorce between art and life without going to the extremes recommended by Cage. When Cage grew interested in mushrooms he quickly discovered that

some knowledge of their botanical classifications was a necessary modification to the practice of eating them at random.[1]
Also, that when somebody arranged a happening in his honour,
which required that he should be physically assaulted, he had to
say that whereas his view was still that 'anything goes,' this was
so only on condition that one could manage to be free without
being foolish. The implied criteria can only derive from the sort
of education which distinguishes between an order and order.
Order turns out to be more comfortable and useful. If our
orientation towards it is not biological, then it is cultural or
educational; and the reason why an order posing as order sometimes seems funny is that it is always presupposing orderly
criteria by which its randomness can be measured; so, having
reduced tradition to absurdity, one makes allusions to tradition
by which the absurdity can be enjoyed as such. Thus silent music
and Void or all-black painting presuppose music which employs
conventional sounds and paintings with colour and shapes.
They are piquant allusions to what fundamentally interests us
more than they do, and they could not exist without it.[2]

Aleatory art is accordingly, for all its novelty, an extension of
past art, indeed the hypertrophy of one aspect of that art.
Virgil Thomson, who has been very sympathetic to Cage, allows
that his random music is not really a matter of pure chance but a
game of which the rules are established by Cage himself. No
matter how much he tries to eliminate his own choices, it is
always a Cage-game, and it involves calculation and personal
choice. Admirers of William Burroughs' *Nova Express* admit
that the randomness of the composition pays off only when the
text looks as if it had been composed straightforwardly, with
calculated inspiration. The argument is too obvious to labour.
Even Duchamp didn't pick up *anything* and sign it. What seems
clear is that a gross overdevelopment of the aleatory element
in art tends to make it approximate to humour; thus the 17th-
century conceit, over-extended, became a joke, and Jan Kott

---

[1] See *Silence*, pp. 261–2 for a gastronomic misadventure.
[2] The *ought* concealed in Cage's *is* is just that this should not be so, because
such an interest is a vestige of the false fictions of order that should die with old
technologies. Thus: 'let sounds be themselves rather than vehicles for man-made
theories in expressions of human sentiments' (*Silence*, p. 10). And the interest of
an all-white painting lies in its shadows, the random change of light upon it.

can turn *King Lear* into an absurd farce. The transformation would be impossible without the theory and practice of predecessors. Its nihilism is meaningless without an assumption of the plenitude of the past. Thus neo-modernists tend to make the mistake they often scold other people for, which is to attribute too much importance to the art of the period between the Renaissance and Modernism. By constantly alluding to this as a norm they despise, they are stealthy classicists, as the palaeo-modernists, who constantly alluded to Byzantine and archaic art, were stealthy romantics.

The point that in theory there is nothing very new about the New, that it is in this respect little more than a reverie concerning the more important and self-conscious theoretical developments of an earlier modernism, was made by Harold Rosenberg himself, when he observed that an Oldenburg plastic pie is not so much art, and not so much a pie, as 'a demonstration model in an unspoken lecture on the history of illusionism,' adding that this kind of thing represents the union of many different tendencies in the art of the past half-century. As to why modernism should tend in this way towards pure farce, he cites Marx's observation that farce is the final form of action in a situation which has become untenable. Like Beckett's hero we can't and must go on, so that going on is bound to look absurd, a very old-fashioned thing to be doing in a situation you have shown to be absolutely new. On rather similar grounds he attacks the fashionable 'aesthetics of impermanence,' saying that the time-philosophy involved is evidently wrong, and that 'art cannot transform the conditions of its existence.'

Such comment amounts to a radical criticism of the theoretical bases of extreme neo-modernism, and it prepares one for the impact of one of Rosenberg's best essays, so far uncollected, which appeared five years ago in *Partisan Review* under the title 'Literary Form and Social Hallucination.' When the subject is literary, this critic seems to see with great clarity truths which become obscure when the topic is painting. He argues that the form of a literary work militates against its ability to 'tell the truth'; that part of its function is in fact to 'tease us out of thought' (an argument employed, though with differences, by Iris Murdoch). From the political point of view this makes form suspect, anti-liberal; for by inducing us to descend into 'out-lived areas of the psyche' it takes our eye off the actual demands and complexities of the world, arms us against the fact. It could perhaps be said that here the criticism is of Form when it ought to be of forms; that the constant researches of the arts into form have as a principal motive the fear that obsolescent *fictions of form* will cause them to be untruthful, or at any rate less truthful than they might be. Thus it is in the popular arts, where the question of fidelity to the world as the clerisy understands it does not arise, that conventions have the longest life. While the highbrows are pondering the *nouveau roman*, the great mass of fiction, which satisfies readers who would never dream of asking that it do more than a token amount of truth-telling, continues to use the old stereotypes.[1] It would probably not occur to the readers of such fiction that truth required the abolition of form, and if it did they might think the point too obvious to mention. Fiction, they know, is different from fact because it is made up. Yet it is precisely this point that, as Rosenberg sees, we need to be reminded of. Theoretical contempt for form in the arts is a fraud.

Formlessness is simply another look and a temporary one at that. In time, organisation begins to show through the most chaotic surface . . . the subversion of literary form cannot be established except by literary means, that is, through an effort essentially formal.

This must be true, despite all the recent anti-formalist researches, aleatory, schismatic, and destructive. In neo-, as in palaeo-modernism, research into form is the true means of discovery, even when form is denied existence. So it becomes a real question whether it helps to introduce indeterminacy into the research, even if it is agreed that this is possible to any significant degree (and it is not). With Danto's remarks in mind we can at least ask ourselves whether dependence on an erroneous or distorted theory cannot be in some measure incapacitating. We need not expect a simple answer, since a great deal that is done in the arts is founded on theoretical positions which are later found to be leaky. We should need to reflect that there

---

[1] It is obviously in order to meet this situation head-on that Robbe-Grillet makes his fantastic claim to have at last found a novel-form acceptable to the man-in-the-street.

is a certain prestige to be had in minorities by professing to concur with what appear to be revolutionary advances in thinking about the arts, so that to find an audience claiming proficiency in a 'new' language is at present by no means difficult.

This is not a problem one can discuss now. What one can do is to say of the theoretical bases of neo-modernism, in so far as they show themselves in relation to form, chance, humour, that they are not 'revolutionary.' They are marginal developments of older modernism. It can be added that disparagement and nihilist rejection of the past are founded partly on ignorance and partly on a development of the earlier modernist doctrine which spoke of retrieving rather than of abolishing tradition, just as the abolition of form is a programme founded on the palaeo-modernist programme to give form a new researched look. A certain extremism is characteristic of both phases. Early modernism tended towards fascism, later modernism towards anarchism. What Cyril Connolly calls the evolution of sensibility is a matter of changing theory, Romantic egotism becoming 'impersonality' and this later turning into 'indifference.' In the same way chance replaces the quasi-fortuitous collocation of images characteristic of earlier modernism. The anti-humanism—if Mr Connolly will allow the expression—the anti-humanism of early modernism (anti-intellectualist, authoritarian, eugenicist) gives way to the anti-humanism (hipsterish, free-sexed, anti-intellectualist) of later modernism. As to the past, history continues to be the means by which we recognise what is new as well as what is not. What subverts form is 'an effort essentially formal'; and the sense of standing at an end of time, which is so often invoked as an explanation of difference, is in fact evidence of similarity. The earlier humanism went in a good deal for the capitalisation of what Mr Rosenberg calls 'outlived areas of the psyche,' and so does the new modernism. For a 'movement' united by a detestation of logic, Modernism has generated an immense amount of theory; this was admittedly much more coherently expressed in the earlier phase. Later it has been scrambled by the babble of smaller voices, and in some aspects has been heavily over-developed, as I have tried to show. In both periods there was a natural tendency (inescapable from the Modern at any period and easier to justify half a century back) to exaggerate the differences between what one was doing and what had been done by the old guard, and this has helped to conceal the truth that there has been only one Modernist Revolution, and that it happened a long time ago. So far as I can see there has been little radical change in modernist thinking since then. More muddle, certainly, and almost certainly more jokes, but no revolution, and much less talent.

That is why, on the one hand, one cannot accept Cyril Connolly's assurance that it is virtually all over, and on the other Leslie Fiedler's claim, recently mentioned in these pages, that we have a new art which reflects a social revolution so radical that he can call it a 'mutation' and its proponents 'The New Mutants' (*Partisan Review*, Fall 1965). Henceforth, he thinks, literature and criticism will forget their traditional observance of the past, and observe the future instead. Pop fiction demonstrates 'a growing sense of the irrelevance of the past' and Pop writers ('post-Modernists') are catching on. The new subject will be 'the end of man' and the transformation of the human life into something else (curious echoes of Mr Connolly, who also thinks of modern writers as post-Modernist in sensibility, and anti-humanist). Mr Fiedler explains that he means by humanism the cult of reason, from Socrates to Freud. This is what is being annihilated, and the Berkeley students were protesting against universities as the transmitters and continuators of the unwanted rationalist tradition. The protest systematically *anti*-s everything: a Teach-in is an *anti*-class, banners inscribed FUCK are *anti*-language, and so on. Actually a teach-in is only an especially interesting class, because the teachers are volunteers and just as engaged with the subject as you are. There is the oddity that this class really works as a 'dialogue' and goes on and on. The banners are no more anti-language than collage is anti-painting; and the absolutely blank banners which succeeded the 'dirty' ones were certainly a very good joke in the new manner, like Rauschenberg erasing a De Kooning, or a Klein Void.

Fiedler's observations on the new life-style of his 'mutants' are more interesting. He stresses a post-Humanist contempt for ideology; a post-Humanist sexuality which has discounted masculinity and developed characteristic patterns of homosexuality, usurpation of female attitudes, polymorphous perversity; and a new range of post-Humanist stimulants (*LSD*, airplane glue, etc.). This amounts, he argues, to 'a radical metamorphosis of the Western male,' a real revolt, unlike our ritual contentions with father. These young people have made the breakthrough into new psychic possibilities, and recognise in Burroughs the laureate of their conquest.[1]

Whether this is nonsense, and whether it is dangerous, is not in my brief. I will only say that the whole argument about 'mutation' is supererogatory; the phenomena should be explained more economically. If the prole has replaced the shepherd, the savage, and the child as pastoral hero, it isn't surprising that those who seek to imitate him should imitate his indifference to ideology and history and sexual orthodoxies. This is not the first recorded instance of libertinage among the well-heeled. Drugs and four-letter words are not new, even among poets, even among the young. The display may seem unusually ostentatious, but it is worth remembering that Fiedler's prime example derives from that highly abnormal institution, the University of California, the unbelievably well-endowed organ of the educational aspirations of a state which is not only very rich but is famous for the unique predominance of the young in its population. In so far as the protest was 'pure' protest, protesting against nothing whatever, it was surely luxurious attitudinising on a familiar undergraduate model but hypertrophied by sociological causes well within the purview of old-style analysis. A thirst for the unique and unprecedented can lead to the exaggeration of triviality or to claims which the record refutes. Thus Fiedler finds in Ken Kesey's (very good) novel *One Flew Over the Cuckoo's Nest* evidence that for the mutants the schizophrenic has replaced the sage as culture hero, whereas by narrating this madhouse fiction from the point of view of an inmate of limited and varying perceptiveness Kesey is using a now time-honoured technique. So with his sociological observations. Even the male behaviour to be observed after midnight on 32nd and 43rd Streets hardly needs to be explained in terms of 'mutation.' To treat such symptoms as unique, as signs that the Last Days are at hand, is to fall headlong into a

[1] It may be worth pointing out that Burroughs himself is far from thinking that drugs will bring this about. His recent *Paris Review* interviewer (Fall '65) asked: 'The visions of drugs and the visions of art don't mix?' and he said, 'Never. . . . They are absolutely contraindicated for creative work, and I include in the lot alcohol, morphine, barbiturates, tranquillisers. . . .'

very naïve—and historically very well-known—apocalyptism.

It is the constant presence of more or less subtle varieties of apocalyptism that makes possible the repetitive claims for uniqueness and privilege in modernist theorising about the arts. So far as I can see these claims are unjustified. The price to be paid for old-style talk about 'evolving sensibility' is new-style talk about 'mutation.' It is only rarely that one can say there is nothing to worry about, but in this limited respect there appears not to be. Mr Fiedler professes alarm at the prospect of being a stranded humanist, wandering among unreadable books in a totally new world. But when sensibility has evolved that far there will be no language and no concept of form, so no books. Its possessors will be idiots. However, it will take more than jokes, dice, random shuffling, and smoking pot to achieve this, and in fact very few people seem to be trying. Neo-modernists have examined, in many different ways (many more than I have talked about), various implications in traditional modernism. As a consequence we have, not unusually, some good things, many trivial things, many jokes, much nonsense. Among other things they enable us to see more clearly that certain aspects of earlier modernism really were so revolutionary that we ought not to expect—even with everything so speeded up—to have the pains and pleasures of another comparable movement quite so soon. And by exaggerating the drawing, the neo-modernist does help us to understand rather better what the Modern now is, and has been during this century.

On the whole one has to say that the older modernists understood all this better. Eliot in his last book, tired and unadventurous as it is, said it once again, and said it right:[1]

A new kind of writing appears, to be greeted at first with disdain and derision; we hear that the tradition has been flouted, and that chaos has come. After a time it appears that the new way of writing is not destructive but re-creative. It is not that we have repudiated the past, as the obstinate enemies—and also the stupidest supporters—of any new movement like to believe; but that we have enlarged our conception of the past; and that in the light of what is new we see the past in a new pattern.

This does not allow for the possibility that chaos and destruction could be introduced into the programme, except by its 'stupidest

[1] *To Criticise the Critics* (London, Faber; New York, Farrar, Straus).

supporters'; but it does seem to make sense in terms of a quest for 'what will suffice.' In the end what Simone Weil called 'decreation' (easy to confuse with destruction) is the true modernist process in respect of form and the past. Or if it is not we really shall destroy ourselves at some farcical apocalypse.

(iii) *Definitions and Variations*

Somebody should write the history of the word 'modern.' The OED isn't very helpful, though most of the senses the word now has have been in the air since the 16th century and are actually older than Shakespeare's way of using it to mean 'commonplace.' The international row about Moderns in the 17th century is terribly well-documented but the historian might find that it only muddied the waters. An earlier usage in the 15th-century *devotio moderna* seems more significant, because it connotes a sharp sense of epoch, and of a reaction against the style of life and thought of immediate predecessors, something rather more than the technical operations indicated by the word 'new'—in the 'new' poetry or the 'new' music. That the Modern is a larger and more portentous category than the New our own usage confirms, or at any rate did so until very lately. The New is to be judged by the criterion of novelty, the Modern implies or at any rate permits a serious relationship with a past, a relationship that requires criticism and indeed radical re-imagining. This sense of 'modern' is the one Mr Spender explored in his book *The Struggle of the Modern*. His is a traditionalist modernism. There is another kind, which Spender wanted to call the 'contemporary,' and which Mr Trilling characterises as anti-cultural. This is the schismatic modernism associated with Barzun's 'clean break' and 'new start,' or, less academically, with the doctrine of The New.

One of the things the historian will have to decide is whether the concept of the Modern, even in its traditionalist phase, isn't open to the kind of attack that is mounted, as a matter of intellectual hygiene, by Ernst Gombrich against any method or set of assumptions that seems to him tainted by Hegelianism, whether of the 'Right,' as in Malraux, or of the 'Left,' as in Arnold Hauser. Another problem is the degree to which the 'traditionalist' sense is merely a specialisation of the academics, related only obscurely to the ordinary-language usage; this, however, seems to reflect nowadays the sense that 'modern' doesn't quite have the up-to-date flavour wanted. The shops call their furniture and curtains 'contemporary,' a word intellectuals dislike, partly because it is uselessly ambiguous, and partly because it is used in this ignorant way mostly of nasty things. However, the historian of the word must be left to sort all this out. On the whole, everybody knows what is meant by modern literature, modern art, modern music. The words suggest Joyce, Picasso, Schoenberg or Stravinsky—the experiments of two or more generations back.

The fact that defining the modern is a task that now imposes itself on many distinguished scholars may be a sign that the modern period is over. We need a language to argue about it, as we argue about Renaissance. The formulae devised will, in the same way, vary with time. A documentary history of the modern would have been different 20 years ago, and will be different 20 years hence, from the one now presented us by Ellmann and Feidelson.[1] They try, in a book of about half a million words, to crystallise the modern sense of the modern—the traditional modern, as their title suggests, for they print not only the 20th-century documents but also what are now regarded as the sources of the modern, as far back as the 18th century. It is fair to say that the book contains a high proportion of material that would have been in any good book of this kind, as well as some things that have only a doubtful right to be there; and of course one can think of omissions, some which may be considered rather damaging.

The editors don't try to define 'modern', saying that it is 'intimate and elusive' and that it is 'not like the reassuring landscape of the past, open and invadable everywhere.' Of course their purpose is to make it reassuring and invadable, to confirm it as part of the past. But they argue that it is more than a merely chronological description because it 'designates a distinctive kind of imagination, themes and forms, conditions and modes of creation, that are interrelated, and comprise an imaginative whole.' These arguments, assuming the discontinuity of the modern mind, are themselves modern, and indicate a degree of sympathy with the material of the book which explains why so

[1] *The Modern Tradition.* Edited by Richard Ellmann and Charles Feidelson. Oxford.

few of the passages included are from writers critical of the conspiratorial element in modernism—the agreement, which can be too easy, that our problems are unique, our world uniquely chaotic, so that we are entitled to mistrust formal arrangements acceptable in the past. They do mention that the modern view of the world—as presenting unheard-of difficulties in the matter of relating imagination to reality, as providing no trustworthy fictions—tempts artists who suffer under it into a familiar historical game, that of deciding when the rot set in: was it with Giotto or with Shakespeare, with Napoleon or the Great War? 'The paradoxical task of the modern imagination,' they say somewhat obscurely, 'has been to stand both inside and outside itself, to articulate its own formlessness, to encompass its own extravagant possibilities.' They allow the modern its cherished formulae, and get one of its favourite paradoxes into the title.

The editors are well-known literary critics, and their book is quite properly centred in literature. 'He makes literature include philosophy?' someone asks Boon in Wells's novel. 'Everything,' replies Boon. 'It's all the central things.' The editors agree, but to document the modern you need to consider purely discursive statements about it, and topics which are not quite literature, though related to it. They have nine topics: Symbolism, Realism, Nature, Cultural History, The Unconscious, Myth, Self-Consciousness, Existence and Faith. The first has bits of Kant and Coleridge, Blake and Goethe, Baudelaire and Flaubert, Nietzsche and Wagner, Pater and Wilde (who most certainly would not have got in had the book been written even 10 years ago). The central documents are from Rimbaud, Mallarmé, Valéry, Yeats, Eliot, Rilke, Pound, Joyce; but Picasso, Arp, Ernst, Duchamp, Klee, Dubuffet and Malraux are also present. The passages may be famous, as with those of Apollinaire, Pound and Klee, or merely useful to make a point, as with Forster's lecture 'Art for Art's Sake.'

This first section, itself the size of a normal book, is very useful. The introduction to it briskly outlines the current doctrine: 'the symbolist is a kind of romantic, one who singles out and develops the romantic doctrine of the creative imagination . . . the image possesses absolute autonomy . . . its maker, the artist, is the truly heroic man.' The history of this group of notions is rapidly traced from Kant and Blake through Flaubert and Wilde and Nietzsche on fictional affirmations, to 'pseudo-statements' and Wallace Stevens, with Cubists, Vorticists and Surrealists chiming in. That the first piece in the book is Wilde's 'Decay of Lying' tells one something about the new modern and about the topicality of this book. But students (basically this is a gigantic textbook) and others will find this way of handling the subject illuminating. There is a point in being rushed from Kant to Arp, from Blake to the Bauhaus—where they also tried, in their way, to prepare a rest for the people of God. In the section on autonomy Baudelaire helps to prepare them for Duchamp, and Apollinaire, announcing that artists are men who above all want to be inhuman, sounds the theme of dehumanisation. Ortega, surprisingly, is left out, although he spent so much time on the concept of the modern, and on dehumanisation. There are such gaps—no Wyndham Lewis, no Worringer, no Kandinsky in this section; but Pound on Vortex—juxtaposed with Dubuffet on zinc oxide—perhaps takes care of that. There is almost nothing about music, either here or anywhere else. Yet this opening section will give many people a clearer notion of the history of the modern literature than they had.

The remaining topics must have been harder to select. 'Realism' is obvious enough, a very modern problem; the editors begin, badly, with George Eliot (the excrescent chapter in *Adam Bede*) but end well with Lukacs (late, unfortunately) and Robbe-Grillet, the prophet of a fully dehumanised realism. One of the great omissions of the book—the relation of art and artists to the modern city and the modern worker—is partly repaired by bits of the Communist Manifesto and Trotsky. No Carlyle, no Ruskin. 'Nature' runs from Darwin and Schopenhauer to Dewey and Heisenberg; the introduction tells us, what I do not believe, that there is 'some analogy' between instrumentalism and the indeterminacy principle, and 'the linguistic experimentalism of the symbolists.' Here axes begin to grind. Heisenberg would not, I think, regard himself as providing material for a waste-land myth of meaninglessness, or confirming Existentialist anxiety; but the editors want to end with Tillich on 'the courage to be . . . when God has disappeared,' and they shape the whole thing accordingly. One sees this in the central position given to Spengler in the 'Cultural History' section. The critics of historicism are not represented, except by Berdyaev.

The section on the 'Unconscious' opens with Goethe, Blake and Nietzsche, has Freud in the middle, and goes on to Lawrence, Tzara and Breton. There is no Diderot, amazingly little sex (which might have had a section on its own) and no neo-Freudians. Dada and Surrealism are here because of their flight to unreason; but Dada is one kind of modernism, capitalising alienation, schism, destruction—the shout into the Marabar Caves—and Surrealism, in spite of the acknowledged links, is another, with implications of social revolution as a reasonable goal. However, as the section of 'Myth' confirms, the interesting aspect of modernism at present is the unreasonable one. I don't know why the quest for a mythology, here represented by Jung, should not equally well have been represented by Madame Blavatsky and Eliphas Lévi. 'Self-consciousness,' one of the odder topics, runs from Rousseau through Kierkegaard and Dostoievsky's Underground to Proust, Gide, Kandinsky and Yeats. 'Existence,' strangely marred by confining the Sartre selections to *Existentialism and Humanism*, has Kierkegaard, Nietzsche at one end and Heidegger and Jaspers at the other. The last section starts with Blake, and arrives, by way of the Grand Inquisitor, at Barth and Tillich.

This list of names is meant to give a notion of what may be found in a rich, inexpensive and useful, if somewhat tendentious book. It tells you what very well-equipped American scholars take the Modern Movement to be; and if the ideas represented are not criticised, and the map a little out of date, that may be because the reader is expected to do some of the work. While I was reading the book I came across Mr Trilling's essay 'The Two Environments,' which quotes Saul Bellow's attack on the complicity of critics in the creation of a dangerous modern waste-land myth 'on which literature has lived uncritically.' Bellow says such critics have helped to 'enfeeble literature.' The editors of this in most ways admirable compilation might, on the severest view, be held not to escape Bellow's condemnation.

Meanwhile, the word 'modern' can still mean something like 'written in the past 10 years,' and this is the way it's used in Mr LeRoi Jones's title.[1] He calls his contributors 'the restorers of American prose.' Their tone is 'non-urban,' belonging to the West of the United States. They are separate men, with an

[1] *The Moderns* (London, MacGibbon & Kee; New York, Citadel).

affinity for the 'non-civilised,' remaining 'outside the mainstream of the American organism.' They study the 'fellaheen,' in Spengler's word—hoodlums, homosexuals, Negroes. Theirs, says the editor, is a 'populist modernism.' The result is grey enough, rather like some *Yellow Book* stories. There is a lot about cities—John Rechy on Los Angeles and Chicago ('savage city'), Kerouac on Seattle and New York. Strip shows are a favourite topic. There is a brisk bit of urban reporting by Hubert Selby Jr, which seemed the best writing in the book. Kerouac describes a Negro cat asleep in the tube. 'I love him,' he confesses. There is some Burroughs. The appendix consists of theoretical pieces, banal for the most part and badly written; one is Kerouac's 'Essentials of Spontaneous Prose,' which ought to be read by anybody who cares about the American future, for it has been recommended to undergraduates as a style-sheet. Burroughs has a piece explaining the cut-up, fold-in technique. Tzara began it, but now, 50 years late, the writer can copy collage and the cinema. 'The best writing seems to be done almost by accident but writers until the cut-up method was made explicit had no way to produce the accident of spontaneity.' Now a pair of scissors will do it.

But this takes us out of the Modern into the avant-garde; and pat comes a book of examples.[1] Burroughs again, a long stretch of Butor, Cocteau (how did he get in here?), and others less famous. There is an editorial introduction of the kind Americans call sophomoric, a display of unmastered terminology, produced with inexplicable heat. 'We have the right to convey the fictive of any reality at all—and there is nothing that is not real—by any method we wish,' Mr Orlovitz boldly pronounces. The whole point is to set forth a demonstration in the fictive that will generate tension even in a reader mystified by the significs, he adds. 'The notion of value belongs to *ad hominen* (*sic*) pleaders,' the man says. Those who suppose that to be avant-garde all you need is to abandon the mind to it, together with the language and the compositor, would doubtless like to think so. Anyway, it shows that there is a difference between 'modern' and 'avant-garde.' But somebody should write a history of that word, too.

(1965–6)

---

[1] *The Award Avant-Garde Reader*. Edited by Gil Orlovitz. Award Books. New York.

Chapter Two

TYPES AND TIMES

II. EDIFYING SYMBOLS

The requirement that art should edify, or at least that it shouldn't disedify, is very old; and although many assume that it is self-evidently an unreasonable requirement, others have always to concern themselves with the difficulties that arise when it is flouted. The patron of the edifying men is Plato; Aristotle is the model of the anti-authoritarians. And the issue is alive wherever you have, as in Russia or in the Catholic Church, doctrinal infallibility and the power to condemn deviations. The difference between Russia and Rome is that the Church has had time to develop much more subtle and considered ways of handling the problem. Obviously you will not find Catholic aestheticians who accept I. A. Richards's account of Doctrinal Adhesion (the eighth of his 10 'chief difficulties of criticism') as 'a fertile source of confusion and erratic judgment.' On the other hand you rarely come across anybody willing to go all the way with Arthur Machen: 'Literature is the expression, through the aesthetic medium of words, of the dogmas of the Catholic Church, and that which is out of harmony with these dogmas is not literature.' In between these extremes there is a range of positions, including those of Aquinas and Maritain, the most frequently consulted of modern authorities.

'Do not separate your art from your faith,' says Maritain. 'But leave distinct what is distinct.' On the other hand art is impossible without love. Love and do as you like; but of course, if you love, what you do will be of its nature acceptable to the Christian God. In practice this means that there must be no Gidian 'collaboration with the demon,' a notion condemned by Maritain as Manichean; and although the artist will be in some degree treating of base or unedifying matters, he must do so in charity, and without collusion. Thus when the artist in question is a novelist, 'the essential point is to know at what altitude he is when he makes his portrayal of evil and whether his art and his soul are pure enough . . . to make it without conniving at it.'

This sounds very judicial, but is surely somewhat removed from the actual experience of reading and judging novels. So it must have seemed, anyway, to Conor Cruise O'Brien, contemplating the fury and the mire of modern fiction as well as the nature and duties of 'the Catholic imagination.' Hence *Maria Cross*,[1] in which he closely examines the work of eight Catholic writers, tackles such questions as the relation between Catholic doctrine and literature, and the extent to which his authors share the same world of imagination.

Maria Cross is a remarkable book: idiosyncratic but civilised in style, cleverly planned, learned and witty. It contains so many good jokes (often preserved in specially built footnotes) that one begins to see how criticism could once have been a gay science. Anyone who has hitherto omitted to read it (as I had) should buy the paperback edition at once. As the main business of this review will be to question the general drift of the book, it is fair to add that the studies of individual authors, considered in isolation, are good enough to deserve comparison with Edmund Wilson at his best. The only serious lapse is the chapter on Graham Greene: only one novel is examined, and that laboriously. On Mauriac, Péguy, Claudel and Bloy, Mr O'Brien is unfailingly perceptive and entertaining.

But it was surely perverse of him to say that this is 'not a book about Catholicism.' It is. It argues that the imagination of Christendom grasps reality only under Catholic forms; that Protestantism is the enemy not only of religion but of art; and that the mess we so often say we are in was caused by an attempt to replace what God and time have made irreplaceable for us, the faith by which alone we were enabled to understand human experience. Arguing this case, O'Brien takes on Freud and the Marxists and all the modern myth-makers, and he does so with a quite rare rhetorical power and variety, mimicking the opposition case, improving their arguments for them, damaging them with

[1] London, Burns & Oates; New York, Oxford University Press.

wit. Whatever the private religious beliefs of the author, this is unambiguously Catholic criticism.

The row about how far a Catholic writer may represent the human condition without a scandalous connivance at sin is, I suppose, largely a domestic matter, and O'Brien's treatment of it is important for infidels only because it earns him the necessary right to discuss works which are not merely edifying. But it is in the course of staking this claim that he goes on to argue for the uniqueness and necessity of the Catholic imagination, the real and only human force for creation and understanding—modern myths and symbols being only shadows of it.

Both stages of argument are sketched in the chapter on Mauriac. First, Mauriac's important novels were harshly treated by the clergy on the ground that they gave scandal in making 'perceptible, tangible . . . the Catholic universe of evil.' But after *Le Noeud de Vipères* he lost his nerve, took these criticisms to heart, and henceforth wrote to illustrate an abstraction, 'the part of faith that is intellectual, not that which is emotional.' What had Mauriac lost, besides realism and intensity? The power to see in the lusts of fallen men images of the love of God, a power without which Catholic fiction is either cut off from its material, or scandalous. The book which best displays this fictional charity is *Le Désert de l'Amour*. Maria Cross is the source of pain for one man who loves her sexually, and for his son, who loves her as a sorrowing mother; the kinds of love are not in the end distinct, and her name unites the varieties of human love and suffering with the symbol by which alone they are to be understood.

Mr O'Brien finds such images of the 'tension between flesh and spirit' essential to Catholic art because 'corruption and the cross are for the Catholic the two central facts.' The Faustian failure of the modern world to hold fast to this is marked by that growth in it of evil curiosity which Bernanos records. O'Brien's writers are exiles both from the rational modern world (which forced some of them near to fascist anti-rationalism) and from their Catholic childhood. They inhabit a cemetery; but to this place of corruption the cross alone gives meaning.

To make his point O'Brien does some brilliant things with the symbolism of his writers, and notably of Péguy, Claudel and Bloy. Rodrigue and Prouhèze in *Le Soulier de satin* spend their wedding night crucified on the same cross: '*La passion est unie à la croix.*' Bloy said 'Woman is the cross.' Man, nailed to his mother, seeks paradise in another woman and 'becomes aware of his crucifixion.' The only way we can understand the suffering of fallen man is by means of this multivalent symbol, which in its universality shares out suffering over the whole Christian community. And the pressure which gives it this human validity comes from below, not from above; all men are born to this cruciform model of passion, and its language, in so far as it is expressible, is 'the Catholic language, the *lingua franca* of suffering.' Protestantism, dead from the waist down, 'conceals the cross, refuses devotion to the mother of God,' and ignores the Communion of the Saints. Hence the vast advantages of Catholic writers; hence also the special advantages of 'warped' Catholic writers, when it comes to expressing the 'tormented unconscious mind of modern ex-Christendom.'

To explain why in my view this work of criticism doesn't at once drive one into the arms of the Church, one need only look at the admittedly fine essays on Claudel and Bloy. Studying the ramifications of gold as a symbol in Claudel, O'Brien has an excursus of Empsonian splendour on the hidden French rhymes for *or* (especially *mort*). This kind of symbolic extensiveness is exceptionally pleasing to O'Brien, who for all his sharpness of mind has a strong sense of the occult. It comes out in his handling of Claudel's water-symbolism. The sea, for instance, is the centre of a complex of occult meanings: *la mère, amer, l'amour, mort.* And so on. Although Claudel is explicit enough about the sexual symbolism of water, this is, as O'Brien explains, not Freudian. It is entirely Catholic, as the scene in *Le Soulier de satin* blending sea, woman man, sun, moon and cross proves. The symbols in the end have fixed meanings; they all meet in the cross. But this seems contrary to what one knows of the operation of symbols in *literature* as against religion. In fact, the mistake which runs right through this book is the assumption that symbols in novels and poems are like symbols in religion, where they are, to a certain degree, fixed: the baptismal water always means the same (admittedly inexplicable) thing, as God intended it to. But every poem or novel creates a distinctive field of meanings, not all of them intended by the author, since he did not, like God, invent his medium, which is the common language.

The error might, if one wanted a label, be called a typological fallacy. It is found in an extensive form in the Catholic aesthetic of David Jones, who says, for instance, that the word 'wood' *always* recalls the cross. But the mistake isn't peculiarly Catholic; and it is also prevalent in much fashionable criticism of Yeats and the Romantics, when the attempt is to discover the exact meanings of poems by reference to the fixed meanings of symbols in a synthetic Neo-Platonic 'tradition.' It seems a hard thing to say of O'Brien, so enormously superior in intelligence and literary sense to most of the 'tradition'-mongers—but he does go some of the way with them in a process which is at once reductive and destructive.

The antiquity of the typological fallacy must be granted, and O'Brien makes much of its extraordinary revival in Bloy. He thought that an exegete should make every sentence in Scripture refer to the Trinity. He held that woman, and specifically her sexual organ, *is* the *paradisus voluptatis* of Genesis, and he shocked many people by observing that the male member was anciently thought of as an image of the cross. The man's emission of semen in the act of sex is a figure of Christ's giving up the ghost (*emisit spiritum*). Similarly, for Bloy, history has meaning only in so far as it can be seen as precisely the suffering by which we 'pay for Mary.' He extended this kind of thinking to economics (money as the blood of Christ). In a sense he is a crazed throwback to medieval typology, very different from, and also much more attractive than, a lot of sophisticated scholarly typologies we now have. He revived 'the symbolism of the Scriptures in the days of the symbolism of the *décadents*,' as Mr O'Brien rightly observes. And far from being merely clinical about this curious archaistic myth-making, Mr O'Brien seems to find it superior to the analogous (but non-Catholic) inventions of Yeats. Moreover he himself employs it. Bloy illustrates for him the truth of the key saying: '*la passion est unie à la croix.*' To anybody who sees no real difference between Bloy's nonsense and the nonsense, say, of a resurrection ceremony at one of Yeats's secret societies, the real and intricate difficulty arises from one's continuing certainty that Bloy and Yeats are worth reading. And the solution has in the end to be subtler than the one which finds the value of a Yeats poem in Porphyry's Cave of the Nymphs, or of a Catholic novel in its *anamnesis* of the meanings of 'passion' and 'spirit.'

Last year in the *Partisan Review* there appeared a story by Bernard Malamud, in which an Italian Catholic girl painter sells an American Jew a share of her studio. All the time she paints abstracts based on the cross. He does abstracts based on the Star of David. She despises and lives off him, and involves him in her superstitions. Seizing a chance to make love to her, he fails, giving up the spirit too early. But one day he decides to paint himself as a priest; she sees him so dressed, pleads for absolution, and is granted it: 'Pumping slowly, he nailed her to her cross.' I wonder what Mr O'Brien would make of this rich story. It uses his symbols, but not in his way; a reading which assumed the exclusive validity of the Catholic 'community of feeling' would surely come out wrong. The fact is that like the Neo-Hermeticists of Yeats criticism, whose discipline was also founded in the age of the *décadents*, Mr O'Brien subtly re-introduces to the business of criticism an old doctrinal adhesion, a claim to exclusive inspiration which is in the end a conspiracy against literature. What makes the Malamud story a good one isn't a community of feeling basically Catholic (or basically Jewish). Nor is it something welling up from below to take form from the fixed religious symbols employed. The symbols are no longer fixed; the business of criticism becomes difficult, inconclusive, delicate and undogmatic in its treatment of symbolism.

Mr O'Brien has a good critic's perceptions of the unique order of a work of art, but, for all his disclaimers, he generalises from them, then moves off into propaganda. Contesting Maritain, he might also have pondered Newman, who said that literature represents men as they are in themselves, 'quite independent of any extraordinary aid from Heaven, or any definite religious belief . . . it is the Life and Remains of the *natural* man.' To bring in the cross on the ground that natural lust is a type of the Passion is to use an archaism in order to bring in by the back door the pious edifying which he himself had thrown out of the front.

(1963)

III. THIS TIME, THAT TIME

The original function of myths, some say, was the maintenance of social stability by the recall of absolutely true stories which explained how things came to be as they were. This is not, in our place and time, a use for myths; and whenever somebody tries to employ them for social or political purposes we expect mischief. As Hannah Arendt observed, the Nazi myth was an instance of something very modern, namely the power of an invention, however absurd on the face of it, to win credence by succeeding in the world. It is no longer necessary for myths to be true. The history of this change goes a long way back, more than 2,000 years in fact, to the point where the word itself began to be associated with lies rather than with truth. But what gave myth its modern prestige? One landmark is Nietzsche's attack on Socrates, destroyer of *die schöne Welt* of the Greek Dionysus by means of his overdeveloped logical power. In a Nietzschean world of fictions, myths regain status; but they have still no real *use*, as they had for the archaic believer.

The story of the rehabilitation of myths for their use in explaining not only archaic societies but the dark side of the modern mind is familiar: it is a different, and essentially post-Nietzschean story. It is still in progress, and the development is multiple; but it's enough to think about the current Freudian and Jungian theories. Modern orthodox Freudians, I gather, have a standard revised version of *Totem and Taboo*: they say that myth, the verbal accompaniment of ritual, has been transmitted continuously by the folk (a way out of the awkward 'memory traces' of the master) and that we have archaic needs and expectations which the myths still, in modern symbolic forms, satisfy. Jungians have not, of course, given up the 'archaic remnants' or archetypes; they use them in the consulting-room and in the study. Both schools are committed to explanation in terms of hypothetical archaic origins, but the Freudians are more rationalist and more tragic, too. They are also, though Jungians argue the contrary, less reductive—they dismiss less lightly the obvious truth that the literature and art they are talking about differ from rites and myths more strikingly than they resemble them, and that much of their value lies in these differences. Nevertheless, a good Freudian might admit that if you had perfect analytical techniques you could do without art altogether, since although it is an honest doctor and tells the awful truth, it is inferior as a healer if only because of its irrelevant interests. Jungians do not say this, which explains their pull.

A yearning for ritualistic satisfactions can have a bad effect in literature as well as in politics, and it is a common enough complaint that the search in novels for mythical order reduces their existential complexity. It remains something of a mystery, this anachronistic myth-hunt. The problems are real enough; they have engaged some good minds, notably Sartre's. Yet the distinction between 'myth: a false account portraying truth' and 'narrative: an account descriptive of events which took place or might have taken place' is 1,800 years old. Why do we mix them up again?

The answer of Mircea Eliade would be that we are terrified of time as we now experience it. Myths take place in quite a different order of time—*in illo tempore*, as Eliade says. *Then* occurred the events decisive as to the way things are; and the only way to get at *illud tempus* is by ritual re-enactment. But here and now, *in hoc tempore*, we are certain only of the dismal linearity of time, the impossibility of re-enactment. Our fictions, as distinct from myths, have a Judaeo-Christian linearity too—beginnings, middles and ends in time. If we are 'dissociated,' it was this change of times that did it; the Bible and Greek reason must be to blame. But anyway that is how things are, and if we long for myth and *illud tempus* it is because we cannot stand the here and now we have. Our fictions are not naturally mythic, and the time they take place in is historic time. This remains true, however they may try to escape time by occult structural devices, repetitions, spatial form. Fictions provide new knowledge; they cognise, myths recognise. If they are dreamlike we require them, in Lamb's phrase, 'to be ratified by the waking judgment.'

Eliade is a most informative guide to the modern mythologies. Two of his books, not previously published in England, are now available.[1] One is an early and exhaustive study of shamanism, the other a summary of his thought and its implications. *Shamanism* must have been the groundwork on which large parts of the later speculative books are founded; though addressed to the non-specialist it carries a huge load of learned references and exhibits great rigour of method. Shamans are specialists in obtaining access to *illud tempus*. From Tibet to Siberia, from

---

[1] *Shamanism: Archaic Techniques of Ecstasy* (London, Routledge; New York, Pantheon). *Myth and Reality* (London, Allen & Unwin; New York, Harper).

North America to Oceania, their ecstasies have much in common. The shaman's vocation involves suffering; he undergoes initiation; his language is secret; his costume is sacred and symbolic; his dream enables him to descend to the underworld, and he climbs a tree in order to ascend to heaven. His ecstasy, a mythical possession, is achieved by a discipline of sanctity, and re-enacts *illud tempus*. The analogues with mystical experience in general, with epic poetry, and with myth and fairy-tale, are obvious. Eliade regards the shaman's 'pre-ecstatic euphoria' as a universal source of lyric poetry, his account of the underworld journey as the source of epic. Even his seance has a primordial dramatic structure, and his secret language is the original language of poetry.

That all this can be true and the fact remain that the shamanic ecstasy tells us very little about *our* life and literature Eliade perfectly understands. His *Myth and Reality* sharply distinguishes myth from history, *that* time from this, the indefinitely repeatable from the once-for-all creation and act. Our beginning, whatever it was, happened and was done with; our end will be total, without renewal. It is harder for us to ruin the great work of time than for the shaman; we cannot abolish and remake the world, all we can do is to remember the origins. Hence our intense preoccupation with history, and our invention of psychoanalysis. We are as much concerned with historical events, whether political or infantile, or even uterine, as primitive man with myth. But history, we feel, is of this time, and a less effective remedy for the pain of the present than myth could provide. So, having de-sacralised the world, we yearn for the myths from which we have dissociated ourselves. Eliade is alert to this situation, and finds it tragic, without, I think, ever saying it is our fault, which dissociation theories usually do. I myself don't see why we should have a preference for archaic over modern in men; the style, simply, is different, as in statues and pots. But Eliade gives the whole subject a valuable and comprehensive new look, and this book could be as influential as Jane Harrison's *Art and Ritual* once was.

To heal the dissociation, to bring together parts of the suffering individual which belong to that and this time, and thus to make him happy, is the aim of the Jungian therapy. It holds, crudely speaking, that we get sick, not so much because of what had to be done to make us civilised, but because we get out of touch with the primitive psychic element that continues to live in the other time. These two aspects of our personalities are so different as to be at times antithetical; the hidden one can register itself in sometimes alarming ways, yet only if we listen to it can we achieve integrity of personality. But this can be done, and the Jungian therapist undertakes to do it. The rewards are great, the integrated man is good. Freud is the Augustine, Jung the Pelagius of psychotherapy.

A vast, extraordinary book,[1] a third of it by Jung, the rest filled in to his plan by colleagues, and the whole strained through Mr John Freeman in his capacity as 'intelligibility filter,' sets out to provide a simple but authoritative outline of the Doctrine. The contributors are assisted by many hundreds of spectacularly good illustrations, which flaunt themselves below and across the text. Serious popularisation is so great a need that one hesitates to criticise, but this diversification by picture and caption can be confusing rather than helpful. When the text is about dreams and painting the pictures are valuable, and the subject being what it is we also need alchemical woodcuts and Hindu objects. But does the point that there is a difference between the lion a witch-doctor in a mask thinks he is, and a real-life lion, need both a picture of a masked witch-doctor and a photograph of the entry under 'lion' in a dictionary? The educational theory involved, that instruction is always better when related to matters more or less remote from the subject, and set up with as much display as is consistent with its conveyance, reminds one of other contemporary educational phenomena: it is for all the world like one of the new universities.

However, the text itself puts the whole matter pretty clearly. Jung, as Mr Freeman explains, had not at first wanted to do the book, but he changed his mind after a dream about explaining his work to a large audience, and undertook to write it with collaborators of his choice. It was his last work. Jung, judging from translation, was not a notable writer of prose, and he was not a gifted expositor. Mr Freeman comments on the typical spiralling argument by which he presents the case that 'man becomes whole, integrated, calm, fertile and happy when (and

[1] *Man and His Symbols*. Edited by C. G. Jung, M-L. Von Franz and John Freeman (London, Aldus; Garden City, New York, Doubleday).

only when) the process of individuation is complete.' The exposition involves rum arguments. The word 'misoneist,' which he
applies to his critics, could be used by the proponent of any
foolishness whatever, and allows the inference that what is new
cannot be false. The notion of 'synchronicity' as here expounded
we can also, so far as I can see, manage without; it distinguishes
significant from insignificant coincidences, but is only a way of
dignifying coincidences you find interesting at the expense of
those you don't. There is, as I see it, a more palpable evasiveness in the part about precognition by dreams—'it was as if
future events were casting' etc. Either they *were*, or the whole
thing is not worth mentioning. The whole discussion of archetypes seems somehow shifty. They occur universally, and with
such sharpness of definition that a patient can be told not to
worry and shown a figure from his dream in a 16th-century
alchemical text he had never heard of. Yet they are various,
interchangeable, hard to descry, 'contaminated by unconscious
contents,' and anyway unintelligible except in the patient's own
psychic context. 'The dream is its own interpretation'—so what
use was the alchemical woodcut? There are difficulties here not
fully explained for the layman, however open-minded, however
much apart from that mysteriously large public who, according
to Jung, believe that 'what we know today is all we can know.'

What comes through strongly is the notion of bringing together the dissociated personality by analysis, and the Jungian
interpretation of dreams. The identification of mythic material
in dreams is interesting but difficult to control, and so are attendant generalisations about the modern world, as when we are
advised to see our own 'evil shadow' behind the Iron Curtain.
M-L. von Franz tells of a girl, a suicide at 26, who had a childhood dream of being pinched in the stomach by Jack Frost.
'From this single dream it is possible to deduce the fate of the
dreamer.' Maybe—afterwards. There is some attempt to share
the prestige of physics by relating the apparent contradictions in
the theory to the Principle of Complementarity, but that is a
principle arising from insurmountable limitations and the
humility these induce in observers, and the less exact sciences
should be chary of imitating it.

This is not the best showing Jung could have had. His
primitive may, like this book, be rich, highly coloured, and

accessible to modern shamans. The reward offered to the diligent is high: happiness, no less. But we must not forget that we live in this, not in that, time.

(1964)

IV. TIME OF YOUR LIFE

Time seems to be in the fashion; having a while ago started to take a special interest in it for what I like to think of as impeccably scholarly purposes, I keep stumbling on books and lecture-series and conversations about 'time's arrow' and so forth, so that it looks as if to be 'Time-haunted,' a word Mr Priestley uses of himself, has become the complaint to have.

The symptoms in his case are copious and graphic; this is a big double-column book[1] with a text, dutifully or compulsively chatty, into which spectacular and more or less relevant photographs irrupt continually. Unperturbed, the author continues with placid thoroughness to discourse on all manner of time-problems; he is a sort of latter-day Addison, an intelligent and urbane middleman with his legs under the coffeehouse table, retailing for the layman his more or less informed views on St Augustine, McTaggart, clocks, and calendars. At one point he humorously observes that the book should probably have been written by somebody else, and it is true that if you are prepared to accept a little less *belles-lettres* in the mix you can do better elsewhere.

All the same Priestley is readable, and he injects a certain urgency by making no secret of the fact that he thinks the subject a matter of life and death. So, of course, it literally is. But it is precisely when he is most serious that he drifts off into quasi-philosophical doodling. Admittedly the difficulties are daunting; some of them are outside the range of everybody except theoretical physicists. But we can cheer ourselves up by believing that all that kind of thing has nothing to do with time as human beings invent or experience it. Anybody can be Time-haunted; the question is, who wants to be, and why?

Sometimes it seems that we may be experiencing, a little prematurely, that convergence of historiographical myths which sometimes happens at the end of a century, and which is sometimes called *fin-de-siècle*, or, in Oscar Wilde's more extravagant

[1] *Man and Time.* Doubleday.

phrase, *fin du globe*. Somehow it seems acceptable to believe that we, of all people, are in the final age of transition before the ultimate count-down, our drab nuclear apocalypse; hence the resurgence of various eschatological myths, such as decadence and imperialism. The beauty of an historical crisis (and it is some time since we have been able to manage without one) is that it gives you a Pisgah from which to observe the predetermined but inscrutable future. Nobody else has ever been so given to screwing up the stuff of chronology into bundles of crisis as we are. And we suppose that we have the right to call ours the real crisis, if only because we can blow the trumpet ourselves. Since we put nothing after the bang—no millennium—we really have a very final end to think about, with possibly only a very short time in between. And over this time we should like to have some prophetic control; not only is it all we have, it also affects our life in the precious here and now.

Do you believe in what Priestley calls 'the F.I.P. effect' (Future Influencing Present)? Of course you do; our apocalypse shapes our lives, whether it's going to happen or not, as apocalypses have always done. And this is, surely, a hint as to the way the future influences the present in less grandiose affairs. We put probabilities to work in the gap between now and the end; we have also images of that end, endowed with more or less of the clarity of a Jesuit meditation. The image we have may turn out to be wrong; we may end unusually, smothered with cassia or shot to death with pearls; but the picture we have—say of an emaciated figure plucking at the covers—has still an emblematic truth, and a powerful F.I.P. effect. Furthermore, the more often you dream about your own or somebody else's death, the more likely you are to get it right, and of course if you have clues—if your husband is a spy or a heavy smoker, for instance—your chance is quite good, you may have an F.I.P. dream any night.

But death, being a certainty, is of small interest if you are looking for a theory of predictive dreaming. It is the trivial predictions that count. And what really interests Mr Priestley, though he spends most of his space rather nobly doing Time, is the improbable dream which comes true. So he tries to put the skeptics' case as fairly as possible, and then comes up with the oddest dreams-come-true he can find. Some are his own, and some are from people whose honesty cannot possibly be challenged. But what we should really need, if we were going to be scientific about this, is a full account of a dream written down and authenticated *before* events confirmed it—in the 'Thirties we were all urged by F. P. Dunne in his then very fashionable *Experiment with Time* to keep a notebook by our beds for exactly this purpose—and this is, alas, hard to find. Even with such an authenticated account one has room left for skepticism. Some dreams discussed by Priestley are rather likely to occur—a driver's dream of killing a child, a vacationing mother's of seeing her baby drowned. We all dream a lot, and that makes millions of dreams, so that some of them working out to the last improbable detail is no stranger than that somebody always wins a lottery. Priestley asked a television audience, presumed to be over a million, to send him predictive dreams, so he was, as it were, buying a lot of tickets. He should have got a few real stunners, and he did; but in no case was the dream recorded before the confirmation, and with the best will in the world people can hardly have avoided reading the event back into the dream.

What struck me about his correspondents was their simplicity. All the letters speak of events exactly like the events of the dream. This is surely a modern naiveté; older dreaming was more complex, more oracular, producing interesting rival interpretations and possessing large symbolic contents. This is true at an apparently unsophisticated level. I remember how my mother, a country girl, would be pleased at some trivial occurrence— say, a pedlar coming to the door—and say, 'Ah, that broke my dream.' It must have been a dream of indefinable significance, which some event could prove trivial and powerless. There is a folk notion, too, of dreams coming true by contraries: if you dream of a wedding there will be a funeral. This suggests at least an inkling that the temporal confirmation of dreams is likely to be obscure and in need of interpretation. Among the learned the whole problem, until quite recently, was considered in terms of the distinction between the good and the evil dream, *somnium* and *phantasma*; so that there is an equivocality built into the tradition. Shakespeare, who knew this distinction, learned the uses of equivocation. In the early history-plays people, Queen Margaret, for example, can prophesy the dynastic developments of the next couple of generations with the uncanny accuracy of seers vouchsafed a glimpse at a proof copy of Holinshed; in *Macbeth* prophecies quiver with equivocation from the first line, and indeed equivocation becomes the subject of the play. Dreams, after all, are fictions; and our most ordinary fictions use this basic equivocation. In its mechanical form you can watch it on *Perry Mason*—somebody will say 'I'll kill you for this,' and the person threatened will surely soon be dead, but not at the hand of the threatener. The odd thing is that Mr Priestley's correspondents fall below this level of smartness, and the only equivocating is in the slight margin of error the dream prophecies seem to leave: you dream your baby drowns, and he very nearly does.

It is about this equivocation that Priestley theorises. Years ago he took Dunne very seriously, but he now rejects the general theory proposed by that interesting figure because he is made giddy by the doctrine of an infinite regress of time-observers. This was actually an attempt to solve an old philosophical puzzle concerning the flow of time: time itself measures a flow of events, so what measures time must be another kind of time, and so on infinitely. Dunne hypostasised this regress as multi-dimensional time, which each of us may experience in any dimension; and so he explained predictive dreams. Priestley turns this down largely because he doesn't like it, and because he can handle three dimensions of time more comfortably. Here he seeks support from the disciples of Ouspensky, who give Time three dimensions to correspond to those of space, calling them the fourth, fifth and sixth dimensions of reality.

Three Times have their uses, no doubt: one for ordinary experience, one for achronic insights, one for the mystic's time, the *nunc stans*. And three is the number time-theorists have lighted on again and again; it clearly is the comfortable number, though large questions are involved in the supposition that it is therefore descriptive of an impersonal cosmos. Three, in short, is no truer, only more convenient, than eight or seventy-two. But it does come in handy when you tackle specific problems such as Priestley's worry about the degree to which action based on prophetic dreams can forestall the evil there predicated; he has workable counters, Times A, B, and C as he calls them, and he uses them to explain not only why we can foresee, but why we can prevent what is to come. Each of us is, if only fitfully, a

Laplace endowed with the power to apprehend a nature in which what is pre-determined may also be prevented; we have, in some curiously limited way, the power to observe what shall have happened and produce a situation in which we can say that it has not happened. I put it thus because, all questions of the validity of the evidence aside, there is much that is merely verbal in these problems, and it seems unlikely that they will be solved by the free invention of categories which serve no other purpose than to solve them.

Although his defence of three-dimensional time is amiable in tone, Priestley occasionally develops a curiously Calvinistic fervour in his comments on those who do not accept it. They are 'trapped in a barren concept of time,' he says, in an impoverished unilinearity. Actually, modern temporal attitudes are extremely sophisticated and various: archaeologists, anthropologists, art-historians, physicists, factory managers, athletes, all use variant models. But for Priestley this is all thin poor stuff in comparison with Indian recurrence theories, which he is willing to take to their vain and repulsive conclusions (a suicide is buying himself not release but cycles of infernal misery). When myths turn into dogmas they become capable of inflicting wretchedness in so far as they can impose acceptance. I don't care who believes that human consciousness survives in Time Two, and that we have access, in Time Three, to *illud tempus* of myth, this is only another fantastic *fin de siècle* scheme, like Mme Blavatsky's. But when Mr Priestley, on the strength of it, sends the 'wicked' to hell, I know this isn't the world I want, or even a fiction I condone. So it is fortunate that, if I may adapt an old remark of Bertrand Russell's, the reasons for believing in Time Two are exactly as good as those for believing in Santa Claus.

One more word, in fairness, about precognitive dreams. The one that stopped me came from Sir Stephen King-Hall, a most reasonable and intelligent man. In 1916 he was officer of the watch in a cruiser steaming into Scapa Flow. He saw an island a mile ahead, and knew a man would go overboard when they passed it. The moment was entirely inauspicious, as they were about to anchor, but King-Hall ordered the sea-boat made ready, and took other precautions; a man fell overboard, not from his ship but from the one behind; and thirty seconds later another from the ship behind that. King-Hall in a sense risked

his career to play a hunch. I suppose everybody knows the kind
of feeling he must have had; what is impressive is its force. There
may have been circumstances, though he did not notice them
consciously, that made the event more probable (it is not altogether uncommon; I myself saw it happen four times in five
years). Still, it defeats me. But I won't believe in six dimensions to
explain it; I'd rather call it simply 'inexplicable.'

(1965)

V. THE OLD AMALAKI

'I must say, you make the whole thing sound crashingly dull.'
This is what the dissolute Paul says to Christopher in *Down
There on a Visit*, in response to the latter's attempt to explain
Vedantist techniques of meditation. In the end Paul properly
launched in holiness by the guru Parr, turns out to be something
of a saint, a very camp saint admittedly, but an Isherwood holy
man needs to be so. Until Susan Sontag wrote about it in
Partisan Review, the standard treatment of camp was the analysis
in *The World in the Evening*, and one foresaw in this new book[1] a
final apotheosis of camp; but it turns out after all to be crashingly
dull.

(It is possible that some readers have missed the Sontag article
and even that they haven't missed it but failed to understand it.
It may therefore be useful to give a brief account of the *locus
classicus* in Isherwood's novel. Stephen has a friend who explains
the word 'camp.' First he says that 'a swishy little boy with per-
oxided hair, dressed in a picture hat and a feather boa' is the kind
of thing called 'camp' in 'queer circles,' but it is 'an utterly
debased form,' or Low Camp. High Camp is: the ballet, Baroque
art—camp about love, camp about religion; Mozart rather than
Beethoven, El Greco rather than Rembrandt, Dostoevsky rather
than Flaubert. 'Camping' is 'expressing what's basically serious
to you in terms of fun and elegance.' The relevant part of the
discussion ends with the observation that you can't really define
camp:

You have to mediate on it and feel it intuitively, like Lao-Tze's
Tao. Once you've done that, you'll find yourself wanting to use the
word whenever you discuss aesthetics or philosophy or almost
anything. I never can understand how critics manage to do without it.

[1] Christopher Isherwood; *Ramakrishna and His Disciples* Simon & Schuster.

It will be obvious that the word 'camp' in this review is used in the Isherwood sense of High Camp, give or take a little inevitable contamination by the feather-boa sense, which may well have been the original, sublimed though it now is by Isherwood's efforts.)

Not that Sri Ramakrishna isn't High Camp, a real Isherwood character. He was called Paramahansa, which means 'great goose,' though as a name of Vishnu it connotes 'divine.' Mr Isherwood doesn't actually mention this, but the mingling of holiness and folly is what attracts him. Ramakrishna was a highly paradoxical figure, reckoned a profound teacher though ignorant of Sanskrit, English, and even of the higher Bengali literature; a man of perfect life though a transvestite, and something of a coquette; and a stickler for the ritual observances and customs of caste, which as an avatar he might have been expected to transcend. He told animal stories and played jokes, yet at any moment might fall into ecstasy. He reminds one that the word 'silly' used to mean 'holy,' and also that there is a strong camp element in Christianity and in the parables. Ramakrishna was strongly attracted to Christianity and had a vision of Jesus. He would certainly have admired and understood the last section of Erasmus's *Praise of Folly*.

Mr Isherwood isn't, in this book, merely 'down there on a visit'; he is deeply involved. Ramakrishna, even if one leaves out the doctrine, is clearly in his sweetness and silliness an Isherwood person, and one might have expected that he would try to give the reader some intuition of the sanctity of this god-man by camping him, however subtly and reverently. But he goes beyond camp; the camera is focused on the official Life and the Gospels, the style sweetly plain and expository. The book is scripture or hagiography depending on your view of the subject. The standard *Life* of Ramakrishna is a five-volume work in Bengali, but there are several authoritative works in English based upon it, and the degree of Isherwood's dependence may be judged by comparing a passage in his book with the parallel in the Adyaita Ashrama *Life* of 1925. The Indian work says of the disciple Totapuri:

Endowed with an iron constitution, Totapuri was never troubled with complaints of the body. He had a good digestion and always enjoyed sound sleep. . . . But after a few months' stay in Bengal he

could feel the enervating influence of its climate, and even his strong
physique became a prey to a virulent attack of dysentery. . . . Even
before the attack he had marked that the climate was not suiting him
and that he must move. But he could not persuade himself to forego
the blissful company of Sri Ramakrishna. . . . But as the symptoms of
disease began to manifest in his body . . . the desire to quit Dak-
shinewar became stronger, but something or other prevented him
from raising the topic before Sri Ramakrishna and asking his leave.
Seeing him get emaciated Sri Ramakrishna arranged for a good diet
and sundry medicines for him, but it was of no use. . . . He got dis-
gusted with his body and thought, 'Owing to this wretched body,
even my mind is not under control. So why should I associate any
more with this rotten thing and suffer its pain? . . . I must sacrifice it
in the Ganges. . . .' Totapuri carefully concentrated his mind on
Brahman and slowly advanced into the water. But what was this!
Was the Ganges really dry tonight? etc.

Totapuri walks across to the other bank and back, meditating
on the freaks of Maya and the power of the Divine Mother. In
Isherwood the whole thing is shortened and revised:

Tota's constitution had always been strong. He had had little
experience of the miseries of physical life, the aches and pains which
distract the mind from contemplation. But now the climate and the
water of Bengal began to affect him; and he had a severe attack of
blood dysentery. At the first warnings of the disease, he decided he
should go away; but he found himself unwilling to leave the company
of Ramakrishna, to whom he had become devoted. Several times, he
made up his mind to go to Ramakrishna and bid him Goodbye; but
as soon as the two were together, they would become absorbed in
talk about God and he would forget his purpose. So he grew
steadily weaker and weaker despite the medicines which Ramakrishna obtained for him. . . . He was filled with disgust for his body.
'I must get rid of this nuisance,' he said to himself. 'Why do I stay and
suffer? I'll commit it to the Ganges.'

Tota does his double traverse of the river; Isherwood adds a
remark by Ramakrishna to the effect that he must have
'chanced to walk along a shoal which ran out from the bank.'

Obviously it is not only the logia that come out more or less
verbatim but the narrative itself, as in the Synoptic Gospels;
there are many other instances, some of them, like the one of
Ramakrishna's trial of Narendra Nath, even more closely
parallel. Yet, as between the Synoptic Gospels, there are

differences, and not only the differences caused by Isherwood's
need to compress. There is, for instance, the rational explanation
of the miracle. Another example of this is Isherwood's account
of the birth of Ramakrishna. In the traditional account the baby,
while the midwife was attending to the mother, 'slipped into the
adjacent oven.' In Isherwood it merely 'rolled across the floor'
and was found 'lying among the ashes of the fireplace.' Still,
Isherwood isn't so skeptical as not to accept Ramakrishna's
parthenogenetical conception, or Shiva's annunciation to the
mother, or the dispute with the Doctors, or the horoscope. In
fact he argues for the credibility of these events, apologising
only for making everything sound 'a little too sweet.'

What makes this different from medieval *acta sanctorum* is
simply that it can't help being sophisticated: *credo quia non
probabile.* When an Isherwood writes naïvely—Ramakrishna's
parents 'worried over their latest child just as much as any other
couple' despite the visions and the horoscope, but 'their anxiety
proved groundless, however'—we can't avoid the feeling that
maya is having a joke with us. The sort of joke Ramakrishna
plays on Durgadas Pyne by disguising as a woman, when 'even
Durgadas Pyne had to laugh at the joke against him.' But the
whole book is written in this for-the-children manner, except
when it gives solemn explanation of the Hindu terminology—
Brahman, Atman, etc.—or social system (caste is not the social
menace you probably think it). It is partly the fault of good
writers like Isherwood that we can't take seriously this pious
Western version of the holy story. It lacks all irony, all criticism.
'Anyone who meditates beneath an amalaki tree will have his
dearest wish fulfilled,' we are assured. When Ramakrishna imitated Hanuman, a monkey devotee of Rama, his spine grew an
inch in length. If you are tempted not to believe this, remember
that Ramakrishna and his disciples thought it vile to lie. For the
same reason you have to believe him when he says he is an
avatar of Vishnu. 'Many people,' observes Mr Isherwood rather
mysteriously, 'meet a Jesus or a Ramakrishna and regard him
as entirely ordinary, because of the grossness of their own
perceptions.'

It is in such terms as these that the book presents the Indian
god-man. He had transcended our grossness, was 'simultaneously aware of God and the universe,' and acted always on

licenses what Arnold called 'the dissidence of dissent.' Yet another reason may be the ambiguities inherent in Hindu doctrines on sex. Ramakrishna is said to have undergone the Tantric disciplines without lapsing into depravity; the dangers of doing so, or seeming to do so, are illustrated by *Lady Chatterley's Lover*, where Mellors's sevenfold arousing of Connie's *kundalini* has often been misinterpreted. Eliade's book shows how the borderline between sexual depravity and high Tantric achievement is as vague as that between yoga and magic. It is one thing to acquire *pranyama*, which has to do with retaining the breath, and another to acquire *maithuna*, the retention of semen in intercourse; the former requires only solitary practice. Lastly, the sheer permissiveness of Ramakrishna's religion blends interestingly with his personal austerity: drugs, sex, kicks of all kinds, can be somebody's 'way.'

Given this permissiveness, this inclusiveness, this interesting ambiguity, one can see how Western irrationalism and antinomianism continue to be receptive to Ramakrishna's kind of religion. I admit that I am incapable of a sympathetic appreciation of the phenomenon Mr Isherwood describes, but somebody, surely, is entitled to address the opposition—the party that believes the West is committed to reason, and that it will never find its salvation by embarking, with however much protective camp, in a ship of fools, however holy.

(1965)

Chapter Three

POETS

VI. ALLUSIONS TO OMAR

'Try to find out why the FitzGerald *Rubaiyat* has gone into so many editions after having lain unnoticed until Rossetti found a pile of remaindered copies on a second-hand bookstall.' This is one of the exercises recommended by Ezra Pound in the *ABC of Reading*. I suppose Pound's answer would adduce FitzGerald's importance as a prosodist, since he includes him in a list of twenty-four poets 'through whom the metamorphosis of English verse may be traced'—among the others, it may be recalled, are Villon, Mark Alex. Boyd, Samuel Butler, Crabbe, Whitman and Corbière.

FitzGerald was certainly an accomplished 'maker.' He could write blank verse, as some of his Calderon translations and the more resonant bits of his *Agamemnon* show. The rhymed pentameters of the Persian *Bird Parliament*, and the lyric stanzas scattered through the other Persian translations, testify to skill, accuracy and taste—qualities which were tested by his experiments with the Omar stanza, which he adapted to English with much subtlety. Pound would have a soft spot for a man who could do that, and who also saw that there was an art of mistranslation, and that a live sparrow is better than a stuffed eagle. His *Agamemnon*, as FitzGerald himself remarks, is a 'per-version' —but he was right in thinking that it proved his 'faculty of making some things readable which others have hitherto left unreadable.' There is a modern version of the *Agamemnon* which I have long kept in mind as a touchstone—I mean, as a way of finding merit in other translations which show themselves to be, at any rate, not as bad. FitzGerald comes out of this very well:

> The wary merchant overboard
> Flings something of his precious hoard
> To pacify the jealous eye . . .

is, without being wonderful, better than

> A due tithe of his corded bales
> From no parsimonious winch
> The pious master to the deep devotes.

Nobody will get a scholar's idea of Aeschylus or Calderon (with whom FitzGerald is very free) or of Jámi from Fitz-Gerald's allusions to them; you can see why he might be held to have given rise to Pound.

For all that, the true answer to Pound's question is quite different. The *Rubaiyat* didn't lie unread for long. The first edition was published in 1859, the second in 1868; by 1872 the book was widely sought for, and Quaritch was asking the modestly anonymous author for a third edition. Its admirers included Ruskin, Swinburne, Burne-Jones, Morris and Rossetti. Charles Eliot Norton had started an American vogue. And surely it fits well enough with a Morrisian view of leisure, of a decorativeness that refreshes amid the nastiness of the real world in the 1860s? The book came out in the year of *The Origin of Species* and Smiles's *Self-Help*; it reached popularity in the decade of *Culture and Anarchy*. These are G. M. Young's 'years of division,' the frontier between two Victorian ages; and the *Rubaiyat* belong to the hither, nastier side, which is, nevertheless, the side of Pater and Swinburne and Whistler and *The Earthly Paradise*. More and more people were in the mood for a Persian garden. 'Omar's Epicurean Audacity of Thought and Speech,' which hindered his reputation in Persia, did not, as the translator's learned friend Cowell feared, upset the English, who are quick to domesticate the exotic. Worse things are heard in the Palm Court, as in the more vigorously antinomian moments of *The Vagabond King*. Besides, Omar, for all his subtlety, is often open to the comment 'How true!' I think I first heard the lines about the moving finger from a Methodist pulpit—not Calvinistic Methodist either—so that the word 'piety' spoilt the relevance, and might have given rise to doctrinal frissons if anybody had been listening; but nobody was. Omar Khayyám simply joins the list of approved burgher escape-myths. The fame of his accomplished translator is an enormous accident.

Miss Joanna Richardson has compiled a FitzGerald anthology[1] with the first and fourth version of Omar, and specimens of his Spanish, Greek, Latin, Italian, and other Persian translations, notably the brilliant *Bird Parliament*. She includes also the youthful dialogue *Euphranor*, and about three hundred pages of letters. There is material, in this carefully prepared selection, for speculation as to what kind of a man it was to whom the accident of Omar happened. Miss Richardson makes rather large claims for the letters, comparing FitzGerald oddly with Keats, and calling him 'disarming' and 'childlike'—this second epithet is certainly odd. He was excessively complicated, it seems to me.

Despite his father's mining speculations, FitzGerald had a good income and a very grand mother, whose house in Portland Place he visited as little as possible. He never took his friends there. Although these were frequently well-known men—Thackeray, Tennyson, Carlyle—FitzGerald had known them at school or at Cambridge or in some context that had nothing to do with their fame. Although he liked the opera and the galleries, he chose to live in Suffolk with a parrot and a housekeeper and—as everybody knows from *Gerontion*—a boy to read to him. This, he said, was the life for him: 'a pirated copy of the peace of God.' He had, he wrote, 'a talent for dulness which no situation nor intercourse could much improve. . . . I really do like to sit in this doleful place with a good fire, a cat and dog on the rug, and an old woman in the kitchen.' He wrote letters and translations, walked and sailed, saw something of his literate neighbours, and had a deep affection for a fisherman called Posh Fletcher. He wasn't, obviously, guilty of any great degree of self-deception. 'You think I live in Epicurean ease,' he says to a correspondent:

but this happens to be a jolly day. One isn't always well, or tolerably good; the weather is not always clear, nor nightingales singing, nor Tacitus full of pleasant atrocity. But such as life is, I believe I have got hold of a good end of it.

The biggest disturbance of his life was marriage, at nearly

[1] *Selected Works* (London, Hart-Davis; Cambridge, Mass., Harvard).

fifty and sorely against his nature, to the daughter of a dead friend. This union ended almost at once. The success of Omar meant very little to him. He cared deeply for his friends, and quarrelled little; it was a consequence of an editorial inadvertency that Browning was mortally offended by his facetious remark about being glad Mrs Browning was dead, and that was years after FitzGerald's own death.

Such a life is treated, not surprisingly, with affectionate mildness by commentators. The standard *Life*, Terhune's, is a long and thorough book, but the whole work conveys less suggestion of unease than a modern reader might get from knowing the source of the opening of *Gerontion*. Yet surely there is unease? Consider FitzGerald's fear of travel, which was almost farcical. At 33 he found the prospect of a journey to Italy delightful but far too alarming. In his fifties he risked a voyage to Holland to see the pictures, found the Hague gallery closed, but could not wait, and after two days sailed back: 'Oh my Delight when I heard them call out "Orford Lights!" as the boat was plunging over the Swell . . . it is the last foreign Travel I shall ever undertake.' How curious that a man so much in favour of art and activity should behave so! For, under his modesty, his air of *dolce far niente*, FitzGerald wasn't at all the usual English learned recluse. His views on education, for instance, as set forth in *Euphranor*, are Gordonstounian: gentlemen should be active and practical and in 'good animal Condition.' He argued that Tennyson might not have gone off had he 'lived an active Life, as Scott and Shakespeare; or even ridden, shot, drunk, and played the Devil, as Byron.' He never ceased to blame his friend Spedding for devoting his time to the unworthy task of editing Bacon. Yet he himself led a deliberately *lowering* existence: from early days he experimented with a reduced diet, drank little, moved little, confined his literary activity to what he thought of as marginal work. Under the mask of kind old Fitz there must have been a very different face.

If more were known of his relation with his mother it might be easier to make guesses about the marriage and the pointless self-denial. But even his verse is part of the mask—all translation, all from an alien mouth. The Omar translation followed immediately on his breach with his wife. He might, behind that mask, have spoken out; but he seldom does so, and when he does foist an opinion into the Persian, it is the Housmanian

> For all the Sin wherewith the Face of Man
> Is blacken'd, Man's forgiveness give—and take.

Perhaps FitzGerald is a type, after all; the name of Housman suggests it, and as I write it occurs to me that E. H. W. Meyerstein, as we know from John Wain's superb memoir, had some of the same characteristics, only in a more tragic mode.

If celibacy and solitariness were a way of suffering, they also provided some of the means of creating. FitzGerald's exceptional taste alone makes him somewhat solitary. He anticipated the Pre-Raphaelite love for Blake, and possessed a *Job*. He was expert in Constable. Once he amused himself by buying an Opie for £4, and repainting it. He played the piano well. His literary taste was idiosyncratic. He respected Carlyle, but thought his depth a matter of seeming, not of reality, and disliked the prose: 'no repose, nor equable movement . . . one labours through it as vessels do through what is called a short sea.' Tennyson, one of his greatest friends, he thought to have wasted his gift. He admired Wordsworth without love. The 'Gurgoyle school'— Hugo and Browning—he detested for its ugly modernity. He thought Jane Austen trivial beside Thackeray, and most admired Scott, largely for his gentlemanly dash or *sprezzatura*. Such a catalogue fails to convey that Spedding was not entirely wrong when he said that his friend's 'judgments on matters of art,' though 'very strange and wayward,' were original, profound and luminous. 'I pretend to no Genius, but to Taste,' he said, 'which is the feminine of Genius.' In a letter to Cowell we find him wondering whether in 1847 poets can possibly compete with scientists in the creation of wonder, finding Lyell's observations on Niagara 'more wonderful than all the conceptions of Dante and Milton.' *In Memoriam*, which tried to get some of this in, he disliked. The age was closing in on poetry; it seemed harder for art to possess that quality he admired above everything and called 'Go.'

'Go' is what he lacked himself; in the midst of the Omar translation he told Cowell 'My "*Go*" (such as it was) is *gone*, and it becomes *Work*.' He certainly laboured over the *Rubaiyat*. Another man might have hoped that they had, as some scholars thought, a mystical meaning to make the labour worth while;

for FitzGerald, rightly as it seems, 'the Wine Omar celebrates is simply the Juice of the Grape.' The mystical allegories of Persian poetry—we see them in other translations of FitzGerald's—are not so alien to us as they might have been if English poetry had not undergone so many attacks of platonism; but they might well have interfered with the establishment of the Persian garden myth that has kept the poem popular.

Anyway, the *Work* of FitzGerald was of a closer, more scholarly kind than guessing at allegory. We learn from Professor Arberry how he tackled the Persian verses, patching and stitching, developing and omitting. Where Omar asks for a loaf, a jug of wine, a sheep's thigh and a pretty boy, FitzGerald omits the meat, substitutes a 'Thou,' and introduces a poetry book (which no Persian scholar would need) and a Bough, which is not a property of Persian wildernesses. When we see that the translator's first prose shot said 'a bit of mutton and a moderate bottle of wine,' we become aware that, having left Persian poetry out, FitzGerald was putting English poetry in, and his changes obscurely touch the heart of a people which rarely reads verses and rarely drinks wine. He is exotic without being foreign.

For all his work, FitzGerald didn't know enough Persian to avoid slips; his 'Angel shape bearing a vessel on his shoulder' should be an old man rolling out of a pub. And what he loses is suggested by Arberry's excellent analysis of the opening quatrain: it is the complex of submerged senses in the original. Yet, as Arberry shows, FitzGerald replaces this by an independent development of the figures, itself of considerable ingenuity and power. The poem is an allusion to the *Rubaiyat*, a product of FitzGerald's good mid-Victorian talent under Persian stimulus. That is why it could eventually satisfy a public indifferent to the finesse of so foreign a poet as Omar.

(1962)

VII. AMATEUR OF GRIEF

Modern interest in the 'Nineties (Mauve, White, Naughty) is largely a matter of gossip, except when, as occasionally happens, somebody notices in them some forgotten but relevant aspect. Thus the well-known *fin de siècle* mood becomes a matter of interest when Mr Bergonzi relates it to a myth of *fin du globe*. This is an old notion, and perhaps because early apocalyptic numerology made the year 1000 such hell for everybody, it flourished at the ends of centuries. Certainly it did so at the end of the 19th in England, partly because there was natural worry about progress, and also a sense that the reign had gone on as long as it could or ought. But the idea that a *saeculum* is ending can occur at other times; Pope felt he lived at such a time, 1666 was a key year; and there is evidently some feeling at present that the age is too absurd to last, and that a new series of times will henceforth begin, with luck.

Half a century hence someone will put an authoritative finger on the names of the thinkers who shaped our *fin de siècle* myth; for the late 19th century this can be done easily, and among the principal figures are Schopenhauer, Nietzsche and Nordau ('there is a sound of rending in every tradition ... things as they are totter and plunge'). As to Schopenhauer, he has suffered a cumulative misrepresentation, and even in the 'Nineties was doubtless more often cited than read, as he is even now. Patrick Gardiner's substantial new introduction[1] is for that reason unusually welcome—not only does it clear away many surviving misconceptions, such as the confusion between Schopenhauer's Will and Nietzsche's will to power, but it also offers a forceful account of what this 'systematic half-thinker' actually wrote. There is a long and admirably lucid chapter on the philosopher's theory of art, central to his own thought and also extremely influential. This theory, and his slightly depressing views on sex, were together the parts of Schopenhauer which interested artists at the end of the century, and Mr Gardiner relates them so firmly to the whole body of his thought that merely literary people have lost their excuse for casual misunderstanding. Mr Gardiner emphasises the importance of Schopenhauer to Proust, but Proust inherited his interest from the previous generation of decadents. Anyway, Mr Gardiner's moderate claim that Schopenhauer's part in the establishment of modern thought is greater than many suppose seems justified.

Nordau, on the other hand, deserved what he got in the way of censure and neglect, though his linking sexual and literary decadence must have seemed plausible at the time; the notion of

[1] *Schopenhauer*. Penguin.

decadence, though of philological origin, easily shaded over into something like degeneracy, and some people may have cultivated, in the manner of the admired Verlaine, an almost deliberately self-destructive way of life. And then they could be written up to make them fit the myth even more exactly. Ernest Dowson is an obvious instance; and even if everybody gave up reading him he would still have this kind of importance, and remain in the picture of the period with far better writers like Wilde and Lionel Johnson.

His life was exceedingly wretched. In his youth the family property, a dry dock at Limehouse, was already going down because of the size of the new ships using the river, and as a patrimony it was hardly more useful to him than the predisposition to tuberculosis he seems to have inherited as well. His father, a man of taste, grew melancholy and died from an overdose of chloral; his mother hanged herself. Dowson as a child had travelled a good deal, but his education—up to his unsuccessful years at Oxford—was apparently random; and although he worked harder than the myth allows, translating for Smithers, writing Jamesian novels and stories, he remained unwilling to know things. This is a bad trait in a poet, partly disguised in this case by the Latin titles and the allusions to Propertius. Plarr, in his genial memoir, says Dowson was under the impression that Red Indians outnumbered white men in the United States. He lived much in France and translated from French, but according to Plarr his own French was 'dim'. Even in literature he was 'curiously incurious.'

However, he read Schopenhauer and Stendhal, Webster (not Shakespeare), De Quincey, Poe, Hawthorne, James, Verlaine, Murger, Swinburne and Pater. These are roughly the authors you would make him read if you were inventing him. Spending so much time with Lionel Johnson, he must have heard a lot about theology (Yeats remembers that Johnson lectured him on chastity out of the Fathers) but his conversion to Rome seems to have been an unintellectual affair, and he said that what Johnson and he had in common was a passion for Catullus and Battersea enamel. He deliberately avoided ideas. One's opinion of Johnson rises when one reads, for example, his critique of Symons ('. . . "we had champagne, and the rest was an ecstasy of shame." That is Symons'); but although Dowson once showed himself capable of enlightened comment by calling Symons 'a silly bugger,' he seems uninterested in criticism. Thanks to Plarr, we know about his annotations of Olive Schreiner's *An African Farm*, done as part of a literary joke, but in Dowson's case quite seriously. Miss Schreiner's account of life as 'a striving and an ending in nothing' he calls 'the conclusion of the whole matter.' 'Self-contempt is respectable,' he notes. On women he simply quotes Schopenhauer. He often expressed his abhorrence of growth and maturity, and even wrote an essay on 'The Cult of the Child.' He admired this aphorism of Stendhal, no doubt applying it as much to himself as to his century: *'Se sacrificier à ses passions passe. Mais à des passions qu'on n'a pas! Triste XIXe siècle!'* Even as a boy he saw he was part of a myth.

Dowson's biographers have naturally tried to sort out his life from the fables attached to it. He didn't take to drugs at Oxford. He wasn't, for most of his life, a drunk (Plarr says so, but his standards were admittedly robust, since he took 'drunk' to mean 'lying in the gutter on one's back'). Later he did drink, not only in the Crown and Henekey's, but in the Limehouse pothouses, where 'the poisonous liquors' of Symons's fancy were, as somebody has pointed out, supplied by the same brewers as catered for the West End pubs. He also drank a lot of absinthe, the subject of one of his best prose poems. As to Adelaide Foltinowicz, the little Polish girl whom he cultivated, he was no Humbert Humbert: his desires and delusions had a Dickensian purity. He wasn't, like Johnson, impotent, but his taste for harlots was probably less depraved than Yeats suggests. So the myth is modified; but he clearly did a lot towards killing himself. At 30 he could speak of being in old age, and his appearance— toothless, scarred by drunken fighting, racked by coughing— made him more than ever 'a demoralised Keats.' He died at 32, of tuberculosis.

The myth began, as Plarr says, at the graveside if not before. Symons, who had started the process while Dowson was still alive, wrote a long obituary which, despite its show of modera-tion, types the dead poet firmly as *maudit*: a drunk, a drug-taker, a lover of squalor, all sensibility and no intellect, like Yvor Winters's description of Pound. Like some chartered accountant of the soul, Symons finds that Dowson spent too much suffering achieving too small a return of poetry; he could have done what he did 'at much less expense of spirit.' But it is with Yeats that the myth achieves historical importance. Yeats preferred Johnson, and is not very accurate about Dowson, but what he says counts because he was the single poet of stature who survived the Tragic Generation and made it part of a modern poet's material. He tells good stories about Dowson, including the funny one about his escapade with Wilde at Dieppe; but the whole temper of *The Trembling of the Veil* (a study in *fin du globe*, as its title suggests) prepares us for the solemn use of Dowson in *A Vision* as an example of the man of the 13th Phase (the others are Baudelaire and Beardsley, who incidentally thought little of Dowson). While such men may be self-absorbed, morbid, corrupted by enforced love, this is a good Phase for poets, provided they can cultivate a passion for truth. But Yeats, though he says he envied Dowson his debauched life, could not have envied him his mind. The poems he liked so well that he set on foot the *Book of the Rhymers' Club* to get them into print pleased him by their delicate rhythms, and lack of ideas— they are as near *romances sans paroles* as can be got. This is their merit, inside and outside the myth.

It is possible, by an effort, to recover something of the mood they pleased. A good number of readers, one supposes, can do so; hence this new edition by Mark Longaker,[1] who also wrote the standard biography in 1944. It is a handsome but somewhat strange book. All the pieces in Dowson's two books of poetry, *Verses* and *Decorations*, are included, and so is *The Pierrot of the Minute*, a Keatsian playlet marked by little deliberate lapses into the ludicrous which remind one that Dowson really did live in a tough world, and worked for Smithers.[2] These we expect; but where are the 50 pages of uncollected poetry given in Desmond Flower's edition of 1934?[3] These derived mostly from the Flower Notebook, and included the 'Sonnets to a little Girl' and 'Against my Lady Burton,' all of which should be in even a selection of Dowson. Mr Longaker refers to them in his introduction and notes, without ever explaining why he has not

---

[1] *The Poems of Ernest Dowson.* University of Pennsylvania Press.

[2] Smithers in fact treated Dowson very well. For information on their friendship, and much more detail on Adelaide Foltinowicz, see the excellently edited *Letters of Ernest Dowson,* edited by Desmond Flower and Henry Maas and published in the centenary year (1967) by Cassell.

[3] Re-issued by Cassell in 1967.

reprinted them. More curiously still, this edition is biblio-graphically almost a twin of the Flower edition, the texts and the layout virtually identical. The notes are different: Flower gives variants, which Longaker withholds, on the grounds that collation 'is neither practicable nor necessary,' and that the variants are mostly in pointing, a matter, he admits, to which 'Dowson attached a great deal of importance.' The new notes are critical and biographical, but Flower attends to these needs also.

As to the poems themselves, they will doubtless seem to many the record of a somewhat nerveless struggle between a genuine talent for purity of diction and an almost involuntary *dandysme*. The long Latin titles, and the in-group dedications of *Verses*, were deliberately provoking; and *The Times* reviewer, mention-ing 'Extreme Unction: for Lionel Johnson,' and 'A Requiem: for John Gray,' felt he must assure his readers that 'there is no reason to believe that the gentlemen in question are anything but alive and well.' Many of the poems deal with golden hair, young girls and death, sometimes with dead young golden-haired girls, and express an affected chastity of suffering appropriate to the author described by Symons as 'a fastidious amateur of grief.' Much of Dowson's best work was done early, in the years of the Rhymer's Club; it is not all in the mood of the Schreiner anno-tations, and there are a few wan *jeux d'esprit*, but the mood is reasonably summed up in the line 'Labour and longing and despair the long day brings.' A touch of sad wit provides an occasional streak of colour, and Dowson is doubtless the nearest thing in English to Verlaine. In fact his translations of Verlaine strike me as extraordinarily good.

Dowson's positive virtues as a poet are a rhythmic subtlety which is well exemplified in the anthology-piece 'Non sum qualis eram'—a poem also serviceable as an example of what Mr Longaker calls the 'sin poems.' There is an epigram which Yeats would have been glad enough to have written 10 years after Dowson's death:

> Because I am idolatrous and have besought,
> With grievous supplication and consuming prayer,
> The admirable image that my dreams have wrought
> Out of her swan's neck and her dark, abundant hair:
> The jealous gods, who brook no worship save their own,
> Turned my live idol marble and her heart to stone.

What in the end tires us is the repeated use of period epithets ('dim,' 'enchanted,' 'dream-like' etc.) and the traces of Dowson's disastrous theory that you can't use the letter *v* too often: 'viols,' 'violets,' 'vines.' The new flexibility of rhythm was the important thing, but these trimmings often take over and make the poetry look like feeble attitudinising. This was Yeats's struggle too, and he was aware that he had to outlive the companions of the Cheshire Cheese to win it.

Yet Dowson passes into modern poetry not only as a myth, but as poetry. Pound admired him, and his rhythms, and his Propertius, whom he modernised. It may not be too fanciful to find traces of him in the poetry of those 'who walked between the violet and the violet. . . . In ignorance and in knowledge of eternal dolour.' Stevens, in such poems as 'Cy est pourtraicte, Madame Ste Ursule, et les Unze Mille Vierges,' adapts the decadent title and ironises the decadent language. For such reasons it is worth undergoing the somewhat lowering experience of reading through Dowson's poems. One might add to them the story called 'The Dying of Francis Donne' and Plarr's memoir. Thus do the 'Nineties survive.

(1963)

VIII. A BABYLONISH DIALECT

In the middle 'Thirties, emerging from my remote provincial background (but we wrote poems and asked whether Browning didn't sometimes go beyond bounds), I at last discovered Yeats and Eliot; and in that bewilderment one truth seemed worth steering by, which was that these men were *remaking* poetry. Although this recognition had very little to do with knowledge, and one waited years before being granted any real notion of the character of such poetry, it was nevertheless, as I still believe, a genuine insight. As one came to know the other great works of the wonderful years, one also came with increasing certainty to see that the imperative of modernism was 'make it new': a difficult but in the end satisfactory formula.

These were the years of Auden, of a poetry oscillating between an inaccessible private mythology and public exhortation, an in-group apocalypse and a call for commitment to 'the struggle.' It was going to be our war; we were committed whether or not we wanted to be; and there were many poems of Auden especially which have by now disappeared from the canon, but not from the memories of men in their forties. Meanwhile, as the war approached, the indisputably great, the men of the wonderful years, were still at work. What were they doing? Their commitment they consigned, mostly, to the cooler element of prose; but we could hardly suppose they were with any part of their minds on our side. 'Making it new' seemed to be a process which had disagreeable consequences in the political sphere. I forget how we explained this to ourselves, but somehow we preserved the certainty that the older poets who behaved so strangely, seemed so harshly to absent themselves from our world—to hold in the age of the Bristol Bomber opinions which were appropriate to the penny-farthing—were nevertheless the men on whom all depended.

The death of Yeats in January, 1939, therefore seemed to us an event of catastrophic importance. The news of Eliot's death immediately brought to mind, in surprising detail, the events and feelings of that dark, cold day nearly twenty-six years earlier. These were the men who had counted most, yet had seemed to have so little in common with us. Yet on the face of it the two events seemed to have little similarity beyond what is obvious. In the months preceding Yeats's death there had been an extraordinary outpouring of poetry—how impatiently one awaited the next issue of the *London Mercury*, and, later, the publication in the spring of 1940 of *Last Poems and Plays*! And that wasn't all: there was the poet himself, masked as a wild old man or a dangerous sage; there was the samurai posturing, the learned, more than half-fascist, shouting about eugenics and war, and this at a moment when we were beginning to understand that the enemy would soon be imposing both these disciplines on Europe. But one didn't hate the poet for what he thought he knew, remembering that he had always held strange opinions without damaging his verse. 'Man can embody truth but he cannot know it,' he said in his last letter; and years before, in a line which gives modern poetry its motto, 'In dreams begin responsibilities.' He made no order, but showed that our real lives begin when we have been shown that order ends: it is for the dreams, the intuitions of irregularity and chaos, of the tragic rag-and-bone shop, that we value him, and not for his 'system' or his 'thought.' The time of his death seemed appropriate to the dream; in a few months the towns lay beaten flat.

History did not collaborate in the same way to remind us of the responsibilities begun in Eliot's dream. His farewell to poetry was taken only a couple of years after Yeats's. It was no deathbed 'Cuchulain Comforted'; it was 'Little Gidding.' Perhaps the Dantesque section of that poem grew in part from Yeats's strange poem; certainly Yeats predominates over the others who make up the 'familiar compound ghost.' The famous lines tell us what we ought to make of our great poetry and of our great poets:

> '. . . I am not eager to rehearse
>   My thoughts and theory which you have forgotten.
>   These things have served their purpose: let them be.
> So with your own. . . .'

So much for the using up of a poet's thought. As a man he continues to suffer and without reward:

> 'Let me disclose the gifts reserved for age
>   To set a crown upon your lifetime's effort.
>   First, the cold friction of expiring sense. . . .
> Second, the conscious impotence of rage
>   At human folly. . . .
> And last, the rending pain of re-enactment
>   Of all that you have done, and been. . . .'

So the ghost speaks of a Yeatsian guilt, remorse, and purgation. The man who suffers is now truly distinct from the mind that creates poems that have to be, as Picasso said of paintings, 'hordes of destructions.'

It is customary now to speak of a 'tradition of the new' in American painting, and it may even be possible to do the same of American poetry. There is no such tradition in English poetry. That our contemporaries on the whole avoid Eliot's influence is probably not important; perhaps it is the case, as Auden said in his obituary notice, that Eliot cannot be imitated, only parodied. But it *is* important, I think, that his insistence on making it new, on treating every attempt as a wholly new start, is now discounted. It may be true, as is sometimes said, that this wholly exhausting doctrine is on cultural grounds more likely to be successful in the United States than in England; certainly much of the evidence points that way. But that does not entitle us to ignore the doctrine. After such knowledge, what forgiveness? The lesson was that the craft of poetry can no longer be a matter of perpetuating dialects and imitating what was well made; it lies in an act of radical analysis, a return to the brute elements, to the matter which may have a potentiality of form; but last year's words will not find it. In consequence, the writing of major poetry seems more than ever before a ruinous and exhausting undertaking, and no poet deserves blame for modestly refusing to take it on, or even for coming to think of Eliot and his peers as Chinese walls across their literature.

This, of course, is to apply to Eliot the damaging epigram he devised for Milton. Sir Herbert Read tells me that the English poet for whom Eliot felt a conscious affinity, and upon whom he perhaps in some degree modelled himself, was Johnson. All the same it seems to me that the more we see of the hidden side of Eliot the more he seems to resemble Milton, though he thought of Milton as a polar opposite. As we look at all the contraries reconciled in Eliot—his schismatic traditionalism, his romantic classicism, his highly personal impersonality—we are prepared for the surprise (which Eliot himself seems in some measure to have experienced) of finding in the dissenting Whig regicide a hazy mirror-image of the Anglo-Catholic royalist. Each, having prepared himself carefully for poetry, saw that he must also, living in such times, explore prose, the cooler element. From a consciously archaic standpoint each must characterise the activities of the sons of Belial. Each saw that fidelity to tradition is ensured by revolutionary action. (Eliot would hardly have dissented from the proposition that 'a man may be a heretic in the truth.') Each knew the difficulty of finding 'answerable style' in an age too late. With the Commonwealth an evident failure, Milton wrote one last book to restore it, and as the élites crumbled and reformed Eliot wrote his *Notes*. If Milton killed a king, Eliot attacked vulgar democracy and shared with the 'men of 1914' and with Yeats some extreme authoritarian opinions.

Milton had his apocalyptic delusions, but settled down in aristocratic patience to wait for the failure of the anti-Christian experiment, 'meanwhile,' as Eliot said in the conclusion of 'Thoughts after Lambeth,' 'redeeming the time: so that the

Faith may be preserved alive through the dark ages before us.'
In the end, they thought, the elect, however shorn of power, will
bring down the Philistine temple; and the self-begotten bird will
return. As poets, they wrote with voluptuousness of youth, and
with unmatched force of the lacerations of age. And each of
them lived on into a time when it seemed there was little for
them to say to their compatriots, God's Englishmen. Eliot can
scarcely have failed to see this left-handed image of himself in a
poet who made a new language for his poetry and who transformed what he took from a venerable tradition:

> Our effort is not only to explore the frontiers of the spirit, but as
> much to regain, under very different conditions, what was known to
> men writing at remote times and in alien languages.

This is truly Miltonic; but Eliot at first moved away and pretended to find his reflection in the strong and lucid Dryden, deceiving many into supposing that he resembled that poet more
than the lonely, fiercer maker of the new, of whom he said that
it was 'something of a problem' to decide in what his greatness
consisted.

However, a great poet need not always understand another;
there may be good reasons why he should not. And Eliot certainly has the marks of a modern kind of greatness, those
beneficial intuitions of irregularity and chaos, the truth of the
foul rag-and-bone shop. Yet we remember him as celebrating
order. Over the years he explored the implications of his attitudes
to order, and it is doubtful whether many people capable of
understanding him now have much sympathy with his views.
His greatness will rest on the fruitful recognition of disorder,
though the theories will have their interest as theories held by a
great man.

Many of the doctrines are the product of a seductive thesis
and its stern antithesis. The objective correlative, a term
probably developed from the 'object correlative' of Santayana,[1]
is an attempt to depersonalise what remains essentially the
image of romantic poetry, and to purge it of any taint of simple

---

[1] In a letter to Mr Nimai Chatterji in 1955, Eliot says he thought he 'coined'
the expression, but discovered that it had been used by Washington Allston.
Eliot adds characteristically that he is not 'quite sure of what I meant 35 years
ago' (Letter in *New Statesman*, 5 March, 1965, p. 361). Allston's usage is in fact
quite different.

expressiveness or rational communication. Its propriety is limited to Eliot's own earlier verse, which is deeply personal but made inexplicably so by the arbitrariness of its logical relations, its elaborate remoteness from the personal, and its position within a context which provides a sort of model of an impersonal 'tradition'—the fragments shored against our ruin. It is neither a matter of 'the logic of concepts' nor something that welled up from an a-logical unconscious; insofar as it has 'meaning,' it has it in order to keep the intellect happy while the poem does its work, and insofar as it has not, it has not in order to distinguish it from poems that 'make you conscious of having been written by somebody.'[1] The 'dissociation of sensibility' is an historical theory to explain the dearth of objective correlatives in a time when the artist, alienated from his environment, *l'immonde cité*, is working at the beginning of a dark age 'under conditions that seem unpropitious,' in an ever-worsening climate of imagination.

Such theories, we now see, are highly personal versions of stock themes in the history of ideas of the period. They have been subtly developed and are now increasingly subject to criticism. The most persistent and influential of them, no doubt, is the theory of tradition. In a sense it is Cubist historiography, unlearning the trick of perspective and ordering history as a system of perpetually varying spatial alignments. Tradition is always unexpected, hard to find, easily confused with worthless custom; and it is emblematic that a father of modernism should call himself Anglican, for the early Anglicans upset the whole idea of tradition in much this way.

He also called himself royalist, and this is an aspect of a larger and even more surprising traditionalism; for Eliot, in a weirdly pure sense, was an imperialist. This may seem at odds with certain aspects of his thought—his nostalgia for closed societies, his support for American agrarianism; but in the end, although he suppressed *After Strange Gods*, they grow from the same root. The essay on Dante, which is one of the true masterpieces of modern criticism, has been called a projection on to the medieval poet of Eliot's own theories of diction and imagery; but it has an undercurrent of imperialism, and can usefully be read with the studies of Virgil and Kipling.

[1] This is from an early essay on Pound (*Athenaeum*, 24 October, 1919) quoted by C. K. Stead in his interesting book *The New Poetic* (1964), p. 132.

This imperialistic Eliot is the poet of the *urbs aeterna*, of the transmitted but corrupted dignity of Rome. Hence his veneration not only for Baudelaire (where his Symbolist predecessors would have agreed) but for Virgil (where they would not). The other side of this city is the Babylon of Apocalypse, and when the *imperium* is threadbare and the end approaches of that which Virgil called endless, this is the city we see. It is the *Blick ins Chaos*.

The merchants of the earth are waxed rich through the abundance of her delicacies. . . . And the kings of the earth, who have committed fornication and live deliciously with her, shall bewail her, and lament for her, when they shall see the smoke of her burning. . . . And the merchants of the earth shall weep and mourn over her . . . saying, Alas, alas that great city, that was clothed in fine linen, and purple, and scarlet, and decked with gold, and precious stones, and pearls! For in one hour so great riches is come to naught. And every shipmaster, and the company in ships, and sailors, and as many as trade by sea, stood afar off, and cried when they saw the smoke of her burning, saying What city is like unto this great city!

Here is the imagery of sea and imperial city, the city which is the whore and the mother of harlots, with Mystery on her forehead —Mme Sosostris and the bejewelled lady of the game of chess— diminished as the sailors and merchants have dwindled to Phlebas, the sea swallowing his concern for profit and loss, and to Mr Eugenides, his pocket full of currants (base Levantine trade) and his heart set on metropolitan whoring. This is the London of *The Waste Land*, the City by the sea with its remaining flashes of inexplicable imperial splendor: the Unreal City, the *urbs aeterna* declined into *l'immonde cité*.

In another mood, complementary to this of Babylon, Eliot still imagined the Empire as without end, and Virgil, its prophet, became the central classic, *l'altissimo poeta*, as Dante called him. In him originated the imperial tradition. To ignore the 'consciousness of Rome' as Virgil crystallised it is simply to be provincial. It is to be out of the historical current which bears the imperial dignity. In this way Eliot deepened for himself the Arnoldian meanings of the word *provincial*. The European destiny, as prophesied by Virgil, was imperial; the Empire became the secular body of the Church. The fact that it split is reflected in *The Waste Land*, where the hooded Eastern hordes swarm over their plains, and the towers of the City fall. And as the dignity of empire was split among the nations, the task of the chosen, which is to defeat the proud and be merciful to the subject, was increasingly identified with Babylonian motives of profit—a situation in which Kipling's relevance is obvious. Eliot speaks of his 'imperial imagination'; and, given a view of history as having a kind of perspectiveless unity, Virgil, Dante, Baudelaire, and Kipling can exist within the same plane, like Babylon and the *urbs aeterna*, or like the inter-related motifs of *The Waste Land*. Thus does the poet-historian redeem the time. His is a period of waiting such as occurs before the apocalypse of collapsing cities. But behind the temporal disaster of Babylon he knows that the timeless pattern of the eternal city must survive.

Some such imagery of disaster and continuity—'that the wheel may turn and still/Be forever still'—lies under *The Waste Land* and is reflected also in Eliot's cults of continuity and renovation 'under conditions/That seem unpropitious.' Yet when we think of the great poem, we think of it as an image of imperial catastrophe, of the disaster and not of the pattern. For that pattern suggests a commitment, a religion; and the poet retreats to it. But the poem is a great poem because it will not force us to follow him. It makes us wiser without committing us. Here I play on the title of William Bartley's recent book, *Retreat to Commitment*; but one remembers that Eliot himself is aware of these distinctions. Art may lead one to a point where something else must take over, as Virgil led Dante; it 'may be affirmed to serve ends beyond itself,' as Eliot himself remarked; but it 'is not required to be aware of these ends'—an objective correlative has enough to do existing out there without joining a church. It joins the mix of our own minds, but it does not tell us what to believe. Whereas Mr Bartley's theologians sometimes feel uneasily that they should defend the rationality of what they are saying, the poets in their rival fictions do not. One of the really distinctive features of the literature of the modernist *anni mirabiles* was that variously and subtly committed writers blocked the retreat to commitment in their poems. Eliot ridiculed the critics who found in *The Waste Land* an image of the age's despair, but he might equally have rejected the more recent Christian interpretations. The poem resists an imposed order; it is a part of its greatness, and the greatness of its epoch, that it can do so.

'To find, Not to impose,' as Wallace Stevens said with a desperate wisdom, 'It is possible, possible, possible.' We must hope so.

No one has better stated the chief characteristics of that epoch than the late R. P. Blackmur in a little book of lectures, *Anni Mirabiles 1921–1925*; though it contains some of the best of his later work, it seems to be not much read. We live, wrote Blackmur, in the first age that has been 'fully self-conscious of its fictions'—in a way, Nietzsche has sunk in at last; and in these conditions we are more than ever dependent on what he calls, perhaps not quite satisfactorily, 'bourgeois humanism'—'the residue of reason in relation to the madness of the senses.' Without it we cannot have 'creation in honesty,' only 'assertion in desperation.' But in its operation this residual humanism can only deny the validity of our frames of reference and make 'an irregular metaphysic for the control of man's irrational powers.' So this kind art is a new kind of creation, harsh, medicinal, remaking reality 'in rivalry with our own wishes,' denying us the consolations of predictable form but showing us the forces of our world, which we may have to control by other means. And the great works in this new and necessary manner were the product of the 'wonderful years'—in English, two notable examples are *Ulysses* and *The Waste Land*.

The function of such a work, one has to see, is what Simone Weil called *decreation*; Stevens, whose profound contribution to the subject nobody seems to have noticed, picked the word out of *La Pesanteur et la Grâce*. Simone Weil explains the difference from destruction: decreation is not a change from the created to nothingness, but from the created to the uncreated. 'Modern reality,' commented Stevens, 'is a reality of decreation, in which our revelations are not the revelations of belief'; though he adds that he can say this 'without in any way asserting that they are the sole sources.'

This seems to me a useful instrument for the discrimination of modernisms. The form in which Simone Weil expresses it is rather obscure, though she is quite clear that 'destruction' is 'a blameworthy substitute for decreation.' The latter depends upon an act of renunciation, considered as a creative act like that of God. 'God could create only by hiding himself. Otherwise there would be nothing but himself.' She means that decreation, for men, implies the deliberate repudiation (not simply the destruction) of the naturally human and so naturally false 'set' of the world: 'we participate in the creation of the world by decreating ourselves.' Now the poets of the *anni mirabiles* also desired to create a world by decreating the self in suffering; to purge what, in being merely natural and human, was also false. It is a point often made, though in different language, by Eliot. This is what Stevens called clearing the world of 'its stiff and stubborn, man-locked set.' In another way it is what attracted Hulme and Eliot to Worringer, who related societies purged of the messily human to a radical abstract art.

Decreation, as practised by poets, has its disadvantages. In this very article I myself have, without much consideration for the hazards, provided a man-locked set for *The Waste Land*. But we can see that when Eliot pushed his objective correlative out into the neutral air—'seeming a beast disgorged, unlike,/ Warmed by a desperate milk'—he expected it, liberated from his own fictions, to be caught up in the fictions of others, those explanations we find for all the creations. In the world Blackmur is writing about, the elements of a true poem are precisely such nuclei, disgorged, unlike, purged of the suffering self; they become that around which a possible new world may accrete.

It would be too much to say that no one now practises this poetry of decreation; but much English poetry of these days is neither decreative nor destructive, expressing a modest selfishness which escapes both the purgative effort and the blame. America has, I think, its destructive poetry, which tends to be a poetry of manifesto; and in Lowell it seems to have a decreative poet. One way to tell them is by a certain ambiguity in your own response. *The Waste Land*, and also *Hugh Selwyn Mauberley*, can strike you in certain moments as emperors without clothes; discrete poems cobbled into a sequence which is always inviting the censure of pretentiousness. It is with your own proper fictive covering that you hide their nakedness and make them wise. Perhaps there is in *Life Studies* an ambivalence of the same sort. Certainly to have Eliot's great poem in one's life involves an irrevocable but repeated act of love. This is not called for by merely schismatic poetry, the poetry of destruction.

This is why our most lively sense of what it means to be alive in poetry continues to stem from the 'modern' of forty years ago. Deeply conditioned by the original experience of decreation, we may find it hard to understand that without it poetry had no future we can now seriously conceive of. It is true that the exhortations which accompanied Eliot's nuclear achievement are of only secondary interest. What survives is a habit of mind that looks for analysis, analysis by controlled unreason. This habit can be vulgarised: analysis of the most severe kind degenerates into chatter about breakdown and dissociation. *The Waste Land* has been used thus, as a myth of decadence, a facile evasion. Eliot is in his capacity as thinker partly to blame for this. Arnold complained that Carlyle 'led us out into the wilderness and left us there.' So did Eliot, despite his conviction that he knew the way; even before the 'conversion' he had a vision of a future dominated by Bradley, Frazer, and Henry James. We need not complain, so long as the response to the wilderness is authentic; but often it is a comfortable unfelt acceptance of tragedy. *The Waste Land* is in one light an imperial epic; but such comforts as it can offer are not compatible with any illusions, past, present, or future.

This is not the way the poem is usually read nowadays; but most people who know about poetry will still admit that it is a very difficult poem, though it invites glib or simplified interpretation. As I said, one can think of it as a mere arbitrary sequence upon which we have been persuaded to impose an order. But the true order, I think, is there to be found, unique, unrepeated, resistant to synthesis. The *Four Quartets* seem by comparison isolated in their eminence, tragic, often crystalline in the presentation of the temporal agony, but personal; and closer sometimes to commentary than to the thing itself. When the *Quartets* speak of a pattern of timeless moments, of the point of intersection, they speak *about* that pattern and that point; the true image of them is *The Waste Land*. There the dreams cross, the dreams in which begin responsibilities.

(1965-6)

IX. AFTERTHOUGHTS ON WALLACE STEVENS

The early letters and journals[1] of Stevens show a most private man, a self-cramped man or a man who gave everything time to

[1] *Letters of Wallace Stevens.* Selected and edited by Holly Stevens. (London, Faber; New York, Knopf.)

mature. Long-breathed speculation preceded decisions: whether to become 'a money-making lawyer,' to marry, or to write poems. He decided, he says, that fact must be met with fact; if 'life is worth living under certain conditions,' these conditions involved the postponement of poetry. As it happened, business success and poetry came together, as if providence were ready to comply with such planning. There is nothing in the letters to explain how Stevens, who wrote no poetry worth preserving before he was thirty, should suddenly have written 'Peter Quince at the Clavier' and 'Sunday Morning.' One can only guess: among the things he wanted most were a home (where he could cackle in the Stevens environment, as 'toucans in the place of toucans') and 'an authentic fluent speech.' Hartford became the place of this toucan's cackling; but any other one place, if well-protected, might have done. Later, as he reasoned of these things 'with a later reason,' Stevens called the 'place dependent on ourselves' Catawba. It was the mind and reality who married there, and 'they married well because the marriage-place was what they loved.' Catawba might be New Haven on an ordinary evening or Hartford in a purple light or the Tennessee in which he invested nothing but a jar; a place where the mind matches the world on equal ground. Catawba 'was neither heaven nor hell,' but it was a good place to start the war or marriage between the mind and sky.

Seen from the outside, Stevens is quietly absurd. The poet of gaudiness, of pungent colour and exotic shape, was a sort of Hartford Des Esseintes. Des Esseintes' trip to London ended with a bottle of stout on a foggy night at Calais. For Stevens, Europe was a daydream about Paris, a postcard from Basel; and China a box of tea or a packet of jasmine solicited from travellers. His ephebes were exotic youths: a Korean poet, a Cuban scholar. He looked forward especially to the letters of Thomas McGreevy, with whom he could share his distaste for 'Ireland's neighbour,' and of Leonard C. van Geyzel, an Englishman expatriate in Ceylon, who might not only feed one's daydreams but supply 'the very best tea procurable.' The plum survives its poems, as Stevens remarked; but whether he, as poet, could have withstood the abrasions of genuine travel without losing his bloom is a question. The world's gaudy Cockaigne for him was Florida, with Cuba and the banana-islands over the horizon. His sense of place—the Rome of the Santayana poem, the Florence of the dead Englishman—have the same reality as Haddam, where the thin men live, or New Haven, or Oklahoma where the firecat bristled and Bonnie and Josie danced round a stump—his sense of place has an accuracy in respect of the imagination only. While his rich friends the Churches divided their year between New York and Paris, he sat it out in Hartford, working through the summer, dictating insurance letters and philosophical poems, lunching at the Canoe Club, and walking home in the evening to whatever might be 'the combination of the moment,' for example Berlioz and roses. After that, whatever books he might choose to read (he says he has time to read whatever he wants) and letters to and from, say, a Paris bookseller, or a Yale student writing an *explication* of 'Sea Surface Full of Clouds.' It might take such a man to see that the final truth about poetry is the fictiveness of the entire world; save for a mythic core of 'reality' the world is poetry, and there to be discovered, as desperate and virginal in Hartford or New Haven as any where else.

Lawrence once wrote remarkably about the umbrella of fictions with which we keep out the intolerable hot diversity of chaos. For him the original artist was the one who tore holes in the umbrella, so that human life and chaos were for a moment in contact; but the rent was soon mended with another more comfortable fiction, and the need is for a succession of umbrella-tearers who will not let us dismiss all that inhuman fortuity from our lives. Stevens is the poet of that umbrella, but also of the *Blick ins Chaos*, to remember which is to be aware of poetry. (The man who so dreaded poverty in its more physical form had an acute apprehension of the more metaphysical poverty which is our lot without poetry: 'money,' he once wrote, 'is a kind of poetry.') In the 'Thirties the 'pressure of reality' was particularly hard on the umbrella, and Stevens' attempt to meet it in the political form it then took was *Owl's Clover*, a self-confessed failure. The letters of the succeeding period, especially in the war years, silently celebrate the increase in reality's pressure by a steady concentration on the theory of poetry. 'The theory of poetry is the theory of life.' These are only apparently hermit musings, and it is not really surprising that Stevens reached his most authentic and fluent speech in poetry at such a moment;

Notes toward a Supreme Fiction belongs to 1942. The subject is
what human beings must add to the plain sense of things, in
order to make of the world something that suffices. The more
desperate the world's poverty, the harder and the more private
the poet's job. A man who does such a job well might be
represented as a rabbi or a soldier, or simply as major man; but
what he makes *is* a kind of poetry, and so, not necessarily but
actually, the task falls to poets, and poetry is the supreme fiction,
major man is a poet. Poetry is as pure and as impure as life, as
reasonable and as unreasonable. Whatever is well said about
poetry is well said about life. So, in his entirely solitary way,
proceeding at his own slow pace towards the truth about human
fiction, Stevens earned the right to regard any meditation, any
half-worked out 'and yet' or 'as if,' as a contribution to the great
subject, the human meaning of an ordinary evening in Connecticut when beyond the mental umbrella there is chaos, the sun is
meaningless except by our gift, and all the gods are dead. The
subject matter of poetry is 'the aspects of the world and of men
and women that have been added to them by poetry': everything
that is human or humanised.

This gives him a right to his arbitrary musing, and as rabbi
(both learned and understanding poverty) he arrogates the
further right to be aloofly allegorical and to go on with his
thinking just so long as he chooses, without regard to the
unschooled who may not follow. If you were puzzled by the
Arabian in *Notes*:

> *At night an Arabian in my room,*
> *With his damned hoobla-hoobla-hoobla-how,*
> *Inscribes a primitive astronomy*
>
> *Across the unscrawled fores the future casts*
> *And throws his stars around the floor—*

you could write to Mr Stevens, and he would write back and tell
you that the Arabian is the moon, adding that 'the reader could
not possibly know this. However, I did not think it necessary for
him to know.' On the other hand, he thinks that when he uses
the word 'tanks' in a context suggesting Ceylon, the reader should
know exactly what he means without being told. Extremely
obliging in his response to letters of enquiry, he often remarks

that his correspondents are mistaken not only in thinking that his poetry is plainer to him than to them but also, and habitually, in thinking that what integrates a poem is *ideas*. 'A poem must have a peculiarity, as if it were the momentarily complete idiom of that which prompts it.' Newton Stallknecht very neatly called Stevens' poetry 'a poetry of philosophical *intention*'—not, that is, of philosophical execution. It is useless to seek in it a simple bonding of ideas. 'One can do nothing in art by being reasonable . . . it is also true that one can do nothing by being unreasonable.' Hence that range of uniquely philosophical poetry—a different thing, as Coleridge noted, from philosophy and also from poetry simply considered—in which he ranges from a kind of intense meditative mumble to a declarative candour which also, on examination, defies paraphrase. Only thus can one do the work of the dead gods, and create the 'Extraordinary Actuality.'

It is unlikely that Stevens ever really felt the criticism that all this is wildly out of touch with what most people have in mind when, 'in the metaphysical streets of the physical town,' they hear 'the actual horns of baker and butcher.' He wanted to be the consort of the Queen of Fact. When Church was still thinking about founding a Chair of Poetry at Princeton, Stevens advised him that the right man to fill it would be someone who could deal with actuality without referring to poetry at all. Such a man, he said, was Hemingway—'a poet . . . and I should say offhand, the most significant of living poets, so far as the subject of Extraordinary Actuality is concerned.' A Hemingway hero must have seemed a much better image of metaphysical poverty than an Appalachian farmer or an Abyssinian 'coon.'

After the 'Thirties Stevens gave up the attempt to compete with other theories of poverty and reality; he simply went on with his own. That is why the letters of 1942 ignore the reality that was going on in Germany, in Russia and in the Pacific, even the warships clustered at New London on his own Connecticut River. He writes instead about 'the order of the spirit' which 'is the only music of the spheres: or rather, the only music'; about how a private press should print his book ('Light tan linen or buckram cover'); about his Dutch ancestors. Just as 'poverty' became for him a purely metaphysical concept, so did war. His was the primal war 'between the mind and sky'; his soldier was simply another figure of the youth as a virile poet. Even his 'fat girl, terrestrial, my summer, my night' is, he explains, the earth, 'what the politicians are calling the globe,' and what he thinks of as the irreducible reality where all poetry (all humanity) begins. Stevens commits himself to the biggest of all as-ifs; he behaves as if poetry and the imagination are everything that is humanly important (and therefore everything that is at all important). Consequently he felt himself to be dealing incessantly with *the real*.

The philosophy of this was not for him to work out, only to brood over. Though he says that 'supreme poetry can be produced only at the highest level of the cognitive,' he also holds that the kind of thinking it required is distinct from that required by philosophising because it is 'a creation not of meaning but of points,' welcoming fortuity and logical imprecision, devoted not to clarity of expression ('what I intended is nothing') but to the blooding of abstractions. It adds to the vulgate of experience an 'and yet.' So does metaphysics; but he insists that his work has 'no serious contact with philosophy.' Stevens acknowledged an interest in Santayana, James, and Bergson, but his reading was patchy and never deep. He knew *about* Heidegger but not, apparently, even *about* Wittgenstein. When Paul Weiss asked him why he didn't take on a full-sized philosopher he replied with his usual epistolary calm, quite untouched by the criticism. Philosophy, like many other things, was his business only when it suited him to make it so. It became a part of his authentic and fluent speech, but it isn't surprising that when he sent his 'Collect of Philosophy' to a learned journal it was rejected.

Many of these letters are written as part of the para-philosophical game. The correspondents are not, as a rule, confidants; there is a certain reserve even with old friends, though the old gaudiness so personal to Stevens flashes out in letters to the young, and there is an occasional letter, like the one to Harvey Breit about the Dutch Church at Kingston which has an uncovenanted and dazzling philosophical wit. Often he is just thinking on paper, as in some poems. The long letter to a congenial correspondent, and the long poem, suited his mental style. 'Some people always know exactly what they think. I am afraid that I am not one of those people. The same thing keeps active in my mind and rarely becomes fixed.' As letters these are not obliged to be agreeable or self-consistent; but for anybody who knows the poetry they are very revealing, they do enhance one's familiarity with the drift of Stevens' meditation—its hidden structure of seasons, fictions, human fear, its bursts of gratuitous and generous happiness, as when a Norwegian girl poet calls at Hartford. They even suggest a queer kind of heroism, as if the refusal to condone poverty, to care for men in the mass, were a necessary aspect of that attempt to identify poetry and humanity, to be 'major man.'

In the long run, I think, these letters will stand as classic specimens of the preoccupations of modern poetry for such reasons as these, rather than for the direct light they throw upon actual poems. When one comes first to the book, the most obviously exciting letters are those in which Stevens, with extraordinary good humour and candour, and against the whole bent of modern practitioners, gives his own interpretations of certain poems; most remarkably there are many pages on *Notes toward a Supreme Fiction.* The interest of these is of course exceptional, and yet the comments are not, in the end, very helpful. Where the language of a poem is extraordinary, arbitrary, Stevens simply incorporates it into his paraphrases, 'practising mere repetitions,' or he says he can't remember, perhaps never knew. There are certainly hints on how to read the poems, but surprisingly little help with detail.

'The object, of course,' he says of 'An Ordinary Evening,' 'is to purge oneself of anything false.' He wanted to get out of the poem and himself all the left-overs of past imagining. In this sense he was tremendously modern; he was not interested in poetry as 'an aspect of history' but as a conjunction, appropriate to its moment, of the mind and its place, a world essentially indifferent. If the gods die, and statues grow rigid, what can be hoped for poems? But against this self-destructive emphasis on the ephemerality of the modern poem he built up his own world, in which there are to be found relations to some extent proof against time. Everything was implicit in *Harmonium*, and he saw it as a programme, wanting to call it *The Grand Poem: Preliminary Minutiae.* When he finally consented to a collected edition he did so only when he felt something had been completed, and he wanted to call it *The Whole of Harmonium.* Having felt a bit chilly towards *Harmonium* in the years after its publication in 1923, he came to admire again in his late years its unpredictable certainties, its strange rightnesses, the way it confirmed later poems. The *Collected Poems* do make a 'total edifice' and an enduring meditation. There is a lot of squiggling, marginalia, meta-metaphysical muttering, pointlessness, wantonness, the tedium of small private sub-jokes and sub-thoughts, and these will serve to defend Stevens' thesis of necessary obsolescence, the inevitable decline of imaginative objects into absurdity. But for all its fortuity and decay *The Whole of Harmonium* looks pretty permanent, indeed 'a shining exemplum of human dignity,' to borrow Allen Tate's word for the poetry of Hart Crane—from 'Plowing on Sunday' to 'The Rock.' An exile from most of the world, and from most of the people about him who would have been equal to his imaginative demands, he showed that exile, if necessary, may be had without departures, without fuss. The letters often show one how the polite hermit kept out the world, hoarded the passions and the poet's scholarship that a more orthodox life such as Crane's had to dissipate. Of course Stevens is not the great modern poet anybody could have predicted, but great poetry has often been surprising in its time. To undervalue him because he seems so wantonly not to fit the milieu or the moment is still a common error, just as it is to overvalue him because he thinks. Rightly seen he is, in his shy, egotistical remoteness, very central to the whole idea of modern poetry.

*   *   *

How *are* we to see him rightly? The signs are, I should say, that the vogue is ending, and the enormous effort to explain Stevens has failed. It is a characteristic failure of our graduate schools.

There is already a considerable number of books about Stevens, and I have not read them all, though to make up for this I have read some that remained unpublished, and have written one of them myself. Although one learns something now and again from the Stevens literature, it is on the whole dispiriting. 'I must have been terribly wrong,' one thinks, 'ever to have supposed that Stevens was any good.' He emerges as a tiresome doodler with a vast but not profoundly interesting body of

Thought, which he has never quite got round to articulating. The disentangling of this Thought from camp titles and periphrases is the self-appointed task of critics. Now and again there is a confluence of comment on some particularly mysterious poem, like 'The Emperor of Ice Cream,' but the ordinary practice has been to ignore the fact that Stevens wrote a great many discrete poems and treat the whole *oeuvre* as one poem from which one takes one's illustrations, usually with a reference to a page number in the *Collected Poems* rather than an individual work.

Here is a passage, chosen almost at random, and written by a professionally competent commentator on Stevens.

The giant of nothingness is referred to elsewhere, most explicitly in 'Asides on the Oboe,' as 'the glass man,' glass in that he is 'the transparence of the place in which/He is.' Since the place is the mind and the mind is characterised by its will to change only a substance whose nature could change with the changes of its environment—change in the light directed upon them, as glass, crystal or diamond—would be logical for the abstraction of the hero. Yet if the man of glass 'in a million diamonds sums us up,' he is also 'without external reference'—just as the mind itself is at once transparent and without external reference. 'Sea Surface Full of Clouds' is an early poem describing the response of the mind to changing light on a seascape—that is, as a transparence of the place in which it is. On the other hand, as we have seen, the mind is 'eccentric,'—a sensibility that is a thing-in-itself characterised by a will to order and a will to change, paradoxical characteristics that reflect a paradoxical reality. The glass hero in a crystal world (the poet's 'fluent mundo') is thus the first idea of mankind in the natural world—a 'human acceleration that seems inhuman,' and, one might add, an acceleration of nature that seems unnatural.

(L. S. Dembo, *Concepts of Reality in Modern American Poetry*, 1966, pp. 104–5.)

Now if this is not the way to do it, and I am sure it is not, it remains true that this passage is not flagrantly inaccurate or silly. What it does is to take the meta-metaphysical mutter of Stevens and make it explicit. Nowadays the advice of Coleridge (and Eliot) to the effect that poetry can appeal strongly when imperfectly understood—advice Stevens took as a basis for his writing—is considered beneath the dignity of scholarship. What the Stevens glass man 'dewily cries' comes out as if treated by electronic recording engineers to take the dewiness out of it, and we hear such things as the man-monster never uttered, in tones remote from his. Where the harmonics of Stevens are heard they are inappropriate; as when a proof-text—'human acceleration that seems inhuman'—is adorned by a piece of pulpit oratory (and, one might add . . .') which is actually an imitation of the rhetoric the poet himself went in for in the Adagia and the essays.

It is as if the Stevens *mundo* had been stripped and re-assembled, not quite in the same order. Worse still, it gives a strong impression, as I mentioned before, that here is a poet we had best not dabble with, since he is so solemnly foolish. The next paragraph is designed, almost, to confirm this rejection. 'Finally, the "auroral creature musing in the mind" is described as "the naked man" who paradoxically becomes the "plus gaudiest vir," a man constantly rejuvenated by "cataracts of facts". . . .' Who could possibly care?

Who could possibly care? It is the easy comment of our enemies. Our business is to see that people care. Yet there is, of course, some justification for this kind of commentary. Stevens didn't altogether disown the element of puzzle in his work, and he did sometimes think of his entire *œuvre* as an attempt at a Grand Poem. But we are surely in a difficult position when our attempts to make a number of discrete poems into a whole harmonium simply discredit our author, and this is what happens. What one ends up with is an argument, more or less convincing, supported by proof-texts that suggest that the original under discussion is unworthy of discussion. The effect is of the deadlier kind of tract, the brainlessly minute column of Migne. Somehow the worst of Stevens is often the most useful for illustration. Stevens' solar chariot is made up of a good quantity of junk; we shall need eventually to admit that. But some commentators reduce it all to junk.

Harmonium has little junk and is hardest to traduce. Even when a poem contains a metaphysical plot Stevens is usually content to let be the obliquity of most *trouvailles*. When there is some sort of argument in process one is never bothered to do more than keep in the right general direction. I note in Mr Nassar's recent book the most useful explanation I have yet read of *Le Monocle de mon Oncle*, including a note by Arthur Mizener on the lines

Why, without pity on these studious ghosts
Do you come dripping in your hair from sleep?

'In your hair' means 'with your hair hanging freely and naturally' like a colonial virgin at marriage. It is good to know this. Mr Nasser goes on to explain that the whole poem is a sort of love-ode to the Interior Paramour. 'From a sleep of dreams the imagination emerges with fictions that belie any absolutist's ("studious ghosts") formulation of reality, and declare true but irrelevant Swift's satirical description that all pleasing images are deception.' Leaving out Swift, who seems to have no business here, we can say that Mr Nasser is sort of right but that it is not especially good to know that. I cared greatly for this poem before I knew anything about the Interior Paramour. What mattered was the absolutely personal assurance, the sense of one poem as able to bear the strain of so many relations, so many *trouvailles* all in tension with each other, a tension of wit and magniloquence, of notions made significant only because they occurred in one spot, Catawba or Hartford, New Haven or Tennessee or Oklahoma or Key West. Stevens' is a poetry that makes its landscape. Elsewhere it is the poetry of hats, of cocks, of angels, of statues; here it is a poetry of hair. 'Le Monocle' is this, and the crickets, and 'If men at forty will be painting lakes'; it is the red bird, the damsel heightened with eternal bloom; it is the accuracy of grotesque:

> Last night we sat beside a pool of pink,
> Clippered with lilies scudding the bright chromes,
> Keen to the point of starlight, while a frog
> Boomed from his very belly odious chords.

The gap between 'Le Monocle' and what can be said about it in commentaries is wide; indeed this gap is always very wide in Stevens. No commentators will say of his own efforts what Stevens said, commenting on one of his poems: 'This is just an explanation.' And few remember this saying: 'A poem must have a peculiarity, as if it were the momentarily complete idiom of that which prompts it.' He used philosophy, and any other kind of thinking, just as it prompted him. This is equally true of his prose. To take a short and splendid instance, his address at Bard College in 1948, in which he speaks of reality as the poet's 'inescapable and ever-present difficulty and inamorata.' He has said that the imagination is false, and then he says that it progresses by particulars, and that this makes the poet 'like a man who can see what he wants to see and touch what he wants to touch. In all his poems with all their enchantments for the poet himself, there is the final enchantment that they are true.' And after this solemn and animated play with the great abstractions that always haunted his mind, he ends by calling the poetic act 'an illumination of the surface, the movement of a self in the rock.' It might be from a poem, rather than from an address of thanks. Certainly it has a kind of argument. The thoughts and images cross, and what gives them their true relation is not argument:

> One's sense of a single spot
> Is what one knows of the universe

means less and more than Whitehead's 'every spatio-temporal standpoint mirrors the world.'

Stevens accepted Wahl's assertion that no idea is poetic, or 'that the poetic nature of any idea depends on the mind through which it passes.' On the other hand—and this is where the trouble starts—Stevens also believed, as I have said earlier, that 'supreme poetry can only be produced at the highest level of the cognitive'—or, as he puts it in the *Collect of Philosophy*, that the 'poem of poems' would have a philosophic theme. This idea is at once made richer and harder by a figure: 'That the wing of poetry should also be the rushing wing of meaning seems to be an extreme aesthetic good . . . it is very easy to imagine a poetry of ideas in which the particulars of reality would be shadows among the poem's disclosures.'

Further he argues that doing philosophy has aspects analogous to doing poetry; a passage from Whitehead proceeds 'from a level where everything is poetic,' and in another Samuel Alexander strains after exactness just as a poet does. ('Je tâche, en restant exact, d'être poète,'—a paradox Stevens found in Jean Wahl.) But 'the probing of the philosopher is deliberate' and 'the probing of the poet is fortuitous.' He might have said that the philosopher invents and the poet discovers. 'When we want to pay final tribute to Planck we say that his thought on causality had poetic nuances.' He might have said this of Wittgenstein, had he read Wittgenstein. Two truths emerge, anyway. One is that Stevens found philosophical thinking akin to poetry, and exciting. The second is that he was not under the impression that his thinking was 'doing philosophy.' He might very well feel about his systematic critics what the poet Morris said of a reciter who read his verses for the sense alone: 'it took me a long time to get that into verse and this damned fellow takes it out again.' If the poem is finding what suffices, we should remember that the examples given are 'a woman dancing, a woman combing'— sudden rightnesses, not deliberate probing; 'a movement of self in the rock.'

The particular problem, then, for his expositors, is this element of cognitive thought. The solitariness of Stevens makes this very complicated: solitariness, literal devotion to the single spot which is oneself, is admittedly an American tradition, but it calls for great critical resource. It asks for a solitary critic. There is probably no way to talk about the 'Metaphors of a Magnifico' without being a little public, a little philosophical. But the point to remember is that when we have read it together we must read it alone: once for the plot, once for the movement of a self in a rock. And yet even this formula won't suffice. Even in *Harmonium* Stevens is at his thinking: in, say, 'The Doctor of Geneva' or 'Another Weeping Woman' or 'Explanation,' in 'Valley Candle,' just as much a philosophical allegory as 'The Comedian as the Letter C':

> My candle burned alone in an immense valley.
> Beams of the huge night converged upon it,
> Until the wind blew.
> Then beams of the huge night
> Converged upon its image,
> Until the wind blew.

The kind of explanation ordinarily given simply destroys this poem's selfhood. How much harder things become when more and more comment, more and more ideas, shadow the poem's 'particulars of reality'!

After *Harmonium* the meditation becomes more continuous; there are more long poems and more trivial annotations on the commentary in the form of short ones. The flash fades, the voice mutters metaphysically: 'The theory of description matters most. . . . It is a world of words to the end of it.' All this is rich in proof-texts. 'Chocorua to its Neighbor,' its magniloquence qualified by joky nonce-words and bloodless finicking dandyism, is a great source of proof-texts. This is Augustinian speech not as 'direct transference' not of thought but of reverie. But we come in the end to those poems where a movement of a self in the rock requires that, in order for the idiom to be complete, the meditation, the metaphysical or meta-metaphysical mutter, shall be there, in tension with the particulars, as in 'Credences of Summer' the hayfields of Oley are the limits of reality. The culmination of this is *Notes toward a Supreme Fiction*, where we could not have had the passionate thinking of the climax without many testimonies of the imagination's truth and mercy: the chattering birds and the sexual blossoms, the ephebe suffering at his window, the lasting visage in the lasting bush, the true *weather* of the poem. Or, if it is not there, the culmination is in the earned, unfaltering meditation of the great final poems, whether long, like 'The Rock' or the poem for Santayana, or brief, like 'The Planet on the Table' and 'As you leave the Room.' The marriage of flesh and air in a particular poet at a particular spot is mentioned in these words about his poems, from 'The Planet on the Table':

> It was not important that they survive,
> What mattered was that they should bear
> Some lineament of character,
> Some affluence, if only half-perceived . . .
> Of the planet of which they were part.

I have said little of how, as commentators on this poet, we are to get out of our dilemma. Always, from the beginning, he teases us into thought; and later he forces thought upon us, or, at his best, uses it as he used colour in his early poems ('before the colours deepened and grew small'), as among the points which make the uniqueness of a poem. He tells us not to think of him as philosophical, but also that if he could write anything approaching the 'poem of poems' he would *be* philosophical. The only answer I can give (and the fact that the question is difficult doesn't make it unimportant) the only answer is to bear down upon the particularity of the poems themselves, the movement of a solitary self in their rock, and its relation to the particularity of their presiding personality. It is better to grasp

'The Idea of Order at Key West' as a single unique occurrence, an invitation to one's own imagination, than to see it as part of a para-philosophical structure. It is better to feel the peculiar lines of force that dominate *Notes* than to fit it into a philosophy founded on all the other poems. But the best thing of all is to know the point where all these forces cross, the unique Catawba in which the mumblings are the local speech, the human focus of all this physical and metaphysical fortuity. That cannot be done by exploding the whole harmonium into fragments, and re-assembling it into an inclusive commentary on its ideas. There are some key issues that, for pedagogical reasons, may have to be talked about discursively: but if you understand what Stevens meant by 'poverty' you know almost enough; if you can see why *Notes toward a Supreme Fiction* was to Stevens a kind of war poem you are nearly there. Then the thinking has to be muted, seen as an aspect of the ventriloquial powers of this great poet. Like all the others he celebrates the marriage of flesh and air, but in a dialect intensely local, like Bonnie's and Josey's.

We first see Stevens not in perspective, in a long tradition, but flat, like one of his early poems, arbitrary relations of colour and shape. Of course Stevens has his traditional elements, the re-incarnated blank verse for example; and the pose of the atomic isolation of his poetry, which is in a sense traditional for America. And if we complain that Stevens was given to smothering simple meanings in grave or fantastic clothing, we should reflect upon the remark: 'Poetry is like anything else, it cannot be made suddenly to drop all its rags and stand out naked, fully disclosed. Everything is complicated; if that were not so, life and poetry and everything else would be a bore.'

(1966-7)

X. ALLEN TATE

Whoever wishes to know what Allen Tate thinks his criticism is like may find out from his Prefaces, which explain that it is 'toplofty' in tone, aggressive because the only other course is to cringe. He looks back over his essays as he might over poems (for he tells us that poets can only thus discover what they think) and he abstracts certain articles of faith. There is 'a deep illness in the modern mind,' it affects poetry, which, denied any 'large field of imaginative reference,' tends to be complex, difficult, and important. But this must not persuade us to treat poetry as something else; it cannot explain the human predicament; rather it apprehends it 'in the mysterious limitations of form.' This is what it *does*; what it *is* is something else, and here at any rate it resembles, as Cowley noticed in *Of Wit*, that 'power divine' which 'we only can by negatives define.' R. F. Foster has recently commented on Tate's habitual negativity in this matter, but one could say that the 'tension' theory is the same kind of hard-won positive that Cowley reached at the climax of his poem: 'In a true piece of Wit all things must be, Yet all must there agree.' Much of the simple gist of Tate's criticism is in the prefaces.

He has also, in a virtually unique essay, told us what he makes of one of his poems, the 'Ode to the Confederate Dead'; and by the standards of modern poets this is a generous allowance of self-explication. So the author of a book on Tate finds some of the work done. Of course, Mr Tate qualifies carefully; in discussing the essays and the poem he is applying a doubtfully licit hindsight. There is not much point in distinguishing here between essays and poetry, for the best of the former, which come near to being the best of all modern critical essays, are in a way works of fiction, composed by the author of *The Fathers*; subtly elicited, formally constructed, ironical in a sense he and his friends taught us to recognise. Mr Foster argues, very sympathetically, that the New Criticism comes in the end to be best not as a strictly methodical kind of enquiry but as a risky, insight-conferring semi-poetry; he thinks first of Mr Blackmur in this connection, seduced, it may be, by the more intense local splendours. Yet Tate's greatest essays are finally more remarkable; they share with the poems a visionary mode, and a tough latinate vocabulary with controlled colloquial interventions—a style learnt from a despair of aristocracy.

Of course he can speak plainly, as in 'The Present Function of Criticism' and 'Literature as Knowledge'; his analyses of Morris and the early Richards are conducted with much precision. He often makes specific representations, concerning say graduate schools or literary quarterlies. And certainly on these occasions he is mindful of a deeper and more personal issue— his defence of the contemplative against the methodical. But neither these pieces, effective as they have been, nor others which owe their permanent interest to their radical relation with the author's practice as poet, are the really great ones. In that class one thinks of 'The Hovering Fly' with its urbane *progression d'effets*, the remote passion of its Fordian climax; and of the pieces in *The Forlorn Demon*, where contemplation is not a topic but a mode, and most of the rest of us (whether or no we would write like that if we had the talent) must feel like the political poets whom Tate consigns to childish voyages in Percy Shelley's paper boats. In this volume may be found the famous distinction between the symbolic and the angelic imaginations, the second characterising an extreme humanist presumption, the hubris accompanying a desire to liberate poetry from its human limitations; I have wondered whether Tate here silently recalled the greatest of all Stevens' poetry, the passage on the angel in the last section of *Notes toward a Supreme Fiction*. Certainly to read the two together is to effect a sublime modern confrontation. In these beautiful and difficult essays Tate finds his full critical voice. Whether or no, as Miss Koch argued, the verse romanticises itself as it goes on, the prose surely moves triumphantly towards the idiosyncratic Thomism of these later essays, and they provide a proof of that communicability of insight asserted in the essay on Longinus.

The mode is contemplative: witness those acts of rapt attention to a few lines of Dante, or to the last scene of *The Idiot*. And Tate knows that most critics, including his own, are likely to be methodical, not contemplative. In the essay on Yeats, which so successfully relieves the poems of the burden of the System, he prophesied that 'the study of Yeats in the coming generation is likely to overdo the scholarly procedure, and the result will be the occultation of a poetry . . . nearer the centre of our major traditions than the poetry of Eliot and Pound.' (It might be remarked, in passing, that critics—apart from Mr Nemerov— have strangely neglected the power of Yeats over Tate as a poet.) The prophecy has, to our cost, been fulfilled, and Yeats is now almost buried under the detritus of methodical investigation. In certain cases the poetry is valued only in so far as it can be perversely said to embody what is called 'the tradition,' a nonsensical occultist jumble which is now being used to justify other poets as well, among them Keats. The practitioners of this

perversion are the victims of that 'positivism' against which
Tate conducted his 'toplofty' attacks; but theirs is the cringing
defence, they abduct poetry, hide it in some grubby cell, and
make it serve as a kind of Tarot pack. In practice, of course,
these critics have just that ignorant passion for Method that
Tate abhors; they savage Yeats with scholarly procedures
divorced from all insight, and honour the gloss above the text.

This prelude is a way of saying that the man who sets out to
write a book on Tate faces many difficulties. The extractable gist
of the criticism, for instance, is already extracted in the Prefaces,
and there will be a temptation to take the whole of the 'thought'
methodically apart and set it up again, as if it were meccano;
for who, constructing a thesis, can allow for the quasi-poetic
mode and for the difference between contemplation and method?
The matter is made more difficult in that the admiring critic
may want to make of the 'thought' something acceptable to
himself. (The best writer on Tate might be somebody who
thought the 'thought' all nonsense but liked the poems.) There is
another special danger in the essay 'Narcissus as Narcissus,'
where Tate himself (though the essay is very fine) sets his critics
a bad example. He dislikes allegory and has not, I think, tried
to get on terms with Spenser; but his study of the *Ode* is
allegorical. The examples for his practice are distinguished
though not, in this area, very successful: Dante and St John of
the Cross. But the commentary on the 'Ode' virtually authorises
explication by free allegory, an easy approach to the poems
which Tate's mind, in a more characteristic phase, resists, if
only because the approach is methodical. Such explications invite
vulgar disaster in another way, by applying the casually conceited language of the graduate school to linguistic constructs of
notable precision (you might say this is caused by a professional
'hunger breeding calculation and fixed triumphs'). As to the
essays, they can be torn apart, their delicate internal stresses
disregarded; the parts reassembled will make theories, and contemplation will be reduced to method.

Mr Meiners[1] is an able and informed enquirer, and his book
is generally intelligent and useful. He is aware of many of the
difficulties mentioned above, affirming for instance that you

[1] *The Last Alternatives: A Study of the Works of Allen Tate.* Alan Swallow.
Denver.

must, in Tate's phrase, 'discuss the literary object in terms of its specific form.' Unhappily this merely tends to sharpen his pre-occupation with method, and—what is much worse—his pleasure in discussing and demonstrating it. Mr Meiners is not a particularly bad case of this methodological obsession, but one notices how prevalent it is in the criticism of a new genera-tion. (I assume, I hope not offensively, that Mr Meiners is young.) My immediate objections to it are not subtle, like Tate's, but perfectly simple. It gets in the way of the works treated; method in criticism is good in so far as it approximates, like the horn on an absey, to transparency. Methodological problems have a real power to excite the serious mind, which plaits the solutions into a sort of fence; then the critic contemplates the fence—all his own work—and not the field beyond. Mr Meiners begins by wondering where he should begin, quoting Alice. At the opening of Chapter 3, on Tate's poetic theories, he has some admirable remarks on the dangers and difficulties of what he is doing, remembering 'Tate's objection to the obsessive neatness of method.' But he does nothing about this, and I would agree that by such standards any book of this kind needs to be a little treacherous, since it has its own readers to con-sider, and must be tolerably shapely, not merely a discontinuous and repetitive commentary. A certain amount of 'faking' is inevitable. Thus one excuses Mr Meiners for this degree of betrayal. Harder to forgive are the transgressions against the simpler principle of methodological transparency, as in the passage which offers a brief history of *explication de texte* and leads up to a credo: the author believes in something like Wimsatt's 'explicative holism.' He could have let us observe him being explicatively holist and omitted this somewhat self-regarding preamble.

In fact, what follows isn't always explicative or wholesome. Mr Meiners, the holist exegete, is not immune from the familiar afflictions of the justified explicator. For example, he says of the word 'green' in the third stanza of 'Summer' in *Seasons of the Soul*, that it 'has overtones of death—witness Sir Gawain's experience. . . . France is here viewed as not only dynamically alive, but, paradoxically, as barely vegetative.' Such are the ways in which explicators can demonstrate their ingenuity in the detection of meanings: 'paradoxically' admits contradictory senses without further resolution, and a familiarity with the English School syllabus does the rest. What shocks me more (perhaps unreasonably) is a mistake in this same passage, where Meiners misdates the German invasion of France. '1939' here rings so absurd to anybody who knows how '1940' *feels* that one can hardly avoid thinking the point of this poem has been lost on its explicator. I hope I am not merely exhibiting the graduate supervisor's routine insistence on accuracy in such details. The poem has to do with a particular paralysing moment; the mistake is not a year but an epoch of feeling. It seems therefore exceptionally intrusive, like the vast tact of such remarks as 'I have some recollection that Christ once said "I bring not peace but a sword",' and 'I mention ambiguity and I do not wish to be understood,' and 'When dealing with the Goddess of Love in her Greek role we have an extremely tricky situation and I will not attempt any complete statement of it.'

What I complain of in short, is not merely egotistical intrusion, not merely 'methodological' opacity. It is a matter of tone. There should not be so great a discrepancy between text and comment without some good rhetorical reason. In Mr Meiners' book with its flashing of tools, its repeated claims to originality and dismissals of earlier critics, this discrepancy certainly exists. Perhaps this is why he does least well with the poems. They are certainly difficult to write about, but it is possible to multiply problems. The *Ode* is surely on any reasonable view an important and central poem, but Mr Meiners says very little about it; he assumes, rightly of course, that anybody who reads his book will know the *Ode* pretty well already, but by outflanking it he omits to attack the most irreducible of the problems Tate sets his readers. For it not only incarnates that contemplated past, but does so in the form of an ambiguous romantic vision which would obviously be patient of a great many different prose reductions. Meiners' assertion that *The Fathers* shares such characteristics is a good one; but the difference is that the novel finds, or improves out of Ford, a technical means clearly correlative to its intelligible purpose. The difference is between a fictional device one can be rational about, and a poetic device which is arbitrary and self-justifying. The *Ode* is the crucial instance of something that often happens in Tate's poetry—defiantly abrupt modulation into dream, and so, for interpretation, into allegory. There is a notably audacious instance at the beginning of 'Autumn' in *The Seasons of the Soul*, where the bathos is presumably intended or allowed for.

These effects Mr Meiners does little to describe, though I do not know that anyone else has done more. They are what would justify one's calling *Ash Wednesday* Eliot's most Tate-like poem, and the Tate's essay of 1931 on Eliot an important veiled pronouncement on his own poetry. He disputes Eliot's distinction of dreams into high and low, and for special purposes prefers what the other would call low ones; but he presumably agrees (or did so; these are hints of 'angelic' imagination) with Eliot's remarks in the essay on St-John Perse, when he says that the reader must be one who can feel the force of obscure relations rather than seek logical transitions, that he must sense rather than understand in any ordinary fashion the collocations of vision and wit. Incidentally, a very good example of Tate's power to give such collocations firm intellectual structure is the short poem called 'Pastoral,' which Meiners mentions only to chide somebody for liking it. It seems to me a very good poem, though I see that its ironies might be called Fugitive; it presents the ancient and well-endorsed desires of the *locus amoenus* in collocation with another sanctified theme—'love's not time's fool'—witty inverted. The potently suggested aphrodisiac ('She, her head back, waited/Barbarous the stalking tide') is in counterpoint with the 'deep hurrying mirror' of the stream, and the poem is resolved by the account of the lover at her 'wandering side'—not 'wondering,' though she must in fact be wondering what has gone wrong, but 'wandering' because she cannot get anywhere she wants to be without him, and he is lost and impotent, 'plunged into the wide/Area of mental ire,' and far from the conventionally sympathetic fields where lovemaking could happily occur. It isn't, of course, impossible to relate this little poem to those areas of concern towards which allegorisation of Tate always points: dissociation, disintegration, considered as characteristically modern and contrasted with a better-built scheme of things. But this, if we allow it, merely strengthens the wit: 'Such meditations as beguile/Courage when love grows tall' is both a glance at *Hamlet* and a perfectly just nonce-revival of the Chaucerian sense of 'courage.' This is a very tense poem, inescapably a dream poem, inescapably witty, an invert' Extasy.'

Donne lies behind Tate's witty dreams, though Tate is no less different from Donne than are his other modern admirers. I do not think he, any more than Eliot, has written well on Donne; but they have both, clearly, *felt* well about him; and Donne is a poet who might well be in a man's mind when he says 'in poetry all things are possible if you are man enough.' As to Tate's own work, I suppose this boldness is greatest in *Seasons of the Soul*, the poem Meiners singles out for specially full treatment. This blend of wit with dreaming wilder than Shelley's sets Mr Meiners great problems: he might well have said, as he considered it, 'anything is possible in explication of poetry if you are man enough.' With a good deal of his elaborate exposition of the poem I see no reason to agree, though it may well be that nobody else could do much better. Having called his predecessors on 'Winter' both 'wonderfully suggestive' and 'pathetically inadequate,' he labours long over Venus and the Hanged God and the *aeternum volnus amoris* of Lucretius; but merely to do so creates a somewhat false impression, and whoever needs elementary help on these points is not likely to get far with the poem anyway. I should have liked more (what there is is quite good, though) on the enormously inflated sea-conceit; the occasionally dandyish diction ('sea-conceited scop'); the faintly Swinburnian deliquescence of 'living' into 'livid'; the growth in the poem of the surrealist coral with its Dantesque tree; above all on the Freudian beast who 'slicks his slithering wiles/ To turn the venereal awl/In the livid wound of love.' Is there a difference between this and what Tate calls modern katachresis masquerading as metaphor? I doubt it; but the phrase is compelling enough, and has to do with the theme of the sexual wasteland discussed by Tate in the essay on Eliot I mentioned earlier. 'Venereal awl' sounds like baroque slang for the colloquial 'tool'—a calculated and sinister joke. These questions do not seem to be the kind that interest Mr Meiners. The explicator has a trade which grew up with modern poetry; yet a poem which so well illustrates Tate's prose points—a walking of the rope over an abyss of error and nonsense, learning as one goes where the next step must fall—yields very little to him. The poem-dream as 'specific' form, as the model for that knowledge which, except as analogue, is merely knowledge of itself, is essential to Tate; one may contrast the wonderful dreams of Donne, so subordinate to an external logic and rhetoric. Tate's explicator has to interpret dreams: so Mr Meiners can say 'On one level the "tossed, anonymous, shuddering sea" is a visual description; on another it is a value judgment and a behavioral description of modern life.' And it must be admitted that Mr Tate led him into this temptation, though he did not teach him this language.

Mr Meiners, one repeats, shows himself aware of the problem; one of his best observations is that Mr Tate's poetry 'depends upon a peculiarly intense vision in which objects and scenes, originally abstract, are forced to exist in a particular perception, a concrete detail, a specific sensation'—a perception none the worse for being approximately upside-down. He sees that the failures in Tate's poetry are usually related to this fact, whichever way you look at it. My only genuine complaint against Meiners is that occasionally, as in the chapter of *Seasons of the Soul*, he is swept away by his explicative fury into practices which imply neglect of this insight and others.

It is time to add that in discussions of general issues arising from the prose and the poetry Mr Meiners is thorough and often perceptive. On 'formalism,' on the saving doctrine of poetry as analogy, on the problem of a poet in a society lacking 'an objective system of truth,' on the myth of the ante-bellum South, and on the 'dissociation of sensibility' in all its aspects, he does a good and lively job of exposition. As an Englishman who came late to the knowledge (and love) of the man and his books, I am grateful to Mr Meiners for some expansion of my understanding of Tate, and regretful only that the demon Method has in some ways distorted the images of the great poems, the essays and the novel.

(1964)

Chapter Four

CRITICS

XI. A MODEST TRIBUTE TO EDMUND WILSON

(i) *Inside and Painentralia*

And this bwings us to liquorary quiddicism. What a wonderful is
liquorary quiddicism! What fastiddily! what intellectual breath!
what unreproachable stammards and crytearia! what inside and
painentralia!

The Three Limperary Cripples (1930)

And it raises the question why Edmund Wilson should be
thought to be, as in my view he is, so pre-eminently the greatest
periodical critic of his time, at any rate in English. The younger
Americans have of late been showing some disappointment with
him, finding him cranky and unwilling to deal with *their* new
things as he had dealt with his own. We have no special reason
to like him, as the English are a source of annoyance and
disappointment to him and he has often said so. He once began
a review thus: 'Mr E. H. Carr is an odd phenomenon—perhaps
a symptom of the decay of Great Britain.' Nor does this remark,
which—leaving aside the justice of the diagnosis—could only
have been made by a very difficult and occasionally somewhat
ludicrous critic, stand alone. Needing to make it clear that
despite his admiration for Marx and Engels he loathes the
Dialectic, he tosses off the proposal that the Hegelian triad, like
the triangle of Pythagoras, the Christian Trinity and the Wotan–
Brunnhilde–Siegfried set, were symbols of the male sexual
organs (*To the Finland Station*, II, 11). This is an emotional way
of saying that he finds the Dialectic and the Trinity extremely
unreasonable, and lest argument should fail to establish this he
throws in a tremendous symbol of irrationality. Much too
often, I think, he uses Freudian explanations in a similar way:

The Wound and the Bow is on re-reading his least interesting book (though it is still a good one) partly because the theory ends the argument prematurely, and the essay on Ben Jonson in *The Triple Thinkers*, for all its richness of reference and structural power, is so busy with the thesis of Jonson's anal eroticism that it neglects to examine his works. *Texture* is important in Jonson, and its examination is not one of Wilson's strong points. I am not saying the thesis is wrong, or even that it is irrelevant, but only that it obtrudes itself, as E. M. Forster once said mysticism might, 'at the wrong stage of the affair.'

This only begins the tale of Edmund Wilson's deficiencies, and we might as well mention one more which has a bearing on his view of the English: this is simply that he is so *echt* American that it shows in some ways which may strike us as inappropriate. Red Bank, Princeton, houses, friends, heroes such as H. L. Mencken and John Jay Chapman, they all become part of a patrician mythology rather like Yeats's, and sometimes Wilson seems to feel a need to Americanise before he can offer sympathetic understanding. An essay on Dostoevsky makes the point that when the Russian is writing on Russian exiles 'a good deal of what he says applies equally to expatriate Americans in Europe.' Fair enough; but two pages later we read this: 'Dostoevsky's instinct was sound: the fact that the American problem seems a particularly formidable one is no cause for fleeing or evading it.' In the same way we feel an unexpected sympathy with Lenin's red hair and Marx's boils and certain Russian country houses. The Jews are translated into New Englanders. Going to America made Auden a good poet; leaving it made Eliot a sort of cultured Uriah Heep. Finally, *Patriotic Gore*, for all its virtues, obviously indulges a nostalgic, bitter Americanism; so does *The Cold War and the Income Tax*.

Good reviewing in the weeklies and monthlies is, as Wilson himself very well knows, an essential element in the hygiene of a literary culture; yet he has done it more or less under protest over a long period of his life; and this from vanity rather than laziness, for he is apparently a tireless reader and writes (judging from the bulk of his work, and the ease with which it is articulated) with as much facility as any one, though this is a quality that casual readers are very apt to exaggerate. It is not surprising, therefore, that his critics notice a decline in the interest and penetration of his journalism between the work of the twenties and 'Thirties collected in *The Shores of Light* and that of the 'Forties collected in *Classics and Commercials*.[1] No doubt a further decline may be found in the new collection from later years, which is called—as if to emphasise a certain inconsiderate isolation, a galloping off in directions that interest only him— *The Bit Between my Teeth*.[2] If the best journalism belongs to the 'Twenties and the best criticism of the more formal kind is in *Axel's Castle* (1931), there is some justification for the view of various commentators that this formidable figure has—for reasons only to be guessed at, though often related to the politics of the 'Thirties—grown less and less useful over the last thirty-five years. And we can at least be sure that Wilson himself unreservedly accepts the criterion of utility in matters of criticism, as in literature itself. Broadly speaking, this is the way Norman Podhoretz talks about Wilson in what is probably the best essay about him. 'From now on,' Podhoretz says at the end of his piece, 'we shall have to look elsewhere for the kind of guidance that it was his particular glory to give.'

It is not difficult to understand Podhoretz's disappointment. A man who had clearly seen, and tirelessly propagated, the right programme for American letters—who had, with serious optimism, insisted upon their relevance to the health of American society—seems to have contracted out, calling himself an alien in his own country, constructing a misanthrope's *Vision*. All that patrician generosity, all that subtle meditation on social justice, were converted into the gloomy execrations of un-American self-exile; like Shakespeare's Poet visiting Timon in the woods, the dependent critic is rewarded with curses and gold thrown in his face. This is how it must seem to the leaderless.

This is of course primarily an American problem, and it is interesting to notice that a new book on Wilson tackles it quite differently. Mr Sherman Paul[3] has, in fact, written a very elaborate study of the large and varied *œuvre* with the intention not of demonstrating Wilson's cultural usefulness but of tracing

---

[1] Both collections, London, W. H. Allen; New York, Farrar, Straus.

[2] London, W. H. Allen; New York, Farrar, Straus.

[3] *Edmund Wilson: A Study of Literary Vocation in Our Time*. University of Illinois Press.

in it the lines of an important writer's personal development. This strategy has its drawbacks, the worst of which is that it gets Wilson's public achievement out of focus; Paul attends just as closely to writings of small public importance as to the major works, and even the criticism is treated as if it were *à clef*. There are other disadvantages. Nobody can write about Wilson without inviting hostile comparisons between his prose and that of his subject. It would have been tactful of Mr Paul to avoid usages formally condemned by his hero, such as *demean* in the sense of 'disparage' or 'abase,' which occurs twice in the book.

All the same, this is a valuable study. From the opening chapter on the critic's youth one gets a perfectly valid slogan: Wilson is finely Puritan, if the word can mean 'concerned with moral precision.' The dominant virtue of the intellectual is a demythologised charity, and if Wilson has often lapsed from this, both by mythologising and by uncharitable behaviour, who among critics working under such pressures has been more faithful? Certainly not Taine, his earliest model, who 'shrank . . . into professorial superiority' when progress came to be associated with vulgar revolution: 'a remote disapproval chills his tone, all the bright colours of his fancy go dead.' Again and again Wilson finds in the career of distinguished writers a similar shrinking: in Eliot, for example, and all the neo-Christians (as Mr Empson calls them), in Anatole France and Bernard Shaw. But even in the days when the rightness of the Marxist diagnosis seemed most dreadfully confirmed by the condition of America, Wilson wanted Marxism without the mythology, wanted people to prove their charitable faith by good works rather than by an abdication of the reason. Whatever the mistakes, he did seek to carry out the Jamesian programme of 'striving to understand everything' about human relations in a world not in itself organised for humanity, and discovering what might be for humanity 'indubitable values.' Even now it is not the values that have changed, but society that has turned out to be less corrigible than he hoped.

In the early days of his career, at Princeton and in Greenwich Village, the constant pursuit of abstract civil virtue and *il ben del intelletto* seem to have set him a little apart even from his brilliant contemporaries. Part of the difficulty was doubtless that for all his excitement at an American renaissance, his superior understanding of the modern, Wilson was always a man for continuity. He remained devoted to his Princeton teacher Christian Gauss, who believed that to adapt to his environment man must master it intellectually. Criticism would ideally be an aid to this; it should try to be 'a history of man's ideas and imaginings in the setting of conditions which have shaped them.' *Axel's Castle*, which acts upon this belief, is dedicated to Gauss; and it is not merely an exceptionally intelligent and original piece of literary history but an attempt to improve the possibility of literature becoming an agent of human mastery over the modern environment. For Wilson literature is always a way of knowing the world, and however much one may say of it as a giver of pleasure it is measured finally by its utility. It will not be useful unless it is fully informed, and neither the writing nor the exposition of imaginative works can, in his view, be worth much unless the author or the expositor has a deep familiarity with his subject and the knowledge to provide broad context. That is why his own programme has involved the mastery of many languages and literatures, and why he despises monolingual and one-subject professors. It is also the reason for his commitment to the past—not only the American past, but to the best in Greek, Latin, Italian, French and Russian literature as well as English and American, and for his guilt about Latin-American writing. His 'adventure on reality,' as Mr Paul calls it, required also an education in politics and economics. Later Hebrew demanded attention. The artist—and Wilson thought of all his work as an artist's—is committed to the past, to the present, and to the community.

Wilson's plays and his fiction, with the important exception of *Memoirs of Hecate County*, belong mostly to his earlier years. In respect of the need of discipline he did not discriminate between criticism and fiction, and there is a sense in which it is plausible to say, with Mr Paul, that *Axel's Castle* and *I Thought of Daisy* belong together: they were worked on at the same time, and deal with the same problem, 'the writer's allegiance to society.' But even Mr Paul, who devotes many pages to the novel, cannot deny that there is in it a programmatic stiffness, a lack of easy invention, which throws into high relief the ease and authority of the critical work; and Wilson's later memoir of

Edna St Vincent Millay tells us more and more movingly about the personal element than the story can, however teased out by interpreters. She fits, as Wilson's heroes do, into a system not so much autobiographical as symbolising the structure of the world as he finds it: with Scott Fitzgerald and Paul Rosenfeld and Mr Justice Holmes and Whitehead and Gauss and Mario Praz.

This personal mythology is important and valuable to a writer, but Wilson speaks best when he speaks out. His prose style is designed for speaking out: his language is in his own terms, 'the language of responsibility,' as men engaged upon decisive action speak it; he is with Lincoln and Grant, not with the non-participants, Henry James and Henry Adams. If his prose has often an antique balance and his diction an etymological exactitude, this is proper enough, for his action is the action of structural thought; and if it sometimes seems pedantic in its cultivation this is because solecism and vulgarism enfeeble the activity of language. Wilson's prose, whether one speaks of it in quite this way or not, is certainly a powerful instrument; despite his own fears it has remained supple and strong over a long and arduous career. One consequence is that, schooled to correct-ness, one is shocked in Wilson by what would pass almost unnoticed in another writer; when he uses *attainted* for *tainted* a bell rings violently in the mind ('Mr Krutch . . . gives some evidence of being attainted with this tendency'). Anyway, there is small doubt that Wilson's style is better adapted to the exposi-tion of literature and ideas than to fiction.

'Participation in public life through literature' is the pro-gramme of *Axel's Castle*; for Mr Paul it is related to the same needs expressed in the novel, which is the author's need to extinguish in himself any symptoms of Axel-symbolist with-drawal and leaving living to the servants. Having written these books, he was ready for the labours of the 'Thirties; Mr Paul quotes with approval a contemporary opinion that 'one could plot a graph of Mr Wilson from Proust to Karl Marx,' and this is what he does, having chosen to make the inward movement of Wilson's mind the theme of his book. Consequently one needs, if one is to seize Wilson's real importance, which is a matter of creative criticism rather than of literary personality, to get some view of the outward as well as of the inward aspects of this as of other periods of his work; and this one can do by reading such books as Daniel Aaron's *Writers on the Left*, Malcolm Cowley's *Exile's Return*, Alfred Kazin's *Starting Out in the Thirties*, anything that, however obliquely, gives one the feeling of that decisive New York decade. Throughout this time Wilson, Trotskyist at least in this respect, maintained the values of bourgeois culture in the classless society, and saw in Marx and E ɪgels poets of the political vision, as Michelet had been, and as he was now trying to be himself.

To the Finland Station was the result of the arduous reading of the 'Thirties. Alfred Kazin reminds us of Wilson's invaluable self-discipline, a 'habit of willed attention, of strained concentration,' essential to work of this kind; and we can also remember his power to organise large bodies of material, to make self-consistent structures and establish large relevances. It is perhaps the noblest of Wilson's books. It appeared, as Paul remarks, too late, when Stalin had put an end to the dream of the 'first truly human culture'; but in so far as it is about intellectual heroism and the role of honest imaginative thinking in the creation of a good society it is a work of permanent value. It is true that the tone is of biography rather than ideology; but this, like the author's tendency to identify his own mind and methods with those of the subjects, gives it an exceptional resonance, and makes it, like *Axel's Castle*, a book of use even to those who can no longer be instructed by it. One notes that the praise of Marx's expository method represents admiration for an ideal the author himself aims at ('the exposition of the theory—the dance of commodities, the cross-stitch of logic—is always followed by a documented picture of the capitalist laws at work . . . we feel that we have been taken for the first time through the real structure of our civilisation, and that it is the ugliest that has ever existed.'). Here I have had to leave out the long and powerful sentence in which the working of the capitalist laws is described; long, but lucid and forceful, as Wilson thinks expository sentences should sometimes be. And I take it that even the expert will not deny the clarity and cogency of the exposition in this book. Engels as a man is treated with affectionate admiration, but with Lenin one senses the author's detachment: just as Marx was 'incapable of imagining a democracy,' Lenin shunned 'gratuitous intellectual activity.' If Marx was psychologically crude, he was in other ways Wilsonian, 'heavily loaded with the old paraphernalia of culture' and making of *Das Kapital,* somewhat unexpectedly, a work which has affinities with the *Anatomy of Melancholy.* Bıt Lenin was not a scholar, not a writer; his style (as Gorky observed) was 'the cold glitter of steel shavings.' He was the New Man, the modernist of Marxism, exponent of an un-Wilsonian break with the past. 'We don't need bourgeois democracy,' he said in his speech at the Finland Station. In an epilogue looking back over the whole story in 1940, Wilson is finely himself; he cannot allow that the failure of Marxist dogma means the failure of all hope for a society without class exploitation. Doing without the Dialectic is only a small part of the challenge, which will 'require of us,' as he very characteristically concludes, 'an unsleeping adaptive exercise of reason and instinct combined.'

From Mr Paul's point of view, which is reasonable but as I say not the only one, there is a link between this book and Wilson's slightly later volume of *novelle, Memoirs of Hecate County,* comparable with that between *Axel's Castle* and *I Thought of Daisy*; on his view that 'to some extent everything he does—and when he takes it up—is a personal index,' the relation is inevitable. In the central story, 'The Princess with the Golden Hair,' Wilson certainly has rather private sources—he is thinking of Engels and Mary Burns, as well as of Casanova—and yet this is one of his most subtle and passionate comments on the evils of a society in which, as he remarked in *To the Finland Station,* 'there is very little to choose between the physical degradation of the workers and the moral degradation of the masters.' Wilson himself calls it his favourite among his works, and one can see why. Also it marked a turning point in his career; the last of the works in which commitment to public life is a central theme. The later books of travel, the bold attempt on the Dead Sea Scrolls, the works on the Iroquois, the Income Tax, the literature of the Civil War, and the culture of Canada, for all their urgent relation to his own unending self-examination and his concern with American culture, are works, by comparison, of exile. Hence the discontent of some compatriots.

But even from this very defective account of his career one can see that a stranger might very well use his privilege to call such criticism unjust. The example of Wilson—discipline, persistence, self-involvement, a willingness to acquire the means with which to practise an effective criticism—has been followed, but not adequately acknowledged, by younger Americans. To make possible an American criticism that would be strong enough for its job, to provide for it the strength, range and subtlety of the French, was the vast undertaking. Wilson himself saw that it meant good reviewing in the periodicals. The job begins there.

It is no doubt impossible [he wrote in 1928] for an English-speaking country to hope for a literary criticism comparable to that of the French. . . . But when one considers the number of reviews, the immense amount of literary journalism that is now being published in New York, one asks oneself how it is possible for our reviewing to remain so puerile. . . . Since the death of Stuart P. Sherman, who was second-rate at best, there has not been a single American critic who regularly occupied himself in any authoritative way with contemporary literature.

He went on to list some of the evils of the situation which strong reviewing might have averted; many of them he himself was to tackle. But he also added, thinking again of himself, that first-rate criticism must come from writers: 'No such creature exists as a full-time literary critic—that is, a writer who is at once first-rate and nothing but a literary critic.' And so the task of providing America with a criticism was difficult even on the mundane level of simply finding time to do it. You had to review a lot but your reviewing would be useless unless you did other things on another level. Sometimes it wasn't possible to do both; during the years when he was reading for *To the Finland Station* Wilson, as he says, lost touch with what was going on. But by working enormously and being provident in the choice of subjects he succeeded remarkably in his attempt to do everything at once. Because he did so there *is* in America literate unacademic criticism.

One should say, then, that the size of Wilson's critical achievement, as the outsider sees it, cannot be measured by the more formal volumes, such as *Axel's Castle, The Triple Thinkers, The Wound and the Bow*, alone; one has to take account of the hundreds of shorter pieces, not merely because many of them were tributaries to these major streams, but also because they constitute in themselves that almost weekly intervention in the literary affairs of the time which probably, in the end, has the more decisive effect on taste, and on what happens next. Wilson has himself described how a career like this can be managed. In a very interesting piece called 'Thoughts on Being Biblio-graphed' (1943) he complains that his kind of person doesn't seem to exist any more, a writer who is a critic and a journalist, free of the oppression and patronage of academics though having of course his own problems.

To write what you are interested in writing and to succeed in getting editors to pay for it, is a feat that may require close calculation and a good deal of ingenuity. You have to learn to load solid matter into notices of ephemeral happenings; you have to develop a resource-fulness at pursuing a line of thought through pieces on miscellaneous and more or less fortuitous subjects; and you have to acquire a technique of slipping over on the routine of editors the deeper inde-pendent work which their over-anxious intentness on the fashions of the month or the week have conditioned them automatically to reject. . . . My [strategy] has usually been, first to get books for review . . . on subjects in which I happened to be interested; then, later, to use the scattered articles for writing general studies of these subjects; then, finally, to bring out a book in which groups of these essays were revised and combined.

Using this somewhat clumsy but necessary system, he tackled the self-imposed task of carrying on the work of Mencken; one part of it, for example, was to bring home to the bourgeois intellectual world the importance of the literature of post-Symbolism and the implications of the Russian Revolution. Now, he says (in 1943), he is too old for all that; and nobody else is doing it, partly because anybody who might have qualified himself is working in a university or having his talent wrecked in a different way by *Time*, *Life*, and *Fortune*. Wilson had a perfect right to say this about people who feel he has betrayed them by refusing to bear the strain for ever. The routine outlined above takes strength, courage, discipline, none of them to be rewarded by the gift of tenure, or by long, gentle sabbaticals. One sees, sadly, why Wilson is so unkind to academics, refusing their honorary degrees, and, if he admires them, as he did New-ton Arvin, Saintsbury, Gauss, Kemp Smith, Whitehead, Praz, assuming that their ability to write creatively simply takes them out of the academic category, and so does not disturb his theory.

It is the routine reviewing, somewhat disparaged by Wilson himself, that gives the best evidence of hard labour and also, often enough, of disciplined commitment. The three large volumes which collect reviews and other fugitive pieces are, what can rarely be said for such collections of periodical criticism, a great pleasure to read; the reviews frequently survive their subjects. As a great professional Wilson knows the ropes, and is willing to instruct. 'The Literary Worker's Polonius,' written in 1935, sets out schematically the duties of editors and contributors, the former obliged in honour to make quick decisions and quick payments, the latter needing to give the editors reasonable time to decide and consult, and to abstain from writing seductive covering letters. A whole section is given to reviewers, classified under five heads: People Who Want Work, Literary Columnists (overworked, don't expect accuracy), People Who Want to Write about Something Else (even if they let the author down, they are often interesting and should not be discouraged), Reviewer Experts (poets reviewing poets, etc., on the whole not a good thing), and Reviewer Critics. These last are extremely rare, and to earn the title an aspirant should 'be more or less familiar, or be ready to familiarise himself, with the past work of every important writer he deals with. . . . He should also be able to see the author in relation to the national literature as a whole and the national literature in relation to other literatures.' And so on. Only Sainte-Beuve, says Wilson, really fits into this category; but of course he does too. And when this paragon gets down to a book he must not shirk the most boring part of the job, the exposition of the contents, the summary: this is absolutely essential. Wilson does it, as a matter of fact, superbly. He really can 'establish definite identities for the books that he discusses.' It takes work, and more surprisingly brains, to do this. Yet it is only the start. In 'A Modest Self-Tribute' (1952) Wilson is again insisting on the need for critics 'to bring into one system the literatures of several cultures that have not been in close communication. . . . I may claim for myself, since nobody so far as I know, has ever yet claimed it for me, that I have tried to contribute a little to the general cross-fertilisation. . . .

To do this you need more than a 'volatile curiosity,' but you need that too. Some of the long essays in the latest book, which may be used to show how Wilson has wandered off in pursuit of his own private interests, are also evidence of his determination to find out what is necessary. Certainly he goes on rather about the Marquis de Sade; but he also explores *Doctor Zhivago* at great length. It strikes me as both typical and impressive that, returning for another go at T. S. Eliot in a review of 'Myra Buttle's' *The Sweeniad*, Wilson took himself off to a library to read the 'hilariously awful' epic, *Cadmus: The Poet and the World*, written earlier by Victor Purcell, the man behind the mask of 'Myra Buttle.' This later activity may not be as important as being the first to present André Malraux or Henry Miller to the American public, but it speaks of an inquisitive turn of mind and a willingness to walk to the library. Also it reminds one that one of the preservatives of Wilson's periodical criticism is that he can be rather sombrely funny. He did not much like writing for the *New Yorker*, but some of the pieces there printed have lasted wonderfully: the analysis of Ambassador Davies' prose, for instance, the attacks on detective stories (notably 'Who Cares Who Killed Roger Ackroyd?'), and the judicious distaste of the article on Lloyd C. Douglas' best-seller, *The Robe*. In fact the pieces in *Classics and Commercials* are inferior to those in *Shores of Light* only if you miss, what had to go, the special excitements of the 'Twenties and 'Thirties. They belong to what Wilson called 'the bleak and shrivelled 'Forties,' and they address themselves to what seemed in need of informed attention at the time: the intellectual position of Archibald MacLeish in relation to the war; the new novelists—Cain, Steinbeck, O'Hara, Saroyan; Aldous Huxley, Evelyn Waugh (two excellent essays); Sartre, Firbank, and so on, with an extended memoir of Paul Rosenfeld at the end, corresponding to the memoir of Edna St Vincent Millay at the end of *Shores of Light*. The new book, as its title suggests, wanders further from the beaten track, and has a lot about Swinburne and James Branch Cabell, but there are some comedy turns too, including Wilson getting lengthily angry about the way people abuse English.

It is, then, true but unreasonable to complain that none of this has quite the bite of earlier work, done when Wilson was in the centre of things. *The Shores of Light* contains an imaginary dialogue between Paul Rosenfeld and Matthew Josephson (one of the original *Discordant Encounters*) which is so absolutely in the centre of the first controversies on modernism as to be even now immediately relevant. It was written in 1924; forty-two years on Mr Tom Wolfe is doing well out of an *aperçu* of Josephson's in the Dialogue, which is that electric signs are nicer than art. Don't talk to me about art, he says—

> How can you set up these trivialities as rivals to the electric sign . . . a triumph of ingenuity, of colour, of imagination!—which slings its great gold–green–red symbol across the face of the heavens themselves . . .! I tell you that culture as you understand it is no longer of any value; the human race no longer believes in it. That is why I am giving my support to the campaign for Henry Ford as President. . . . Vote for Henry Ford! The Master Dadaist of the twentieth century!

In those days Wilson, not long down from Princeton, was living in the Village and learning his job. As a critic he did most things—vaudeville, the galleries, music, theatre—but he did them as a writer, and with a growing sense of the commitments to the modern and to politics, or rather to the task of making a literature and a criticism which would not simply exclude these. His interests narrowed, perhaps, but never before each had reached fruition in a book; perhaps he forsaw a time when literature and politics would be as inextricably blended in America as in *The Triple Thinkers* he saw them to be in Russia; or a time when a new biographical criticism would profit by the thesis of *The Wound and the Bow*. But of course he changed, moved on, a stranger in a changing world. It is sometimes said that behind every criticism there is a philosophy; Wilson's is steadily pragmatic.

> All our activity, in whatever field it takes place, is an attempt to give meaning to our experience—that is, to make life more practicable.

This is as true of the fictions of Sophocles as of Euclid.

> Art has its origin in the need to pretend that human life is something other than it is, and, in a sense, by pretending this, it succeeds to some extent in transforming it.

This last remark belongs to 1922, and I suppose Wilson would have no reason to withdraw it now. The transformation of the world, as Wallace Stevens remarked, is the transformation of ourselves, and we do it with reason and imagination. What needs to be transformed, how transformations have historically occurred, and what is wrong with present attempts at transformation, are the legitimate and exhausting tasks of criticism. Wilson has worked at them as no other critic in his time. He dislikes my profession and my nationality, but if no American has yet claimed this for him I offer it as the most modest of tributes.

(ii) A Note on *Memoirs of Hecate County*

Edmund Wilson, one of the greatest of living men of letters and a leading character in a most interesting chapter of American literary history, advises the reader in the reissue of *Memoirs of Hecate County* that it is his favourite among his books. 'I have never understood why the people who interest themselves in my work never pay any attention to it.' The reason is, presumably, that Wilson's powers are most impressively exhibited not in fiction but in books which more obviously embody his great intellectual energy, and that range of learning which, in its diversity and order, testifies to the integrity of the mind that assimilates it. But this is also a reason for taking the fiction seriously, for it will give one a chance to observe the activity of this mind when it is freely inventing as well as ordering its material. If only because this book provides an insight into the author's situation at a critical moment in his career it will have its place in the story. But it is in fact rather more than a mere supporting document.

One of the constants in Wilson's literary character—its native American quality—is well expressed in one of the lesser stories here reprinted. The narrator, himself newly returned from Europe, brings with him a conviction that American artists, however much Europe may rub off on them, depend for their continuing vitality on their 'native American base.' Wilson has always been a connoisseur of the vital American tradition, and a patrician connoisseur at that; it is the American 18th century that speaks in his expertises of furniture, women, language. Superimposed on that base is an easy understanding of all that has happened since to alter the cultivated mind—the Russian novel, the colours and shapes of modern painting, Marx and Freud, shifting social patterns and new judgments of manners. The mind is cosmopolitan, equipped for criticism, but deeply American still.

The narrator of the earlier novel, *I Thought of Daisy*, demonstrates its way of working when, back from France, he notices 'with a new attention the way Americans talked,' and read 'with astonished gratification, the first books of those American writers who seemed to be making a new literature out of that sprawling square-syllabled speech . . . a language fit only, it had seemed, for the uses of trade or of a plebeian extravagance and irony.' He takes a critical delight—'an interest self-conscious and pedantic'—in the new slang, classifying it as 'Village' and 'Broadway.' And at the same time he sees sickness in American society—people like Hugo in *Daisy* who seem 'a human penance for the shortcomings of a whole class and culture'; the new life is built on corruption, injustice, sterility. Like many others, though more thoroughly than most, Wilson studied the Marxist diagnosis and the Russian cure. But *Hecate County* is mostly about the sickness.

It is a collection of six stories and *novelle* (one long enough for a novel, but still, in method, a *novella*). They are written in that characteristically fastidious prose, at once masculine and sensitive, and all are satisfying, though not all are strong enough to justify Wilson's preference for this book over the others. 'The Man Who Shot Snapping Turtles' is a mildly Westian extravagance; 'Ellen Terhune,' an exercise in the manner of *The Turn of the Screw*. There are examples of satirical demonism, touches of Scott Fitzgerald. A certain slight poverty of means (endless drinks, parties, conversations) makes itself felt, without great harm to the intellectual elegance of the work; it wouldn't be worth mentioning except that the author's own standards are so high ('If you begin recommending the second-rate . . . you're not gradually educating people . . . you're simply letting down the standards and leaving people completely at sea.') These minor tales don't matter much, considered in relation to the whole output of a major writer. But the centrepiece, 'The Princess with the Golden Hair,' does.

This is the story that caused all the fuss when it came out twenty-three years ago. The trouble was caused, I take it, by the descriptions of lovemaking. These passages, which are absolutely essential to the structure of the piece, are so refined and periphrastic that it is hard to imagine how anybody could be wickedly stimulated by them. The other shocking thing was that the narrator, a cultivated art expert, contracts gonorrhoea. But that too is sedately expressed, and, in the story, quite as functional as the parallel infection in *Bubu of Montparnasse*. It seems unlikely, given the changes in the climate of literary sexuality, that any of this can now get in the way of the reader, or even cause the book to be read for the wrong reasons.

In respect of its form, the story has the patrician elegance; its matter, however, is less mandarin, since it deals with the 'mechanical tyranny' of the 'dying social system' as observed in the Depression years. The narrator deals obliquely with this contrast in a passage about his rejection of the doctrine of 'significant form'—stimulated by a new and fruitful contact with proletarian life, he sees the intense formalism of painting after Cézanne less as a triumph of art than as a symptom of 'human decadence.' But he cannot entirely give way to these feelings, and the distortions of life, reflected in some painting and brought about by capitalism, become the material of an elegant fictional argument.

The substance of the book lies in two contrasting love affairs. There is a bourgeois beloved, long untouchable and wearing a brace because she thinks she has tuberculosis of the spine. In fact the condition is hysterical. Her bogus pre-Raphaelite remoteness, and later her selfish sexual performance, are represented as deviant from a healthy American norm. Imogen is Beauty chained (by her self-induced disease) to a couch, a decadent, unhealthy teaser. Her beauty is real enough; she is perfect in form, and even the distortion of a breast by the unnecessary brace seems luxurious in its perversity. In her dealings with vulgar life she shows a streak of commonness. This is a very adequate image of the social disease of a bourgeoisie lacking the fineness that should accompany privilege.

The other girl is a second-generation Slavic-American, one of the good poor who have fallen into a feckless underworld life because of 'the badness of the times,' a victim of the system. She brings the narrator into contact with what is left of the good life of the poor, and he thinks of this as human reality in contrast with the spuriousness of Imogen. She also introduces him to the infections of that life; the gonorrhoea, unlike the tuberculosis, is real. It lingers in him, a reminder of the problems of class.

The proletarian–pastoral is notoriously a genre which promotes sentimentality and simpleness. Wilson's critical faculty is on duty here to prevent disaster. The narrator's love for the girl is critically presented. Was he perverse, seeking underworld excitements, deceiving himself? He decides not. She gave him 'the life of the people,' which transcended what infected and defiled it, and had more reality than the 'infantile fairy tales' of Imogen.

The delicacy and strength don't come through in summary. The story has to be read. In its subtle joining of American patrician and American plebeian the book itself is a moment in the history of American culture.

(1965-6)

XII. FRYE RECONSIDERED

The one thing certain about modern criticism is that there is too much of it, and it is only rarely that one can say of a practitioner that he cannot safely be left unread. But one has to say it of Frye; ever since the publication, in 1957, of *An Anatomy of Criticism*, we have been trying to come to terms with him, and he has been writing a succession of shorter books to help us do so. Shakespeare's final plays have always been important to his theory, and he has now devoted to them a series of lectures which should enable us to make up our minds.

One striking aspect of Frye's system is its theological rigour. He insists that his theory, however primitive in its present form, is the only true one, that you must accept or reject it *in toto*. This new book, *A Natural Perspective*, is lucid and self-explanatory (Frye writes excellent prose); but it implies the dogmatics of the *Anatomy*, and readers who cannot find the time to absorb that vast and surprising book should at least read two of the essays reprinted in the collection of 1963 entitled *Fables of Identity*; these give the gist of the doctrine under the rubrics 'The Archetypes of Literature' and 'Myth, Fiction and Displacement.' They will then notice that this new book, freshly thought out as it undoubtedly is, is an application, to works Frye regards as crucial, of the general theory. I may as well say right off that I look for a way of saving some of the special insights without accepting the doctrine; exactly what Frye regards as an impossible compromise.

According to Frye, we must not confuse the experience of literature with criticism. In this book he 'retreats from individual plays into a middle distance, considering the comedies as a single group unified by recurring images and structural devices.' The reader 'is led from the characteristics of the individual play . . . to consider what kind of a form comedy is, and what is its place in literature.' This is what he calls 'standing back,' the way you stand back to look at a painting. One step back gives you the view of Wilson Knight or Bradley—occult thematic or psychological patterns—and the second enables you to see the object in its genre: *Hamlet* as a Revenge Play, for example. One more step and you have Frye's view: *Hamlet* as myth, probably multiple: the *Liebestod* and the leap into and out of Ophelia's grave. From this distance you see a work of literature as frozen in space, devoid like myth, of temporality, and fit for inclusion in an all-embracing mythical system. 'It is part of the critic's business to show how all literary genres are derived from the quest-myth . . . the quest-myth will constitute the first chapter of whatever future handbooks of criticism may be written that will be based on enough organised critical knowledge to . . . live up to their titles.' Criticism is a progressive system of description. It cannot value literature, but by describing its mythical fundamentals it can enable us to deduce its political role, which is identical with that of myth: 'the central myth of art must be the vision of an end of social effort, the innocent world of fulfilled desires, the free human society.'

This is not the whole of Frye, but it is, I think, the essence. And before disputing it one must insist that the mind which gives it embodiment, whether in the glittering structures of the *Anatomy* or the various and resourceful inventions of the present book, is well-stocked, cogent, and sane. Some of its principles deserve to be regarded as laws: 'there is no passage in Shakespeare's plays . . . which cannot be explained entirely in terms of its dramatic function and context . . . nothing which owes its existence to Shakespeare's desire to "say" something.' Or, to take another instance, Frye's denial of allegorical readings applied to such works as *The Winter's Tale*. The argument is dubious (there is no room for allegory because the drama does by 'the identity of myth and metaphor' what ritual did by 'the identity of sympathetic magic') but the conclusion is right: 'the meaning of the play is the play,' and abstractions from it are all false.

Nevertheless, all critics proceed by abstractions from that meaning. Some of them, however, seek to stay as close as may be to the 'total experience of the play'—as W. K. Wimsatt once put it, they work out *pi* to as many decimal places as possible. Frye abstracts by *standing back*, and finds strength in his analogy with looking at a painting: but, as Philip Hallie has pointed out, the analogy is useless, merely a way of dignifying Frye's generalities. What could be more abstract than the observation that the heroines of the romances are Andromeda-types; unless it is the observation that the hero of them all is Orpheus? The method can produce insights, as it does when Frye discusses the wedding 'masque' in *The Tempest*—a passage that has always seemed to fit rather loosely into an otherwise tight play. The accumulation of such insights is in fact an important part of the true history of criticism, though Frye does not think so; for him, of course, their value is determined solely by their adaptability to his total system. He is the polar opposite of Blackmur, who was essentially a very unsystematic critic and believed, dangerously but correctly, that criticism is mostly anarchic, though dependent on a difficult act of submission and then on the critic's having a mind with useful and interesting contents. The insights are quite unsystematic; their history is certainly not that of a 'progressive' system. And of course the general history of criticism very powerfully suggests that it isn't progressive; which is why Frye has had to strike such a revolutionary pose, representing himself as being to Aristotle the critic what Linnaeus was to Aristotle the biologist. The cost of the system is fairly faced in the opening pages of the *Anatomy*, which deny the critic the right to make judgments of value. What is more serious is the assumption that the farther he gets from the work the more accurate his descriptions will be.

These are the issues that arise once more in *A Natural Perspective*.[1] Characteristically, they have to do with Frye's

[1] *A Natural Perspective: The Development of Shakespearean Comedy and Romance*. Columbia.

system rather than with Shakespeare's plays. How, to borrow Frye's neat quote from *The Comedy of Errors*, should we 'entertain the offered fallacy?' Frye is saying that the romances, rather than the tragedies, are the culmination of the 'logical evolution' of Shakespeare (one of those disguised value-judgments one often finds in his work) because tragedy pays more respect to the reality principle, whereas romance deliberately moves back towards myth: 'the story seeks its own end instead of holding up the mirror to nature.' In other words, the more a work deviates from the reality principle the better he likes it, just as he believes only in criticism which has backed so far away from literature that all the little things that make one work different from another drop out of view. The closer it gets to myth, the more completely the story identifies itself with ritual magic, as Shakespeare must have known when he regressed at the end to the 'childlike and concrete' romance conventions, and so lent himself more easily to a criticism which 'deals entirely with literature in this frozen or spatial way.' At the stage in his evolution marked by *Pericles* Shakespeare is ready for the full Frye treatment.

'Drama,' says Frye, 'is born in the renunciation of magic'; but instead of drawing the more obvious conclusions from this sound observation, he goes on to show not only that magic was never totally renounced, but that the best drama is always trying to get it back. When Shakespeare isn't returning directly to ritual origins he is at least getting back as far as the New Comedy, stock characters of which recur in the Romances under very ingenious disguises: Leontes, for instance, is the jealous *senex*. It is true enough, though probably too general to be very useful, that Shakespeare's comedies are like the Latin ones in that they show the reformation of an anticomic society and the festal inauguration of a comic one. But Frye's real purpose in so arguing is simply that a general resemblance between Shakespeare's plays and the Roman comedies is a large step back towards myth and ritual. In taking the step Frye argues well and makes many interesting points; but the essence of the situation is precisely that he is the critic of regress, writing regressive criticism about plays he finds to be regressive.

There is nothing new, of course, about treating the romances as a group; and to do so is at once to begin the regression, to lose sight of the differentiae. If one holds one's ground for a moment it will be clear that few plays could be different from one another in more obvious ways than *Pericles* and *Cymbeline*, the first and second of the series. To forget that the mythic patterns of *The Winter's Tale* are qualified by the actuality of Leontes' putrid talk and the sexual realism of Perdita: or that the play of multiple recognitions, *Cymbeline*, is also one in which the talk of the characters achieves a new level of ratiocinative complexity; or that Prospero's insistence on the need for magical chastity and the total obedience of his inferiors colour his language with prurience and fuss—to forget such obvious facts is to sacrifice the plays to a satisfying generalisation, and this seems no more acceptable in Frye than in Dowden or Strachey. And to prefer the romances to the tragedies, at any rate on these grounds, is to dismiss as irrelevant everything that constitutes the personal presence of a work of art, its existential complexities, all that makes it mean something *now* to a waking audience.

And here, I think, is the clue to what finally invalidates Frye. If literature does the work that ritual and myth once did, the arrangement is providential, for myth and ritual can obviously no longer do it. What makes literature different is, roughly, a different reality principle, appropriate, in an expression of Eliade's which Frye himself quotes, to *this* time as myth was appropriate to *that* time. The difference between *illud tempus* and *hoc tempus* is simply willed away in Frye's critical system, but it is essential to the very forms of modern literature, and to our experience of it. I do not mean simply that in the literature of our own time, which is itself considerably complicated by the prestige of myth, we are made aware of the conflicting claims of rigorous fact and comforting fiction; in my generalisation I include Shakespeare, and especially the Shakespeare of the tragedies. King Lear dies on a heap of disconfirmed myths, and modern literature follows Shakespeare into a world where the ritual paradigms will not serve, and magic does not work; where our imaginative satisfactions depend on a decent respect for the reality principle and our great novels are, in the words of Lukacs, 'epics without god.'

And even Shakespeare's romances belong *in hoc tempore*. We do not accept their conventions as we accept those of popular tales, simply as given for our ease and comfort. The tough verse forbids that, and so does the particularity of what happens on the stage. The statue that moves might enact the Pygmalion myth, were it not that Perdita in all her vitality stands motionless beside it; and that it is shown how no chisel could ever yet cut breath. It is the breath of Hermione, the presence of Perdita, that are lost to view as you stand back; you sacrifice them to a system and a myth. The conclusion seems obvious: when you hear talk of archetypes, reach for your reality principle.

(1965)

Chapter Five

NOVELISTS

XIII. D. H. LAWRENCE AND THE APOCALYPTIC TYPES

Writing novels is more like writing history than we often choose to think. The relationships between events, the selection of incident, even, in sophisticated fictions, the built-in skepticism as to the validity of procedures and assumptions, all these raise questions familiar to philosophers of history as problems relating to historical explanation. One such problem is explanation by types. They are obviously important in novels, for without them there would be no 'structure.' How do they work in history? How do we recognise a revolution? The events of a selected series cease to look random when we assimilate them to other selected series which have been identified and classified under some such term as 'revolution.' Similarly for series which can be filed under 'crisis,' or under 'transitional epoch.' There is the complication that personalities involved in the events under consideration may very well have done the typing themselves, as revolutionaries generally do, and this means that historical, like fictive events, can in some measure be caused to occur in conformity with the types. Furthermore, since everybody's behaviour is indeterminately modified by the conviction that he is living through a crisis, it might be argued that history can, though with unpredictable variations, be prepared for such a conformity, even without the intervention of conscious theory. But the element of indeterminacy is so gross that we can perhaps forget this.

There are, very broadly speaking, two quite distinct and mutually hostile ways of considering 'typical' explanations. One is to assume that, with varying and acceptable degrees of 'displacement,' histories and fictions cannot avoid conforming with types, so that the most useful thing that can be done is to demonstrate this conformity. However sophisticated and cautious the exponent of this doctrine may be, his thinking is likely, in the last analysis, to be sentimentally ritualistic and circular. He is nowadays much more likely to be a critic of fiction than an historian. Historians and modern theologians nowadays employ typology in a much more empirical way, a way consistent with a more linear notion of history. The historian will agree that the discovery of a motive in some action or series of actions involves classifying it as belonging to a certain type. Unless that is done it will not appear that a motive has been discovered. Of course he will also, as a rule, agree that the material available is not always so classifiable; and so will the novelist. The distinction between these kinds of event is roughly that defined by Bultmann in respect of biblical history as a contrast between what is *historisch* and what is *geschichtlich*.[1] The novelist, as a rule, has rather more interest than the historian in the latter, that is, he more completely ignores the multitude of events that might be supposed to have occurred along with the ones he chooses to treat as specially significant. His position is neatly put by Conrad: 'Fiction is history, human history, or it is nothing. But it is also more than that; it starts on firmer ground, being based on the reality of forms.' Forms are systematised typological insights; they are, or should be, always under very critical scrutiny, because they can tempt us into unjustified archaism.

The modern theologian is forced to understand the difference between sentimental or archaistic typology and the kind which is appropriate to a belief which has had to emigrate, like the Jews, from myth into history. He professes to use the old scriptural types only as indices of the contemporaneity of the New Testament, and not as elements in a miraculous plot, devised by the Holy Ghost, to keep Old and New Testaments, and the whole of history, in a condition of miraculous concord. Of course there are atavistic theologians as well as atavistic historians, literary critics, and novelists, though it is to me an interesting reflection that modern theology got really deeply

[1] I have borrowed some notions and terms from A. C. Charity's *Events and Their After Life* (C.U.P., 1966). For a fuller discussion see *Novel*, Summer 1968.

into de-mythologising at about the time when literary critics began to go overboard for mythology.

I will not pursue that, but ask why literary people should be so liable to this atavism. One reasonably simple explanation is that our immense skepticism, our deep concern with the nature of the tools we are using, is only one of the traditions to which we are heirs. Another is a tradition of mythological primitivism which has branches of many kinds: occultism, Frazerian Cambridge anthropology, and of course Freud and Jung. In the period which was formative for us there was also a fashionably circular historiography, provided by Spengler; a revival of primitive art; and, a large and seminal literature which was in various ways primitivistic and favourable to archaic typologising. Thus, when novels are closest to history we may still ask whether their fidelity to certain types is wholly consistent with a just representation of human history.

I begin with this dogmatic introduction in order to make it clear in what relations I am considering D. H. Lawrence. Among the reasons why he continues to be thought of as a particularly important novelist is this: he believed himself to be living in a time of cosmic crisis, and partly justified this conviction by archaic typologising. History was for him a plot devised by the Holy Ghost, and 'scientific' explanations (which would first examine and then reject this as a fiction) he found hateful. Unlike George Eliot, a predecessor in The Great Tradition, he could not separate the intuition that he lived in the great age of transition from explanations devoid of empirical interest but interesting enough to all primitivists, and indeed to historians of ideas. He knew a great deal (anti-intellectualists need to) and was exceptionally aware of the nature and history of his typologies; for example, he was a great student not only of mystery rituals but also of Apocalypse, and commentary on Apocalypse. This essay is about what he knew, and how it is expressed in various books, notably *Women in Love*.

In the 'Study of Thomas Hardy,' which belongs in time to much the same period as *The Rainbow* and *Women in Love*, Lawrence observed that a man can only view the universe in the light of a theory, and since the novel is a microcosm it has to reflect a micro-theory, 'some theory of being, some metaphysic.'

Of course this metaphysic mustn't obtrude and turn the novel into a tract, nor must the novelist make himself a metaphysic of self-justification, and then 'apply the world to this, instead of applying this to the world,' a practice of which he found a striking instance in the ascetic Tolstoi, whom he describes as 'a child of the Law.' The fact is that Lawrence was at the moment when he wrote that passage troubled about the 'metaphysic' of the work he had in hand. That he should use so curious an expression of Tolstoi—'a child of the Law'—gives one a strong hint as to the character of that metaphysic.[1]

Lawrence was obsessed with apocalypse from early youth, and he remembered the chiliastic chapel hymns of his childhood. During the war the apocalyptic coloration of his language is especially striking; sometimes it strongly recalls 17th-century puritanism. He considered the world to be undergoing a rapid decline which should issue in a renovation, and expected the English to have some part in this, much as Milton put the burden on God's Englishmen; Lawrence, however, dwelt more on the decadence, and seemed to think the English were rotting with especial rapidity in order to be ready first. He spoke of the coming resurrection—'Except a seed die, it bringeth not forth,' he advises Bertrand Russell in May, 1915. 'Our death must be accomplished first, then we will rise up.' 'Wait only a little while'; these were the last days, the 'last wave of time,' he told Ottoline Morell. There would be a new age, and a new ethical law.

The nature of Lawrence's pronouncements on the new age and the new ethic is such that he can very well be described as a 'moral terrorist'; Kant's term for historians who think that the evident corruption of the world presages an immediate appearance, in one form or another, of anti-Christ. But he was also what Kant, in the same work (*The Disputation of the Faculties*) calls an 'abderitist,' namely one who explains history in terms of culture-cycles. More specifically, and perhaps more recognisably, he was a Joachite.

---

[1] It is worth remembering Lawrence's capacity for having things both ways. He balances his more extreme metaphysical and occult fantasies with a sophisticated pragmatism; the effect in his fiction is to have passages that jeer at Birkin's doctrines. This hedging of bets I occasionally refer to, but it gets in the way of exposition, and the reader might like to re-introduce it into his reflections if he finds something that seems unexpectedly and positively absurd in my account of Lawrence's crisis-philosophy.

Where Lawrence, who was to call himself Joachim in *The Plumed Serpent*, got his Joachitism from one can only guess. A possible source is Huysmans' *Là-Bas* ('Two of the Persons of the Trinity have shown themselves. As a matter of logic, the Third must appear'). But Joachitism is a hardy plant, and as Frank E. Manuel says in *Shapes of Philosophical History*, it was particularly abundant in the literature of the French decadence and so could have formed part of that current of occultist thinking to which Lawrence was so sensitive. The doctrine varies a bit, but broadly it postulates three historical epochs, one for each person of the Trinity, with a transitional age between each. The details are argued out of texts in Revelation.

It is hardly too much to claim that the vague and powerful assumptions we all make about historical transition have their roots in Joachism; in Lawrence, however, the relation is much more specific. The wartime Hardy study speaks of our having reached an end, or a 'pause of finality' which is not an end. It is the moment of Transition. There has been an epoch of Law, and an epoch of 'Knowledge or Love,' and out of the synthesis of the two will develop the new age, which will be the age of the Holy Spirit. As in some early Joachite sects, the sexual implications of this are especially important. Lawrence holds that the principle of Law is strongest in woman, and that of Love in men (which is worth remembering when one considers Ursula and Birkin). Out of their true union in 'Consummate Marriage' will grow that ethic which is the product of Law and Love but is a third distinct thing, like the Holy Ghost. Although there is every sign that we have reached the point of transition, the art which should reflect it has not yet been invented. Obviously the big double novel he was working on was to be the first attempt at this appropriate art.

Now I daresay that some admirers of Lawrence will go a long way towards allowing one to speak of his thought, on sex and other matters, as having a strong apocalyptic colouring, yet draw the line at this very schematic and detailed application of the idea. Yet it is, I think, incontrovertible. When Lawrence spoke of 'signs' he did not mean only that everything was getting very bad, he meant that there *were* apocalyptic images and signs in the sky. The Zeppelin was one: 'there was war in heaven. . . . It seemed as if the cosmic order were gone, as if there had come a new order. . . . It seems our cosmos has burst, burst at last . . . it is the end, our world has gone. . . . But there must be a new heaven and a new earth.' This is from a letter to Lady Ottoline Morell, in September, 1915. A few days later he again calls the Zeppelin 'a new great sign in the heavens.' When he came to write the famous chapter 'Nightmare' in *Kangaroo* he again remembered the Zeppelin, 'high, high, high, tiny, pale, as one might imagine the Holy Ghost.'

In *Kangaroo* the Holy Ghost is patron of a new age which will dispense with democracy and bosses and be dominated by 'vertebrate telepathy' from a leader. As always in apocalyptic historiography, this renovation is preceded by a decadence; the 'new show' cannot happen until there has been some smashing. Lawrence's image of the transitional smasher was the terrible 'non-metal' mob, often symbolised by the troglodyte miner, one of his recurrent figures and an object of hate and love, fear and admiration. Continually reflecting on the apocalyptic types, Lawrence produced his own brand of Joachitism, as distinctive as that of Blake in *The Everlasting Gospel*, but easily identifiable, just as one can readily see the conformity between his more general apocalyptic thinking and the whole tradition. For convenience one can identify three aspects of this, in addition to the specifically Joachite notion of transition and crisis. They are: the Terrors (the appalling events of *dies illa*, the last day); decadence and renovation, twin concepts that explain one's own discontent and one's own hopes for another Kingdom, somewhere; and finally what I call clerkly skepticism, the reluctance of the literate to credit popular apocalyptism in its crude forms, with consequent historiographical sophistications.

In Lawrence there is a very personal ambiguity in these matters; he was a clerkly writer, but the popular apocalypse fascinated him just the same. He had a doctrine of symbolism which helped him to bridge this gap, and sometimes his allusions are so inexplicit that only if you are a naïve fundamentalist (in which case you probably wouldn't be reading Lawrence) or are on the lookout (in which case you are reading abnormally) will you pick them up. A good example of this is the passage in *St. Mawr*, which is in general an apocalyptic story, where Mrs Witt discusses with Lewis 'a very big, soft star' that falls down the sky. Lewis is led on to talk about the superstitions of his countryside, and finally to explain what the star means to him: 'There's movement in the sky. The world is going to change again.' When Mrs Witt reminds him of the physical explanation of shooting stars, mentioning that there are always many in August, he just insists that 'stones don't come at us out of the sky for nothing.' Whatever Lewis has in mind, Lawrence is certainly thinking of Rev. vi.13, 'And the stars of heaven fell unto the earth,' which happens at the opening of the sixth seal, when 'the great day of his wrath is come.' Lawrence is explicit enough about the general apocalyptic bearing of the horse itself, and perhaps too explicit about the decadence and the possibility of a new show and Lewis's superior understanding of the situation, but in this little episode there is a set of variations on a hidden apocalyptic symbol which is in some ways even more characteristic.

What we have to see, I think, is that, explicit or inexplicit, this, the apocalyptic, is the chief mould of Lawrence's imaginative activity. In the work of the 1920s it grows increasingly explicit, for example in the Whitman essay, or in the study of Melville, where the sinking of the *Pequod* is called 'the doom of our white day.' There had always been a racial aspect to his apocalyptic thinking, as we shall see; even in his essays on Dahlberg and Huxley's *Point Counter Point* he affirms the exhaustion of the white racial psyche, the disintegration that will lead to a new show. From 1923, mostly in letters to Frederick Carter, he was offering elaborate interpretations of *Revelation*, based on a study of conventional exegesis (which he despised) and on less orthodox treatments, such as those of James Pryse, Madame Blavatsky, and Carter himself. In 1924 he wrote some articles on the subject, and in his last years worked hard on *Apocalypse*, his own commentary.

In *Apocalypse* Lawrence acknowledges that the book of Revelation, and other parts of the Bible, with which he was saturated in childhood, remained in his mind and 'affected all the processes of emotion and thought.' But in the meantime he had come to loathe it, and his long essay is an attempt to explain why, consciously and unconsciously, this 'detested' book could play so large a part in his most serious work. It has to be separated from mere vulgar credulity and subjected to a clerkly skepticism that is still not mere rationalism. Years of labour went into Lawrence's theory that the version we read in the Bible, the hateful book, 'Jewy' and 'chapel,' meat for underdogs, was a horribly corrupt version of an earlier work which must have related the ritual of an authentic mystery religion. What he tries to do is to remove the 'Judeo-Roman screen' and penetrate to the fundamental rite, as it was represented in the imagery of the original pre-Christian text. This rite would be a guide to 'emotional-passional knowledge'; the editorial sophistications stood for the non-vital Christian universe. The original was quick, though the corrupt version was dead. And of course Lawrence found in Revelation his mystery ritual. There was the Great Mother, whom the Jewish and Christian editors had dissociated into one good and one bad, the Woman Clothed with the Sun and the Scarlet Woman. There was the ritual descent into hell, and the rebirth. And this *katabasis* was the type of the one the world was at present undergoing. As in the mystery rite, the contemporary harrowing of hell is to be accomplished by a sexual act. In the epoch of the Holy Ghost we shall revert 'towards our elementals,' as Lawrence put it in that curious homage to the Paraclete, *Fantasia of the Unconscious*; to Adam reborn, love will be a new thing; the man–woman relationship will be remade. But first there has to be death and rebirth.

Although his commentators pay very little and then only embarrassed attention to it, *Apocalypse* is ideologically a climax of Lawrence's work. But because he never ceased to feel that it was not enough merely to describe the crisis, the terrors, the death and rebirth, he wrote over the same years a novel, a novel which should be impregnated with this sexual eschatology. That novel was *Lady Chatterley's Lover*. As I tried to show in an essay published four or five years ago, that book enacts the sevenfold descent into hell and the climactic rebirth by sex. I shan't dwell on it now, because I want to talk about better books, and especially about one in which the apocalyptic types have a peculiar historical force, namely *Women in Love*.

Ritual descent into hell, followed by rebirth—that is the character of Lawrence's transitional period. The reason why the world misunderstands what is happening is that it knows only a corrupt Apocalypse—it sees, with Mellors, that 'there's a bad time coming, boys,' but thinks that the smashing-up will be a way of dislodging the proud, and setting the underdogs up instead. Actually the beneficiaries constitute an elect, isolate in a new consciousness, synthesising Law and Love. A mark of this elect will naturally be the new man–woman relationship; for the woman was law and the man love, and just as these two epochal ethics will be transformed in the third, so will the two Persons, Man and Woman, be, under the new dispensation, merged in a new relationship, and yet remain distinct. The obvious image for this sexual situation is the Trinity, of which the Persons are distinct but not divided. And this epoch of the Holy Ghost has no time for underdogs.

As we have seen, this programme, already implicit in the Hardy study, requires not only a new ethics and new philosophies of culture, but also its own art; so it is not surprising that the novels Lawrence wrote during the war have much apocalyptic figuration. *The Rainbow* came to represent the Old Testament (Law) and *Women in Love* the New Testament (Love). The rainbow at the end of the first novel is the symbol of the old Covenant; the apocalyptic climax of the second reflects the structure of the New Testament. *Women in Love* is an end, where *The Rainbow* was a beginning; it represents the destruction of the old, and enacts the pause before the new world. It projects a kind of Utopia; but it is subjected, like the rest of the apocalyptic material, to Lawrence's own brand of skepticism.

The Rainbow is deliberately rendered as a kind of Genesis. The opening passages have a sort of Blakean gravity, like the illustrations to Job—the gravity is patriarchal. Allusions to Genesis punctuate the book. The death of old Brangwen, drunk, after a flood, makes him a sort of distorted antitype of Noah. George Ford's extremely interesting book on Lawrence (*Double Measure*) makes these and other connections with Genesis, including the references to the coming together of the sons of God and the daughters of man, which establish a typical basis for Ursula. *The Rainbow* also contains some faint but characteristic premonitions of the apocalypse to come: as when Anna sneers at the lamb-and-flag window of the church, calling it 'the biggest joke of the parish.' The lamb and flag constitute a traditional icon of apocalypse, but Anna is sneering at her husband's interest in such symbolism, as her daughter will later deride Birkin's more sophisticated apocalypse. Women are skeptics, they cling, like Anna, 'to the worship of human knowledge,' they hanker after the Law. In fact Brangwen is a sort of decadent typologist, with an underdog chapel apocalypse; we are not surprised when we meet him briefly in *Women in Love* and find him grown insensitive, proletarian, obsolete.

The lamb-and-flag window is one of those glancing allusions, like the falling star in *St. Mawr*, which show how these figures possessed Lawrence. The great chapter of the horses is more explicitly apocalyptic; Lawrence's discussion of the horse in *Apocalypse* establishes a direct connexion with Revelation; and in the same section he once again quotes that text from Genesis, earlier used in *The Rainbow*, about the sons of God visiting the daughters of men, adding that according to Enoch these angels had 'the members of horses.' The passage is extremely complicated, as always when Lawrence's imagination is fully extended on this theme. These horses stand for the lost potency of white civilisation; (and specifically of England: this is the gloomy patriotic element in Lawrence's eschatology); they also stand for sexual terrors of the kind he associated with them in *Fantasia of the Unconscious*. Of course sexual terror and the racial decadence were closely related subjects, as one sees most vividly in *Women in Love*.

In fact *Women in Love* exhibits all the apocalyptic types in their Lawrentian versions—decadence and renovation in a painful transition or crisis, elitism, patriotic fervour, sex and mystery. Its subject, like that of *Lady Chatterley*, is, basically, England, and by extension the decline of 'white' racial culture to be unimaginably redeemed in a sexual mystery. The characteristic pattern occurs with peculiar clarity in a letter of 1926: 'they've pushed a spear through the side of my England,' means, superficially, that the country round Nottingham had been ruined and disfigured by 'miners—and pickets—and policemen' during the great strike; but underneath there is the imagery of death and a new love: dancing, disciples, a new 'England to come.' There is a sort of Blakean patriotism, even in *The Rainbow*; but Ursula in *Women in Love*, *is* England, for her, as for Connie, that other sleeping beauty, there is a programme of renovation by sexual shock. We find her, after the water-party, 'at the end of her line of life,' her 'next step was into death.' This death, she finds, is preferable to mechanical life. But the death-flow of her mood is interrupted by the arrival of Birkin. At once she hates him. 'He was the enemy, fine as a diamond, and as hard and jewel-like, the quintessence of all that was inimical. . . . She saw him as a clear stroke of uttermost contradiction.' The life-flow of love and the death-flow of law here clash. Birkin contradicts death, personal, national and cosmic. He himself often meditates on the necessary death of England; 'of race and national death' at the wedding party near the beginning; of the death of England when he and Ursula buy the old chair; of the necessary disappearance of England in the chapter 'Continental,' when Gudrun sneers at him and calls him a patriot. But death is for him a preparation for the new life; so he must contain and overthrow Ursula's skepticism; and because she is England he must work the renovation on her body.

This intermittent equation of Ursula and England gives some indication of the means by which Lawrence matched his apocalyptic types with history. For *Women in Love* is an historical novel. Like *Middlemarch*, to which it owes so much, *Women in Love* is a novel about a modern crisis; and it deals with it, partly, by concentrating on the condition of women question, the answer to which, as George Eliot once remarked, had been from the time of Herodotus one of the most important symptoms of the state of a society. Unlike *Middlemarch*, however, Lawrence's novel contains no positive allusion to actual history. 'I should wish the time to remain unfixed,' he wrote, 'so that the bitterness of the war may be taken for granted in the characters.' I shall postpone discussion of this radical difference of method, because the immediate need is simply to assert that *Women in Love* is nonetheless an historical novel, a book about a particular historical crisis. When Dr Leavis observes of Lawrence that 'as a recorder of essential English history he is a great successor of George Eliot,' he is thinking primarily of *The Rainbow*; but he adds that '*Women in Love* has . . . astonishing comprehensiveness in the presentment of contemporary England (the England of 1914).' *The Rainbow* has 'historical depth,' and studies the past in which the crisis germinated. *Women in Love* concerns itself less with evocations of a lost world than with a moment of history understood in terms of a crisis archetype. The random events of history assume the patterns of eschatological feeling and speculation.

'The book frightens me: it's so end of the world,' said Lawrence in 1916. George Ford points out that among the early titles proposed for *Women in Love* were *The Latter Days* and *Dies Irae*. And this eschatological preoccupation touches everything in the book. Consider, for example, the social aspect. Lawrence's apocalypse, as I have said, is elitist, and like the elite of the medieval Joachite sects, for instance The Brethren of the Free Spirit, his chosen ones exclude the profane from their mysteries. Birkin often remarks that people don't matter; or they matter only in so far as they may produce the terrors, the great mindless shove into the last days. The mood is reflected also in Lawrence's own letters and in *Kangaroo*. The mechanical mob has nothing to do with the true sexual mystery-religion of apocalypse; it was in their name that the Jewish and Greek bottom-dogs corrupted the text of the original Revelation. They have a false, lesser mystery, no true katabasis, but merely a parody of it. These *profani*, destructive, even chthonic, were associated in Lawrence's mind with colliers, the 'blackened, slightly distorted human beings with red mouths' who work for Gerald. To Gudrun, who has an instinctive sympathy with them their debased power—Lawrence writes several passages to make this point including the very fine one where the workmen lust after her in her fancy stockings—to Gudrun they are 'powerful, underworld men' in whose voices she hears 'the voluptuous resonance of darkness'; she desires them, related as they are to the kind of evil found in the waterplants of 'Sketchbook,' and the decadence of Halliday's statue. If Ursula is the Magna Dea in her creative aspect, Gudrun is Hecate, a Queen of the Night. But in the renovated world there is to be no place for her, or for her underworld men.

The real descent into hell and rebirth Lawrence can signify only by sex. The purest expression of it is in *The Man Who Died*, but in some ways the love-death undergone by Ursula and Connie is a fuller image because it amalgamates heaven and hell, life-flow and death-flow, in one act. The act is anal. Lawrence is never explicit about it, whether in the novels or in the essays where one might have expected some explanation of the Holy Ghost's electing so curious an epiphany. But he has in mind what he takes to be the basic figure of the mystery behind revelation—this is the point, for Connie and Ursula and for England also, where life and death meet; when the shame induced by Law is defied and burnt out. 'How good it was to be really shameful. . . . She was free.' This participation in 'dreadful mysteries beyond the phallic cult,' enacts death and rebirth at once, is decadent and renovatory at once.

As the literature shows, this is not easy to discuss. One cannot even distinguish, discursively, between the sex Gudrun desires from Loerke, which is obscene and decadent, and that which Ursula experiences with Birkin, which is on balance renovatory. The first comes straight out of Nordau, the second is darkly millennialist, again like that of some medieval sects in their Latter Days; yet in practice they presumably amount to almost the same thing. It is an ambivalence which may have characterised earlier apocalyptic postures, as Fraenger argues in his book on Hieronymus Bosch. Decadence and renovation, death and rebirth, in the last days, are hard to tell apart, being caught up in the terrors.

Does a new world—created in the burning out of sexual shame, in the birth from such an icy womb as in that of the last chapters of Lawrence's novel—does such a world await the elect when the terrors of the transition are over? Do the elect rightly look forward to the epoch of the Holy Spirit? The myth in the book says yes. It says so throughout—in image after image and in a long series of antitheses: in 'Rabbit' and in 'Water-Party,' in the water-weeds and butterflies, in Gerald's death journey to Gudrun's bed and in Birkin rolling naked in the pine-needles; in the flow of death and the flow of life, the imagery of *fleurs du mal* and the rose of happiness. But the book also obscures the myth. Between the flow of life and that of death there is 'no difference—and all the difference. Dissolution rolls on, just as production does . . . it ends in universal nothing—the end of the world. . . . It means a new cycle of creation after. . . .' Birkin is glossing his earlier remark that Aphrodite 'is the flowering mystery of the death-process.' He cannot tell Ursula quite how their Aphrodite is dissociated from that process. And here he invites her skepticism.

As Magna Dea committed to continuance, as woman the voice of Law, and as modern clerk, Ursula is repeatedly the voice of that skepticism which always, in history, attends apocalyptic prophecy. When Birkin rants about the disappearance of England, she knows it cannot 'disappear so cleanly and conveniently.' It is part of the historical tension between myth and history (the long record of disappointed apocalypse) or between what Birkin thinks of as life and death. The novel fights back at myth, and where the myth says yes, the novel and Ursula often say no. The novel, as a kind, belongs to humanism, not to mystery religion; or in terms of Worringer's contemporary distinction, it cannot, because of the society that produced it, abandon empathy entirely in favour of abstraction. Thus our white decadence can never take the obscenely abstract form of Halliday's statue. And Lawrence knew this. Whereas *The Rainbow*, which looks back to a pastoral Genesis, can end with the archetypal sign of the covenant, *Women in Love* must have a modern conclusion in which nothing is concluded, a matter of disappointed love, a pattern incomplete. It allows history some ground unconquered by the types.

'Has *everything* that happens universal significance?' It is Birkin's question, and the novelist's question always. For Birkin it arises out of the repeated assertion that Gerald's type is Cain. Gerald's shooting of his brother is to Gudrun 'the purest form of accident.' But Birkin decides that he 'does not believe there was any such thing as accident. It all hung together, in the deepest sense.' Hence the subsequent death of Gerald's sister, his own visit to the depths of the lake, the region of death, and finally his death in the ice, may be seen as pre-determined. At any rate Lawrence wants us to ask questions about the truth of the types in a novel. The New Testament shows them all fulfilled, in the 'fullness of time.' Can there be such a novelistic *pleroma*, in which no event is random? If so, all the apparent randomness of the book must have significance: cats, rabbits, jewels, floods. This kind of realism finds its *figura* in random event. So the mythic type returns powerfully to its ancient struggle with history. But Lawrence never in fact allowed history to lose altogether, even in *The Plumed Serpent*, even in the narrowly schematic *Lady Chatterley's Lover*. He headed dangerously towards a typological predominance, and paid the price; the more he asserted the fulfilment of preordained types, the less he could depend on that randomness which leaves room for quickness and special grace. Mrs Morel locked out of her house, experiencing fear but burying her face in the lily—that is the kind of thing that is lost. We still have it in *Women in Love*—in a relevance altogether strange, in unique configurations. There are the naked white men round the African statue, an image not subordinated to the element of doctrine involved; or the eurhythmics and the cows in 'Water-Party.' One of Lawrence's powers was a capacity for stunning verisimilitude, a thing precious in itself—one thinks of the passage in *The Rainbow* in which Will Brangwen picks up the factory-girl at the music-hall. There are always untyped graces of this sort in Lawrence; they belong to history, and they are what all good novels ought to have. Lawrence never lost the power, but it must have seemed that its relevance to what he was doing progressively diminished.

Women in Love is the last novel in which he kept the balance. Its radical type is apocalypse, used as an explanation of the great contemporary crisis; for 'it was in 1915 the old world ended' and the great transition began. The great feat is to confront what Auerbach calls 'the disintegration of the continuity of random events'—reflected in the technique of Lawrence's novel—with the unchangingness of the types, and to do it without sinking into a verisimilar discreteness on the one hand, or into a rigid, flux-denying schema on the other. *Women in Love* studies crisis without unforgiveably insulting reality. Its types do some of the work which historians also do with types.

Perhaps we can get a clearer notion of the kind of balance Lawrence had to struggle for if we look at that earlier historical novel to which he was so much indebted, *Middlemarch*. Lawrence grew discontented with George Eliot, but *Women in Love* is nevertheless his *Middlemarch*. The opening pages of the Victorian novel were in his mind when he made Ursula throw the jewels at Birkin, and again at the end when Gudrun gives the stockings to her sister—a curious dissociation of the Eliot scene, which stuck in his mind partly because of Dorothea's priggish allusion to the use of jewels by St John in Revelation. There is an important typological recall of the great passage in *Middlemarch* when Dorothea returns, desolate, from Rome: near the climax of Lawrence's book Gudrun passes a terrible night, alone with the ticking clock, in bondage to time, to the horrible mechanical

Gerald, and half thinks her hair may have turned white. 'Yet there it remained, brown as ever, and there she was herself, looking a picture of health.' The slightly perfunctory nature of the prose here may be a consequence of Lawrence's feeling behind what he was doing the extraordinary strength of George Eliot's moment—Dorothea also desolate, also against a background of ice and snow, 'incongruously alive,' 'glowing . . . as only youthful health can glow.' It is in the same scene that Lawrence allows Gudrun to think of herself as a modern Hetty Sorrel, and of Gerald as a modern Arthur Donnithorne. It is a thought full of irony and the recognition of a change in the patterns of sexual tragedy. The very concept of the big double novel, earlier called *The Sisters*, is owed to Eliot: not only the contrasting sisters, but the deep study of two marriages at the end of a world. Ursula is his modern Dorothea, Gudrun his modern Rosamond. Ursula's mistake over Skrebensky, as George Ford says, is founded on Dorothea's mistake over Casaubon. From the start her crucial relationship was to be with Birkin, as if Lawrence had decided to shift the focus to the second union; but he knew, as he remarks in a letter, that Ursula needed this earlier barren experience also, and, with some difficulty, got Skrebensky into the story-line. Finally, he remembered that George Eliot had researched *Middlemarch*, as if to write history, and he researched *Women in Love* similarly, doing a lot of intensive reading for it in the early months of 1916.

Middlemarch is the novel of another crisis. It was begun in 1867. The 'Sixties were thought then, and are thought now, to have been critical, a transition between two worlds. They opened with the American Civil War and ended with the Franco–Prussian War. *Essays and Reviews* come at the beginning, *Culture and Anarchy*, the First Vatican Council and the dogma of Papal Infallibility, at the end. The Education Act, which did as much as any single statute could to alter the whole character of society, became law in 1870. The source of the Nile was discovered in 1860, the Suez Canal opened in 1869. Various post-Gutenbergian techniques were taking hold: the telephone was invented, and ironclad warships, and the dynamo, and dynamite. For the first time you could telegraph to India and travel by tube. In the very year of dynamite and the telephone, Marx published the first volume of *Das Kapital*, a genuinely revolutionary event to which hardly anybody in England paid the slightest attention, and Disraeli got through his Reform Bill, an event thought by a great many people to be as fraught with revolutionary possibilities as the passage of its predecessor thirty-five years earlier. It seems not only that a world we know well was struggling to be born, but that people felt strongly, as they often do, that there was a crisis in their vicinity, even if they did not always agree with us as to where, exactly, it was.

In the year of the Reform Act, the telephone and *Das Kapital*, George Eliot began to plan *Middlemarch*. Writing began in 1869, 'simmered' for a long time, and got properly under way in 1871. Then the story formed a union with an independently conceived story called *Miss Brooke*, and was published in eight parts between December, 1871 and December, 1872. Throughout these vicissitudes two factors remained constant. One was that this novel was to deal with 'contemporary moral history' (to steal a phrase used by the Goncourts of their own *Germinie Lacerteux*, published in 1864). The other, which seems to indicate a programme different from that of the French realists, was that from the earliest stages George Eliot set her story very firmly not in the decade that was ending but at the beginning of the 'Thirties. Her notebook lists political and private events, which were to be cross-referenced in the narrative, and modern scholarship has illuminated this oblique historical accuracy. The author not only copied out lists of events from the *Annual Register* but also got up medicine, hospital management, scientific research. Bible scholarship, which is equally important to her design, she did not have to get up. She was particularly careful about medicine, as the notebook shows; and we must guess that this was not only because her principal male character was a doctor, but because 1832 is the date not only of the first Reform Bill, but of a catastrophic event, the arrival in England for the first time of the Indian cholera. It is a reasonable guess that, in the early stages of planning, she meant to have a cholera epidemic as well as an election in *Middlemarch*. It would be a great test not only for her doctor, but for the well-disposed gentry with their interest in sanitary dwellings.

Cholera was a disease unknown in England before this time, though there were of course later Victorian epidemics. This first onslaught of the disease must have seemed a new plague for a new age, much as syphilis had been for the period of her previous novel *Romola*, and it coincided exactly with the ominous political upheavals of the months preceding the passage of the Bill. She made a note to the effect that the preamble to a bill in Parliament spoke of the disease as an infliction of Providence, and that six members of the Commons voted for the exclusion of this phrase. The coincidence of these events is a sufficient explanation of her fixing upon the years preceding the Reform Bill's passing, and her choosing an advanced young doctor as her principal character in the 'Middlemarch' part of the book. Other details fell into place; in the 'Thirties but not in the 'Sixties she could have a serious biblical scholar who yet remained ignorant of the advances of the New Criticism. After all she herself had translated Strauss in the 'Forties.

So she turned to earlier crisis-years, the years when the civilisation she knew, and which seemed in its turn to be on the brink of radical change, was being born out of great political and scientific events. Of all English novelists she came closest to accepting the Goncourt programme for using novels as means of prosecuting *les études et les devoirs de la science*, though in making one crisis the model or type of another for the purposes of the study, she was, though with a new scientific seriousness, adopting a device not uncommon in English fiction she knew, and which is of course a characteristic of all narrative explanation. George Eliot was in any case not interested in radical formal innovation; her attempt is rather to explore and modify the existing novel schemata. Thus she maintained, despite a conviction early on in the writing that the novel had 'too many *momenti*,' the several continuous, elaborate and interrelated plots to which readers had become accustomed.

Middlemarch has nothing in it quite like the famous intrusive chapter in *Adam Bede* ('in which the story pauses a little') but it is not without authorial interpolation, and there is one passage, uneasily facetious as George Eliot sometimes was when she felt she was being self-indulgent, which must cause pain to post-Jamesian purists. Yet it tells us something useful about the book. Mr Standish has just been reading old Featherstone's will, and we have heard how vexed the family is at Joshua Rigg's inheriting. The conclusion is that no one in the neighbourhood could be happy at this turn of events; nobody could prophesy the

long-term effects of Rigg's arrival. Whereupon the novelist
adds:

> And here I am naturally led to reflect on the means of elevating a low
> subject. Historical parallels are remarkably efficient in this way. The
> chief objection to them is, that the diligent narrator may lack space, or
> (what is often the same thing) may not be able to think of them with
> any degree of particularity, though he may have a philosophical
> confidence that if known they would be illustrative. It seems an easier
> and a shorter way to dignity to observe that—since there never was a
> true story which could not be told in parables where you might put a
> monkey for a margrave, and *vice versa,*—whatever has been or is to
> be narrated by me about low people, may be ennobled by being
> considered a parable. . . . Thus while I tell the truth about my loobies,
> my reader's imagination need not be entirely excluded from an
> occupation with lords. . . . As to any provincial history in which the
> agents are all of high moral rank, that must be of a date long
> posterior to the first Reform Bill, and Peter Featherstone, you
> perceive, was dead and buried some months before Lord Grey came
> into office.

That this is facetious, muddled and evasive does not entirely
destroy its value. It is one of the few places in which the novelist
openly adverts to a matter which, on other evidence, she had
incessantly in mind as she planned and wrote *Middlemarch*. She
is merely pretending to be sarcastic on a well-worn issue, the
right of novelists to concern themselves with low characters—
the sort of thing she did in *Adam Bede* when she remarked
correctly, though with an evil emphasis, that 'things may be
lovable that are not altogether handsome, I hope.' It is the
attitude controverted by Ruskin in his observations on *The Mill
on the Floss* ('the sweepings of the Pentonville omnibus').
Perhaps the question had not entirely lost importance—certainly
George Eliot herself had not entirely solved it, as we shall see;
but it is very unlikely that she here states it with any real seriousness. For in *Middlemarch* the problem is not so much to justify
one's rendering of a provincial society for its own sake as to
make that society serve to illustrate a great historical crisis. The
point is not that you can read lord for looby, or George IV for
Featherstone, as she ironically proposes, but that if the novelist
has got the detail right you can find in the book a 'parable'

concerning these events in the mind and the conscience of society which, at a particular historical crisis, signal the birth of a modern age, that great theme of the modern novel.

And that is what the paragraph is trying to say. It tells us to relate the events of the novel to Lord Grey's Act and the other great changes of that time. The period of the novel is precisely the years and months before the Act. The notebook contains not only lists from the *Annual Register*, but precisely dated events for the unwritten novel. Thus the marriage of Lydgate is timed to coincide with the dissolution of July, 1830, and the height of the cholera in Paris; Mr Casaubon's death coincides with the last days of the Parliament whose dissolution in 1831 led to the General Election in May of that year, the election at which Mr Brooke failed to win his seat in what was to be the Reform Parliament. Not all these dates eventually coincided, but the book retains, as Mr Jerome Beaty has shown, a good many delicate cross-references to political events, to the vicissitudes of Peel and Wellington, the death of Huskisson, and so on. The final illness of George IV, mentioned in relation to that of Featherstone, was enough, if you coupled it with the dissolution of Parliament on the Reformism, and a general election, to make Mr Vincy ask whether all these were not signs that the world was coming to an end. But this overt though facetious allusion to the apocalyptic archetype of crisis is not repeated; the author is content with unspoken allusions and parallels. Lydgate's efforts at medical reform are specifically related to the political struggle after the dissolution of 1831; Chapter 84, of which the main business is the family's opposition to Dorothea's re-marriage, begins with an allusion to the rejection of the Bill by the Lords. And many other events are sketched in thus. The book ends a few weeks before the final enactment of the Bill. In the narrative there are a few major crises—those of the two marriages, and the attendant crises in the reformist activities of Lydgate and Dorothea; there are also minor ones, relating to religion and business, Fred Vincy's attitude to Holy Orders and Bulstrode's disgrace. But these personal crises are shadows of the historical crises, of the 'new life' struggling to be born in 1832; they are parables, to use George Eliot's word, of that crisis which is in its turn a model for the modern crisis of 1867, the leap in the dark, the end of another world. For in some ways we are all, even learned historians, Vincys. A crisis date gives history structure, and provides ways of talking about it.

This is the larger issue—crisis as a mode of historical explanation. The present point is that *Middlemarch* is a novel concerned with the end of a world. But it was expressly intended to inculcate 'a religious and moral sympathy with the *historical life of man*,' and it issued from the hands of an author who was done with all manner of explanations requiring a mythology of transcendence. Such divinity as may occur in *Middlemarch* must be humanised in the manner of Feuerbach; the history must be human also, Comtian not Christian. Thus the types of Dorothea are Antigone, Theresa, even the Virgin Mary (an extravagant observation of Lydgate which the author partly endorses), but they are systematically Feuerbachised, qualified as human. Rosamund's 'confession' is another instance; it is sacramental only as to efficacy, not as to mystery. The Joachite elements in George Eliot's history belong, like those of Comte, to an age in which apocalypse has been positivised. This humanised apocalypse is what we are all familiar with, for we habitually allude to it when we consider our own historical crisis.

The type of apocalypse, however transformed, is still operative in *Middlemarch*. The word may seem very strong; it only means apocalypse of the kind Feuerbach might have contemplated had he given his attention to eschatology—a 'Copernican' apocalypse, brought down to its true level, the human crisis. It is a good many years since Mark Schorer discovered in the novel what he calls 'metaphors of . . . "muted" apocalypse,' mentioning the figures of light, fire, transfiguration, epiphany, fulfilment, and the deliberate antithesis between *Middlemarch* and the New Jerusalem. He found prophecy and pseudo-prophecy, vision and growth. This is a muted apocalypse, certainly: the jewels of St John's Revelation are mentioned early, but the context seems to make them serve only as a way of noting Dorothea's priggish attitude to Celia. Schorer quotes a passage from Chapter X in which Dorothea's hopes of revelation from Casaubon's learning are given a strong though of course ironical apocalyptic tone. Above all, the historical events mentioned in the novel—again in a muted way—serve to emphasise the fulfilment of a time, and a renewal; though that, since the novel is set in the past, can be left to retrospective prophecy, the kind we, as historians, are best at. These are the last days; humanly speaking, the last days of an epoch, which is a Feuerbachian equivalent of the mythical apocalypse. The myth abandoned, this is still part of the structure of our historical thinking. And one reason why we relish *Middlemarch* still is that we understand the muted eschatology of its design.

For example, the crisis in bible criticism seemed at the time catastrophic in its implications. Casaubon, firmly planted on the wrong, mythological side of it, is typed in the same way as other characters—his name relates him ironically to the great Casaubon; he is a Milton, he is a Locke—all great men associated with major crises in the history of thought; but Casaubon's relation to them is ironically qualified, as Dorothea's is to hers, or as Lydgate's to Vesalius and the other great medical men whose names and dates George Eliot copies out so carefully into her notebook. They stand for virtues or certainties thought to be in decadence at this turn of time; though they also, by implying the meliorist scientific achievements of the succeeding age, suggest also renovation, always in apocalyptic thought the obverse side of decadence. Middlemarch itself, as Schorer says, silently proposes its antitype, The New Jerusalem.

If Casaubon's biblical methodology illuminated the historical crisis, so did Lydgate's medicine. The opposition between Lydgate and the older provincial doctors is not the whole story: the parable is incomplete if it does not include allusions to modern differentiations between typhus and typhoid, the new treatment for delirium tremens (which becomes the material of an important narrative crisis), the general theory of fever, and indeed modern developments in 'cell-theory.' Of course part of the point is that to know about all these things is not enough; that in the new dispensation as well as in any older one the virtues, under whatever demythologised form one knows them, must be preserved. A spot of commonness, a failure to apply the proper kind of attention to another person, a neglect of duty, a cheapening of love, will bring disaster. Lydgate's 'commonness,' as it happens, is associated with his caste—it proceeds from an inability to treat as true persons his sexual, social and intellectual inferiors—and so derives from a system that was beginning, with the Reform Acts (and perhaps more with the Education Act of 1870) slowly to collapse. In much the same way the dryness and sexual impotence of Casaubon reflect the sterility of a world-view that lingers on in survivors of the older ruined order.

The historical antitheses of *Middlemarch* go beyond scholarship and medicine, and are far from simple. It is not only, we see, a matter of one age, characterised by myth and ignorance, yielding to a new, of history and science, or of a supernatural giving way to a natural religion. Religious beliefs of many kinds—Fairbrother's, Fred Vincy's, Tyke's, and especially Bulstrode's—are ironically exposed at this historical crisis, but their forms survive that crisis, as fiction survives religious belief. Bulstrode's error is to suppose too exact a relationship between plot (providence) and the random actuality on which it is imposed. He takes his prosperity as a figure of his justification, as arising from divine but mechanical plotting; his God knows nothing of contingency; the logic of his plots is the logic of myth, not of everyday life. The tide of plausible human events is not in accordance with his Calvinist prediction, and his discomfiture is proof of the obsolescence of another mythology, one that was still in favour among some of the novelist's contemporaries. George Eliot has her own Feuerbachian version of predestination, worked out many times and most explicitly in Tito Melema; this and the erroneous old version play against each other in the Bulstrode crisis. That which works through Raffles is not, any longer, God; but neither is it mocked.

Many incidents are invented to strengthen the sense of an historical transition. There is the talk of new building and improvement, the tone of political dispute, Brooke's inability to command the respect of the labourer Dagley, even—great Victorian symbol of the division of time—the railway; and Garth, that wondrous necessary instrument of capital, suppressing resentment at its progress through midland meadows. This critical balance is characteristic even the minor crises of the book. Casaubon's scholarship hangs posthumously over Dorothea in her decision to marry Ladislaw. Lydgate voting for Tyke is voting, he thinks, in the interests of progress, but they turn out to be the interests of Bulstrode; he accepts Bulstrode's saving loan, and Raffles is given medical treatment acceptable in current obsolete medical opinion, but to Lydgate's new knowledge dangerous. A good deal of the corruption, impotence and ineffectiveness of characters in *Middlemarch* is imposed upon them by a dying but stubborn past, and they are part of the price one pays for living in 'an age of transition.' This is what Dorothea means, really, when she says she will 'find out what everything costs.' She takes on the new world. Lydgate finds himself cursed by the old; he must take Bulstrode on his arm; he is not one of the elite in any new world, even in a new world of which the millennialist ideal is so severely chastened by contact with a powerful sense of reality. The scientific figures which, as has often been observed, penetrate the texture of this novel are not arbitrary reflections of the author's own interests: they establish the modernity of the problem, and they also, by indicating the tone of the future, judge the moral effectiveness of the characters who faced it then as we must now, and suggest the consequences of a failure such as Lydgate's. The eschatology is humanised, but the old judgment remains, as to type, applicable: 'I know thy works, that thou art neither cold nor hot . . . so then because thou art lukewarm and neither cold nor hot, I will spew thee out of my mouth.'

Thus *Middlemarch* arranges itself as an image of crisis, and a study of the moral obligations of men in transition. Its typology relates it to the archetypes of crisis, and this is one of the ways in which we understand human history. As I said at the outset, such terms as *crisis* and *revolution* describe to our satisfaction what it is in the utter particularity, the randomness and disparateness of events, that we can recognise and understand; indeed people concerned in the making of history have often shaped it in conformity with such types, just as novelists do. Real events comply with archetypes of this kind; why should not fictional events? At the centre of this novel is a great and typical historical event. But it is only the nucleus. Round it accrete all these other images of crisis. The manner in which the basic apocalyptic figure permeates the texture is strikingly demonstrated in one of the greatest passages of the novel: the frustrated Dorothea contemplates Rome, the eternal city a wreck, a marble confusion, St Peter's and its statues disfigured by red drapery, as if seen by a diseased eye: the vision of the *urbs aeterna* blighted. 'Images are the brood of desire,' says the novelist at the opening of the fourth chapter (in which Lydgate is on the point of marrying a woman he has presented with a whip). The image of Rome is the brood of desire that fails. To balance the scene, there is the wonderful moment of Dorothea's return to Lowick and the blanched winter landscape, when the fire glows incongruously and she, seeking confirmation in the glass for her sense of deathly defeat, finds an image of health and vitality, the human and perhaps specifically female strength that comes through these crises. Lawrence—who saw so clearly that the novel must make *this* kind of sense and not fob us off with papers stuck into brandy-flasks, meticulously rendered lawsuits—Lawrence not only learned from the good and the bad in Eliot's figures, but, as we have seen, remembered and reproduced this one at the climax of *Women in Love*. He meant that Crich, like Casaubon, belonged to death, to an old order.

However the relation between story and apocalyptic type is visualised, it presupposes an imaginative feat and a large degree of intellectual control. Occasionally this fails. There are lapses: for instance in the climactic interview between Dorothea and Rosamond, by which George Eliot set so much store. This was to be a flow of Feuerbachian feeling, confession and all, and so warm and spontaneous that she claimed to have refrained from thinking about it till it happened, and then to have written it entire, without revision, a claim which the manuscripts show to be untrue. However, it has virtual truth: it suggests a deliberate letting go, a kind of moral failure (nothing in Dorothea gives her the right to be even a Feuerbachian confessor to Rosamond) and redeemed only at its end, when Lydgate, dismissed from the elect, takes up his meaner burden. This is a failure of spiritual pride, like Bulstrode's.

There are more serious faults proper to be mentioned here. One is, if one may so put it, that George Eliot runs out of love; or we could say, she too has her elite. I mean that she cannot sustain that special love by which a novelist knows and preserves the identity of characters. The indications of this are her slipping away into caricature or humour-characterisation when she moves out of the sociological middle area. At the extreme edge is Mrs Dollop, in the pub, but Trumbull the auctioneer is only good for a laugh and as a handy pneumonia patient. The Garths, even, are honourable pastoral prigs about whom one wants to know no more. As one moves out from the central figures, the two married couples, towards the periphery, the figures are increasingly distorted. In a certain sense, she is interested most in the good bourgeoisie and a little above it, the Vincys to the Brookes. The others she more or less deprives of moral reality much as Lydgate deprives Rosamond, and with similar results. What happens is that an authentic relation of type to history is distorted by adherence to novel conventions which are meaningless except as reflections of a caste system. Possibly the degree of distortion is as little as could be managed in the England of the time. But one sees why Arnold Kettle can attribute the failures of *Middlemarch*—a novel about change—to a view of society and morality 'somewhat static,' not incorporating 'a dialectical sense of contradiction and motion.' This is overstated, but it does locate, in this novel of crisis, a spot of commonness. Lawrence, we saw, had his own problem arising from a conscious elitism, but he contrived, partly by formal innovation, to keep it out of his novel.

Another fault of *Middlemarch* is in the plotting: or so it must seem to us. We are not, for various reasons too complicated to enter into now, so interested nowadays in what Beckett, praising Proust, called 'the vulgarities of a plausible concatenation' as our great-grandfathers, or even our grandfathers, but we cannot excuse George Eliot so simply, because in this respect she was obviously on our side, and admired narrative with a strong thematic aspect. Yet she wrote a good deal of unnecessary plot, not so much in *Middlemarch* as in *Felix Holt* and *Daniel Deronda*, but still too much. The Bulstrode affair is an instance. In its elements this is impeccable 'thinking with the story'— Lydgate's association with the banker contaminates him with an odious pre-scientific religion, and the climax turns upon an issue between old and new medical practice. The conduct of Mrs Bulstrode is a grace, one of those favours that drop upon a writer because he has worked hard for something else, and not been a slave of the types. Yet in order to get to the point of Bulstrode she invented all the perfunctory business of Rigg and Raffles, the note stuffed in the brandy-flask, the unnecessary relationship with Ladislaw. In the notebook she laboured over the elaboration of all this in such unusual detail that, as Mr Beaty very credibly suggests, it looks as if she was not interested enough to carry such essentially extraneous material in her head. And this plotting damages the modernity of the novel. It is regressive, it takes us back to a more naïve kind of novel, in which it is assumed that the mere delights of concatenation are enough, in which serious thematic or typical interest is largely a matter of luck. Such plots are anti-historical, destructive of the crisis-'set.' Of course we have many later books to be wise by; yet there is no reason why we should not say that this kind of thing diminishes the critical force of the book, given its historical theme. Once again, Lawrence knew better, but it must also be said that the comparisons are not all in his favour.

I have been re-arranging familiar elements of *Middlemarch* because I want to make it possible to think of the novel as having various aspects in common with other kinds of narrative. *Middlemarch* is, to admiring eyes, a novel explanatory of crisis, and it achieves its explanations by means which may be called historical and typological. On the whole it does this without undue violence to persons or to probabilities, remaining true not only to the aims of historical narrative, and to the typological bent of our minds, but also to our sense of fact. Looby Event serves Lord Crisis. *Middlemarch* achieves all manner of consonances between past and present, the before and after of the crisis; but its Transition, its Terrors, its decadence and renovation are thoroughly secularised; apocalypse here has emigrated out of myth into history.

I hope one can say that it is now clear how much *Middlemarch* and *Women in Love* have in common, though even when one considers the similarities the differences insist on their presence. Each deals with a topic, absolutely central to the modern novel, namely what Lawrence described as 'woman becoming individual, self-responsible, taking her own initiative'; and each associates certain bad kinds of sex with an older order, an order of death—though Lawrence did not need Casaubon's impotence, for it was clear that this had become too limiting a symbol for sexual disconnexion, and Skrebensky and Crich are more than ordinarily virile. But both use marital crises as figures for vast and impersonal historical crises and revolutions; at the heart of the books there are the two couples, Casaubon and Dorothea, straddling their historical crisis, Lydgate and Rosamond not even worthy of the ordeal of initiation; Ursula and Birkin representing the mysterious struggle for a new epoch, Crich and Gudrun increasingly excluded, left to set up their own universe of death, with Loerke as its satanic priest. From this basic resemblance many others follow, which it is unnecessary to spell out.

On the major differences in the manner of representing historical crisis there is more to say. We noticed that George Eliot assumed a need for historical particularity, and therefore chose as a model of her own crisis another which she could investigate as thoroughly as she liked. Lawrence chose to write about the one that was going on all around him, and deliberately stripped it of contemporary reference. An historical novel, meaning an exploitation for the purposes of the moment of a set of events long past, is something that it is very hard to imagine Lawrence ever writing. So he 'detemporalised' his book, avoided mentioning that its events belong to the war years. The war was to be any war. Gerald had a commission, but has resigned it, as he could not do in wartime; the Pompadour is the pre-war Café Royal; and so forth.

One reason for this is simply that George Eliot was powerfully under the influence of demythologising Germans, notably Feuerbach, whom she persistently regarded as the leaders of modern thought. Lawrence was, though uneasily, a re-mythologiser. 'The myths begin to hypnotise us once again, our impulse towards our own scientific way of understanding being almost spent,' as he observed in the *Fantasia*. He lived after that great literary and academic and clinical revival of mythology with which we associate such names as Frazer and Harrison, Freud and Jung; with which we associate a whole movement of modern thought which is far from exhausted now. Consequently he associated the old demythologisation with an outmoded rationalism, and so far as it was consistent with his revised version of realism he gave his age of crisis the minimum of historical particularity and the maximum of mythical, or typological, or symbolic, reference. The very character of his narrative involves a recoil from mere history and from 'the vulgarities of a plausible concatenation.' He will have none of that plotting which in George Eliot soaks up so much authentic, thematic interest—no Raffles (compare Raffles as a plot agent with Loerke!) no papers wadded in brandy flasks. He will not make up stories which *explain* how one thing leads to another. There are concessions to contingency, for without them we should hardly recognise the book as a novel, but we move with the minimum of formal continuity from one crux to the next. It is true that the book starts in the traditional mode common to George Eliot and, say, Bennett in *The Old Wives' Tale* or even Tolstoi in *Anna Karenina*, but we soon see that the scene at Halliday's, for instance, exists *for* the image of the African statue and the naked men, and that 'Rabbit' is an entirely new refocussing of the novel on to a symbol of large and ultimately indeterminable significance, related by many thematic ties to the general order of the book. When the older Crich, ordinarily right outside the narrative, is needed to make a point, he is worked in, made to symbolise the dying Age of Love; actually his business is only to die, for Gerald must run from his deathbed to make love to Gudrun. Loerke is introduced and given elaborate development much too late for a major character in a more orthodox narrative. There is a good deal which receives no formal 'explanation' at all—the relations between Birkin and Crich (especially after the cancellation of the Preface), the relevance of the long discussion between Loerke and Ursula on the autonomy of forms in art. The death of Gerald's brother, and later of his sister, are related only thematically to the general design; they are certainly not tributes to contingency, but neither are they given narrative 'followability'. Lawrence does not force discontinuities on one's attention, but everybody observes them, and notes that they are much sharper here than in *The Rainbow*. The change reflects the break with the past which happens between the first and second novels of the sequence; the new manner is what Lawrence described in a famous letter to Garnett as 'futuristic,' not only in narrative but in the conception of character liberated from an established set of expectations which include not only a 'certain moral scheme' but also satisfactory explanations. A new deeper concept of personality required a narrative manner more dependent, as he says, on intuition, on illogic; and it also rendered very undesirable any sharpness of historical definition, allusions to specific event of the sort found in *Middlemarch*.

If we now consider these similarities and differences in the light of what we think novels ought to be, it will, I suppose, be clear that each writer, and all writers of the same degree of seriousness, had to contend with the special pressures of their particular moments upon an essentially atavistic form; the novel tells a story. The pressure on George Eliot was of an age of scientific morality, an age too which made the first onslaught on what used to be called the concord of the canonical scriptures, and discredited the old version of the plot of the Bible, and the plot of comparative religion; she boldly chose that as an important part of her theme. Lawrence, on the other hand, lived in a time when the scientific criticism of her German heroes had not only spread out into politics, history and literature, but had bred a formidable counter-movement, that anti-positivism of which we still hear so much. Because it seemed important to break with pseudo-scientific categories that had lost their relevance—the traditional ideas of character, indeed of order— Lawrence abandoned plot and radically altered traditional characterisation; because the truth lay in the blood and the darkness of the mind, and not in positivistic inferences from detail, he went more directly to the basic mythologies. Whereas she could assert fixed points in the historical flux without direct recourse to apocalyptic figures, which she would have thought, in their naked form, uninverted by the Feuerbachian dialectic, obsolete and irrelevant, he short-circuited conventional representations of the historical course of events and drew much more nakedly on the complex imagery of apocalypse that was maturing in his own mind.

Either way there is a good deal of waste and loss, and neither book can I suppose quite match our own typologies of crisis and change. But they do touch us, and one reason why they do so is surely that under our impressions of change the explanatory types persist. These books reflect our terrors, our contrary yet complementary types of decadence and renovation, even if they lack the peculiar quality of our own fears, and of our own ironies and reserves. We recognise that these books have tensions and problems essentially modern, in the sense that they grew out of an appalled sense of what it means to be modern; and this is true even though our modernism is on the surface so different from theirs, because they rest their whole weight on crisis and modernity, on modernity and history, and they seek our *kinds* of explanation for the pain of being where they are.

(1967)

XIV. COLETTE

We Anglo-Saxons, as the General indiscriminately calls us, have special problems with Colette, and I think the way to sort them out is to argue from the premise that she is a great writer (not, that is, a merely interesting or charming or odd one) and see what happens. Getting close enough to her to do this well is a further difficulty, obviously because she is not an easy writer to translate, obviously again because there is so large a body of work, and less obviously because the alien eye is especially likely to confound what is really impressive with what is more or less strictly for the members of the Colette cult.

By and large the translators have served her well, especially Antonia White and Roger Senhouse. And there seems to be a very fair amount of Colette at present available in this country. Farrar Straus have a programme to publish translations of the whole Fleuron edition, which has fifteen solid volumes, and there are many books in print, of which six have been collected in a Modern Library edition. The indispensable *Break of Day* (*La Naissance du jour*) is now available. Finally, no Anglo-Saxon should nowadays take on Colette without the help of Margaret Davies' excellent short introduction (Oliver & Boyd, London; Grove, New York). Thus equipped, he can pursue the inquiry suggested above, and face the third difficulty, that of sorting out the really valuable from the merely chic or adorable.

At this point I might as well say which books I myself think the ones to be reckoned with if you believe (as I do) that Colette ought to be considered with the same kind of attention given to her most distinguished contemporaries: both of the *Chéri* stories, *The Ripening Seed*, *Break of Day*, *The Cat* (at present, it seems, hard to find), *Julie de Carneilhan*, and some short stories. About one or two more I cannot make up my mind, and there are moments when I have doubts about some of these. But it is a working list.

The newly translated *pensées* called *The Blue Lantern*[1] don't change the picture substantially. This is a brave and gay performance by an old woman in pain, a kind of unaffected tribute to herself, a book by a brilliantly intelligent member of the Colette cult, rather as if Jane Austen should have survived to

[1] Translated by Roger Senbouse. New York, Farrar, Straus.

take part in those learned and adoring games played by devoted Janeites. But this sounds much too harsh. Years before, Colette in her strangest book had celebrated, as a woman of fifty, her liberation from the sharper lusts, partly for the reasons which caused Sophocles to rejoice similarly (but at eighty) in *The Republic*, partly because that masculine directness and hardness —which she thought women really had more of than men— could now be allowed a larger share in the arrangements of life. Now she faces another change, death; she writes about the progressive fading of the senses, accepts it, and values what remains behind: sights, sounds, smells, animals, and old friends. She speaks with love of Jean Marais, of Cocteau and Moreno and the dying Fargue; she is charitable to the most egocentric of the young, remembering her own youthful 'shudder of repugnance at the touch of old people.' She watches children at play in the garden beneath her window, and writes of them with the unillusioned toughness she showed in the music-hall stories of long before. She writes of animals with an unsentimental anthropomorphism we Anglo-Saxons may have trouble understanding, because our culture precludes the unsentimentally anthropomorphic.

Colette combines a strong sense of the total otherness of plants and animals with an equally strong assumption that they have their real meaning in terms of a human world; thus the final cause of flowers is the art of the gardener and the florist, of rustic foods, Parisian *haute cuisine*. Her intensely civilised attitude to the wild reports of sense distinguishes her clearly from Anglo-Saxon nature-mystics, Wordsworth or Thoreau, as we can see in this book from her accounts of painful visits to the *vendange* at Beaujolais, or to Provence for the scents of the hills behind Grasse. She is the inheritor of that great French 19th-century enterprise which was devoted to the confusion of nature with art. Out of it springs a delicate veneration for the cosmetic but also a grossness, the grossness of the *belle époque*. Colette has them both, is as much at home in the reeking scent factories of Grasse as in the hills; a parody of her manner would have to concentrate on her cult of odours, which is alike responsible for much that seems tedious and affected and for such marvels as the conclusion of *The Ripening Seed*.

On the whole, then, one sees *The Blue Lantern* as an agreeable act of self-indulgence, a cultist tribute to a writer whose notoriety has merged into her fame, whose grossness time and the worshippers have sublimated into a unique delicacy. The books have been part of an experiment in living conducted as if there were no evidence to work with except what living provides; thus the conclusions—that the passionate senses beget their own temperance, the mind its own heaven—are what we extract at our own risk from books which never offer a moral formulation and are variously and unpredictably gross and delicate.

Anglo-Saxon attitudes to Colette may be further contorted by our lack of ease with the French concept of the woman writer as *homme de lettres*. We think, maybe, of some burly suffragette, made more formidable by a native French arrogance, as of Colette's own *grandes cocottes* in their contempt for alien whores. And to have got rid of this feeling is not to have abolished altogether that obscure discontinuity of understanding which intervenes between French and English, and in which, notoriously, flourish such reputations as that of Charles Morgan. The very career of Colette is likely to promote fruitless wonder in us. Her first books were no more than tricks done at the bidding of an unscrupulous husband; she wrote herself out of mere naughtiness into the relatively serious Lesbian plot of *Claudine Married*, and out of mere whimsical compliance into a vocation. Leaving him, she became a music-hall dancer, and some of her best stories come out of this episode. Still dancing and writing, she was next the hostess wife of an amorous diplomat. Her third marriage was marked by a new combination of interests: actress, dramatic critic, owner of a beauty shop, novelist. She moved about in worlds to be realised and made concentric only in Paris. Not very like Virginia Woolf, or the modern lady campus-novelist.

And throughout there is this unfamiliar sensual empiricism, expressed most often as a completely open mind on love. She herself was involved in a scandal about a music-hall kiss with another woman; one of her heroes, a lover of young girls, comments on the natural sensual depravity of a rustic fifteen-year-old and describes the smell of her sweat (like 'rest-harrow' in this story; in *Le Blé en herbe* Vinca's is 'pink cammock or crushed green wheat'). The most cultivated life of the senses (food, scent, clothes, the country) is easily associated with venal

sexuality, the remote language of botany with a physical innocence that only full experience can restore. Colette would have
understood up to a point the New England hedonism of Wallace
Stevens, his Florida with 'mornings meet for the eye of the young
alligator,' but not the usurping metaphysics, not the poetry
which says 'It is not in the premise that reality is a solid.' In *Le
Blé en herbe* the boy, newly promoted to manhood by an older
woman, sees his girl and thinks, not 'how innocent!' 'how
beautiful!' but *'Comme elle est solide!'* Hardness, truth to natural
instinct, are the qualities for which she values people and
animals. To be so confidently rooted in the senses is egocentric;
yet one sees why André Billy told her, 'Beside you we are all
little boys.' Men have less solidity, a less certain grasp of things;
this *homme de lettres* is entirely female, and in her total freedom
from grand male notions and theories is perhaps the first great
woman writer, as distinct, of course, from woman *writer*.

We return, then, to the problem of how to be seized of this
greatness without joining the cult. The best thing is to avoid
Gigi, merely a throwback to naughty Claudine, and tackle the
Chéri books. *Chéri* begins in the *belle époque* manner, a piquant
study of a boy educated by *grandes cocottes*; but with a great
technical and moral leap Colette invents a mode, the mode of
hedonist tragedy. Chéri's beauty and taste, his meanness about
wine and gasoline, the eternal awareness that luxury and beauty
have to be hoarded against extravagance and time in a fashion
more bourgeois than a banker's, are all part of a severely
rendered social milieu. The detail is characteristic: 'Have you
noticed,' asks one ageing lady of another, 'that as the skin gets
less firm, the scent sinks in better and lasts much longer?'
Chéri's leaving his older mistress Léa to make a proper marriage
is a normal event of this world; but it projects the story into a
dimension where the will confronts unknown and terrible
possibilities, and the passions assert themselves as imperious
enemies of ease and content, the allies of time the destroyer. In
each book Chéri has, by means of a faint, to flee the world of
sense. The postwar *Last of Chéri* is a great book, surely; Colette
is here in the position of Piranesi cutting deeper into the plates of
the prison etchings made years before. It is still Chéri and Léa;
but the man, symbolically wounded, carries a paralysed will into
a life of pure misery. These are two episodes of exceptional

power: the scene in the opium flat where Chéri, under great photographs of Léa, suffers dreams which are ambiguously of her and of the world before the war; and the properly famous peripeteia when he comes to her in despair, as if to regain lost time, and finds an old woman, masculine and derisive, wearing age like a natural costume; obese, pure, life-accepting, whereas he carries death with him; she is a Falstaff who rejects the prince.

The Chéri books are a triumph of time. Chéri progresses from beauty and vitality, from the world of death-denying artifice and irresponsibility to an intolerable world of corruption and ennui, and so to suicide. Between the two parts there appeared the more limited yet more perfect *Ripening Seed*. The adolescent lovers long for the end of innocence, inhabit an artificial paradise closed to their lifeless, shadowy parents. The boy escapes, and is seduced by an older woman, so exchanging an anguish rich in revery for a known and limited pleasure. But Phil is the soft male, wincing at the girl's easy cruelty when fishing; and now even more vulnerable, he has discovered a sense that life is shared throughout nature, and this gives him the right and duty to tremble '*devant la vie délicate des bêtes et le sang échappé à ses sources.*' Returning from his woman he sees in the glass not the face of a new man but of a murdered girl. Vinca soon forces him to take her out of innocence also; but she is solid, and the morning after she loses her virginity Phil is astonished to see her happy on her balcony, singing and watering a fuchsia. The end reminds us of the hostages given to time and nature: in a few weeks the singing girl may be terrified and condemned, the boy may need to revise his new estimate of himself as the giver of only small pleasures, small pains. The fact is that in this book, with its delicate Breton beaches, its extraordinarily strong and accurate love-scenes, Colette invented not, as somebody said, 'a new way of being sad,' but a way of telling the truth as a woman of civilised eye and sex and pen can feel it; and the truth is again tragic. It is in such works that what she herself began by treating as a trivial stock-in-trade is worked into great literature; and they are the best guide to the reader facing the problems I mentioned earlier.

'Death does not interest me,' Colette once said: and in spite of evidence to the contrary in such stories as 'The Sick Child,' it seems generally true that it interested her mostly as an aspect of love. Perhaps the most remarkable instance of this is the climactic scene in the first *Chéri*, where love is represented as an almost intolerable loss of personality, a closing of the other senses at the command of one grown gluttonous. *Break of Day*, of which Miss Davies rightly says that it is the one work without which Colette's work cannot possibly be seen in perspective, enacts a psychic rebirth by the renunciation of sexual life; the return of the fully adult to the garden where children name the beasts and flowers. The long conversation which is the heart of this book has its *longueurs*, but they are justified by the conclusion. And Colette isn't, hereafter, going to sell love short. *Julie de Carneilhan* is a sombre record of the shabby middle-age of a twice-married and fastidious woman who, like Chéri, abandons the world of the rotten; in another splendid conclusion she polishes her riding boots and sets off through the autumn woods with her taciturn horsy brother, back to where she belongs.

The major Colette is tragic, and *The Blue Lantern* is strictly not so; it is brave, amused, charming. Yet the aged hedonist, almost happy in her pain, experiences the last stirrings of that spirit of rebirth which is the other side of tragedy. 'If I am lying here motionless tonight, there is good reason for it, for I can feel stirring within me—apart from the twisting pain, as if under the heavy screw of a winepress—a far less constant turnscrew than pain, an insurrection of the spirit which in the course of my long life I have often rejected, later outwitted, only to accept it in the end.' When the aged *homme de lettres* passed in her wheelchair through a hotel lobby, everybody stood up. We shall not understand her quite so deeply as her countrymen, perhaps, but we can try to sort out the unique hedonist tragedies from the mere fluff; and we shall then know at least enough to see that to stand up was the proper and inevitable thing to do.

(1963)

XV. JONAH

I can't imagine that anyone will ever write better than Orwell on *Tropic of Cancer*.[1] Miller, he said, was 'the only imaginative

[1] London, Calder; New York, Grove.

prose-writer of the slightest value who has appeared among the English-speaking races for some years past.' He believed that Miller was important in the only way a writer could be in such times, 'a mere Jonah, a passive acceptor of evil,' who demonstrated the '*impossibility* of any major literature until the world has shaken itself into its new shape.' He saw that *Cancer* really belonged to the 'Twenties, was in some ways already old hat by 1934; but he urged everybody to read it because of Miller's often rich and muscular prose, and because he used a selection of language of real men.

'Inside the Whale' is itself a period piece, belonging to Orwell's 1940: the world about to succumb to totalitarian dictatorships, writers, with the iceberg of liberalism melting under them, had nowhere to go but into the whale. Re-reading the essay, I think the judgments which are still absolutely valid are the limiting ones, and that much of the commendation derives from Orwell's obsessive interest in extreme poverty and such relaxations of language and conduct as might be thought to attend it. Who now, for example, could honestly endorse the view that the language of Miller's characters is that of 'an actual majority' of ordinary people? It is certainly not an unfamiliar dialect, but it is spoken not by ordinary people but only by men without women: sailors, for example, or possibly men in heavy industry. Miller's Americans in Paris have a different girl every night, but they are still men without women. There is no real objection to the use of the four-letter word for the female organ in a proper context (bearing in mind all the connotations of fantasy and insult) but men *with* women—sharing a society with them—don't use it metonymously for 'woman.' As 'skirt' is deliberately cheap, 'cunt' is deliberately solitary, and reduces sex to an activity which, as one of the characters discovers, might as well be performed with a cored apple. It makes no difference that the girls in the book are all whores, since Miller regards them as persons, and even seems to prefer them to other women. Similarly, for someone who thinks sex has potentially a paradisal function, it's odd that he should—like many people who don't— explain his low valuation of something by saying he doesn't give a fuck about it.

Certainly Miller's language is closer to one that is actually spoken than the ridiculous upper-class chatter about 'going off' and so on in *Lady Chatterley's Lover*; but it is the language of grossly limited groups, and is not, as Orwell thought, a language of acceptance but of rejection. It rejects half of the population. The stated purpose of the author is to put down 'all that is omitted from books' and we know this is a great deal; but much of what Miller puts in is simply what every sailor knows. The book is often like a very long night in port, late, when the money's spent—a topic of reasonable but limited interest.

The Tropic of Cancer rejects as venal not some but all kinds of living that have any pretence of *mesure*, the quality he hates most also in art. Thus the book is a messy account of mess, as Miller intended it to be, believing that this is the way to produce sudden and fragmentary greatness, the wisdom of 'splinters, toenails.' The rejection of *mesure*, of art in a pejorative sense, had been an avant-garde convention for quite a time, and this is the only reason I can find to explain why some of the early sponsors of Joyce and Lawrence came out in favour of *Cancer*. The 'modernist' family resemblance between Miller and these writers is entirely superficial; Joyce was a life-long student of *mesure* in one way and another, and Lawrence would surely have loathed Miller's book. History ('obscene love of the past') is rejected along with art, because it is simply a record of man's self-betrayal, the long trek from Eden.

Miller is, then, primarily a rejector; in this book there flowers that germ of nihilism present from the beginning in the Romantic culture. What, it may be asked, are those positive, moral, vital-ising suggestions that so many persons of authority have found in his book? They seem to amount to repeated assertions that the ecstasy of artists can bring health to the cancerous mass he describes; that out of the modern jungle in which he says he walks, 'a lean and hungry hyena,' may come a new Jerusalem. His Paris is a Babylon big with this apocalyptic city; in fact, since it serves as a symbol of these two antithetical establish-ments, Paris has in the book an ambiguity which Miller, so far as I can see, does nothing to resolve. Often it sounds like Baudelaire in a bad translation:

Night after night I had been coming back to this quarter, attracted by certain leprous streets which only revealed their sinister splendour when the light of day had oozed away and the whores commenced to take up their posts.

Under its Jerusalem aspect the tone suggests a talentless amateur copy-writer: 'God knows, when spring comes to Paris the humblest mortal alive must feel that he dwells in Paradise.' The trouble with this is not that Paris won't stand up to such symbolical usage but that Miller simply hasn't made the effort.

What other good things grow out of the 'muck and filth'? There are the surrealist celebrations of Romantic joy which even Orwell throws out; and there is the private ecstasy, which was to recur in later books and with genuine splendour in *The Colossus of Maroussi*. Miller observes that *The Tropic of Cancer* is not concerned with 'sex, nor with religion, but with the problem of self-liberation,' and he speaks of the need to be picked clean by life before one can know reality. The man who achieves this rebirth will be 'a pre-Socratic being, a creature part goat, part Titan.' There is nothing intellectually disreputable about this familiar atavism—'deep in the blood the pull of paradise'—nor about Miller's war on time, his search for its 'meridian,' where 'there is no injustice.' But all such quotations have to be drawn from the many passages in which Miller is outlining his programme, talking about the book he is writing rather than writing it. The book doesn't seem to have much to do with this programme. Curiously enough, it ends with the story of how a friend of the narrator's was able to escape from a tricky Parisian situation by fleeing to America, not exactly one of Miller's paradises. Admittedly the narrator, who momentarily has the cash to do likewise, prefers to stay with the mess; we leave him enjoying a moment of *calme* and *volupté* beside the Seine. This last section is, I think, much the best in the book, but I say so because I see in it obvious formal virtues, and I doubt if people find their guru in Miller on the strength of these.

Miller, obviously, can write, as Orwell claimed; but he rarely bothers to. Whether or not you think it worth rummaging through *Cancer* in search of those golden pages ('splinters,' 'toenails') really depends upon how you like your wisdom served. To my mind, the scattered *logia* which the Millerite view prefers to more formal communication amount anyway to a group of second-hand attitudes only occasionally galvanised by some happy audacity of phrase. I don't feel life in this book which is so famous for having it; and I sympathise with those friends of the narrator who made him feel 'a sort of atavistic remnant, a romantic shred, a soulful Pithecanthropus erectus.' Orwell admiringly calls Miller 'Whitman among the corpses' (Whitman accepted life in a world which still permitted him to do so; Miller accepts death, which is all our world has to offer). I don't think this is quite right. Whitman, after all, spent some time among real corpses, and seems to have known the difference between them and the living.

(1963)

XVI. HEMINGWAY'S LAST NOVEL

This[1] is about how Paris was in the early days when Mr Hemingway was very poor and very happy and handling himself very carefully because he knew there were going to be some rough contests, not only with Mr Turgenev and Mr Stendhal but also with life, 'the greatest left-hooker so far, although many say it was Charley White of Chicago.' The sadness of the book comes at the end because it explains that something got lost and the author was no longer making love with whom he loved, an activity to which he attached much importance. But it also speaks very happily about Paris, which is the best place in the world to write in. It explains writing carefully: the great thing is not to describe but to make, not to invent but omit. And to be a good writer, as Hemingway has formerly explained, you need a built-in shit-detector. With one of those, working well, you can purge not only your prose but your acquaintance; so this book tells how Hemingway detected Ford Madox Ford and Wyndham Lewis and even Gertrude Stein, though it also tells how and why he put up with Scott Fitzgerald. It also tells about skiing, horse-racing, and fire-swallowing; about fishing in the Seine and the troubles of waiters, and how the Kansas City whores drank semen as a specific against tuberculosis. If I make it sound a little as if the figure of Lillian Ross's Papa must be casting a shadow over the book I do it no wrong.[2] But I do it wrong beyond question if I seem to suggest that it could have been written by any but a great writer. This is, in some ways, Hemingway's best book since the 1920s and that makes it altogether exceptional.

[1] *A Moveable Feast*. Scribner.

[2] This, needless to say, was written years before Mr Hotchner's further revelations.

At the beginning we have him sitting in a café on the Place St Michel writing 'Up in Michigan'; he names the streets he walked by to keep out of the wind, as elsewhere his route is determined by the need to avoid food-shops. A girl waiting in the café provides a kind of emblem of what he is feeling, and gets into the act; he sees her when he breaks off to sharpen a pencil, and she belongs to him as he to his craft. Finishing the story he feels 'empty and happy, as though I had made love.' This passage, which is about writing, is written not only with the skills but in the manner acquired during the period in which it is set, and so is the book as a whole. Some of the older attitudinising Hemingway has got into it, certainly—a sort of sentimental understanding of his own gifts and problems. But the book has that sharpness and suggestiveness which Hemingway means to achieve when he pursues his famous policy of omitting the known, the familiar links with other experience. And the power of it comes from its being a return—though by a man still sentimentally engaged in the struggle for style—to the time when he first made that hero's effort. The old writes about the young Hemingway, but in the prose of the latter.

The coexistence in this writer of technical and personal ambitions which seem at odds with each other has attracted much comment. Technically he intends to purge his prose in the interest of accurately representing the structure of experience and the texture of the world. It is the getting rid of *littérature*. The young Hemingway was dedicated to this effort. He had been a fluent journalist, and had had to learn that the good thing is the thing done with difficulty. So he went hungry when he need not have done, and 'learned how to make a landscape from Mr Paul Cézanne'—the hardest kind, demanding strict technical application, like boxing and shooting. And he listened to Stein and Pound. 'Isn't writing a hard job, though? It used to be easy before I met you,' he wrote to Stein. 'I certainly was bad, gosh, I'm awfully bad now but it's a different kind of bad.' He learned how to leave things out and get right the things he did not. To all this he returns at length in the new book, telling how he took up Cézanne in Paris where he had left him in Chicago, 'learning something from the paintings . . . that made writing simple true declarative sentences far from enough to make the stories have the dimensions that I was trying to put into them.'

And when the light went in the Luxembourg he called on Gertrude Stein and watched her 'alive, immigrant hair' as she told him 'many truths about rhythms and the use of words in repetition.' It was taking him a morning to write a paragraph, but he was in training, like a fighter.

This book is in the manner then acquired. But it is far from bloodlessly insistent on purely technical feats. It is explicit that a living man, a natural heavyweight, was involved in these cerebral experiments, and they are accompanied by beer, whisky and oysters. The technique involved a technician, human material which felt itself involved in the demands of harsh difficult skills. And the behaviour of this material under stress came to interest him more and more. Perhaps we remember best of all the stories in his first book *Big Two-Hearted River*, with its concentration on a sporting technique and a sportsman's life. But Hemingway moved on, as he had to, from paragraph to story, story to novel; and he moved also into larger attitudes—the hero and not his skill became the focus. This is probably why Gertrude Stein could say that in her view he wrote nothing so good after 1925, the date at which this book ends. It is certainly why he began to lay the foundations of the heroic Hemingway myth.

This myth has often been characterised as self-indulgence, as something very different from the genuine dedication with which he went about making a style. In life it produced the insecure toughness ridiculed by Stein and rendered more sympathetically, a quarter-century later, by Lillian Ross. In prose it produced a writer who, in Lionel Trilling's words, 'put away the significant reticences of the artist' and 'opened his heart like "a man".' The ethics of Jordan, the aesthetics of Cantwell, the cult of honour in defeat, too rigidly expressed, loosen and trivialise the writing, which invites harsh comparisons with the rigorous truth-telling and uncompromised structures of the earlier work.

This is a not unfamiliar line of argument. And yet this book strongly indicates something that was always there to be seen; only this hero, for all his self-indulgence, could have developed the manner of *In Our Time*. It is the same man throughout. The difference between the pre- and post-Stein Hemingways, as he himself represents it, was the difference between a man who could do a lot easily and a man who could do a little only fairly well, and with great irritation and pain. He was learning a difficult craft and learning to do it with one hand. He thought it heroic, and perhaps it was; anyway the man who did it became the suffering hero of the novels. It is worth noticing that Barnes's wound in *The Sun Also Rises* is a very literary wound, and is obliquely compared with the mysterious accident of Henry James. After that the wounded writer is replaced by all those other sportsmen-technicians who have to hold the line of maximum purity in the utmost exposure: the bullfighter who, incapacitated by an accident, has to kill his bull with one good hand; Morgan's last fight, one-handed against an evil world; Cantwell's wounded hand, which the perfect contessa loves; and finally the Old Man and his bad hand. Once he had beaten a powerful Negro in an all-night hand-game at Casablanca; but now his hand betrays him. 'If he cramps again, let the line cut him off.' When he sleeps after returning with his skeleton fish, the boy sees his hands and weeps.

So the years in Paris were not only a time in which Hemingway was learning how to do it, but how to be heroic in doing it, one-handed. And there is an intelligible relation between the self-denial of the writing and the self-indulgence of the attitudes, between finding out how to do it 'so it will make it without you knowing it,' and being the big game man, the *aficionado*, the marksman, the fisherman, the DiMaggio of the novel. The style is a painful stripping away of all that is not declarative. What goes in must have the same kind of authority as a manual of instruction in some manly technique. Now the man who makes such prose is affected by it, and develops an increasingly simplistic theory of manliness. Hence the attention paid to the life of honour ('this honour thing is not some fantasy I am trying to inflict on you. I swear it is true') or the life of pure timeless and mindless love, even the life of the mystic. But above all, as we see when the lines of the literary diagram grow sharper, it is the life of the heroic and gifted peasant.

Hence the cultivated fellow-feeling for proletarian heroes— bakers, bullfighters, fishermen, all possessing techniques to be maintained in purity by imperfect human equipment. The theme is most diagrammatically proposed in *The Old Man and the Sea*. There the hero speaks as Hemingway's Spaniards spoke, an invented language, common and pure, evading the transience of refinement or of slang. It is not spoken English any more than

the language of the characters in the Civil War book is Spanish.
It is the language of Wordsworth's Michael, resettled, after all,
in the tropics. It is very understandable that *The Old Man* was at
first taken to be an allegory of some personal disappointment,
perhaps over the reception of *Across the River and Into the
Trees*. It is simply the fullest representation of a pastoral myth,
the myth of the author reduced to the simplicity of a one-
handed struggle against the world, saying everything by saying a
little accurately.

In the meantime, what happens to the reticent, heroic prose?
The truth, it seems, can be known only by simple men who cannot
speak English. One consequence is a sort of bombast, for Great
Ideas can be mooted and discounted at the same time, as when
the Old Man argues that you are entitled to kill a fish if you love
it, but at once reproaches himself with thinking too much. This
is certainly a difficult line to hold without falling into self-
indulgence, and the later Hemingway is marred by a great deal
of this disingenuous *simplesse*. Only one sees how it is related to
his virtues, and developed from them.

So, if we consider this posthumous book *ad hominem*, it will
strike us as very moving. It was written by a man who thought he
had, over the years, disciplined his technique to the point where
he could deal with what he called the fourth and fifth dimensions;
who had, year in and out, fought his handgame with language
till blood came from under his nails; who knew that he could do
it any length, yet published nothing in the last decade of his life
except a *novella* of the crystalline variety, very different from the
arduous prose of the first heroic period. And a few years later he
began to write this book about the heroic apprenticeship. It
opens with a passage which equals in subtlety and power anything in the great stories. 'Then there was the bad weather' is the
first sentence—what was omitted before he arrived at this
declaration?—and before the end of the first page we are in the
midst of a painter's description of sewer wagons in the moonlight
on the rue Cardinal Lemoine. Then he tells about the girl who
got into 'Up in Michigan,' and goes right on to a description of
one of Stein's lessons. He wants it to be clear that this book is
about writing, about the heroic apprenticeship.

Much of what he says of Paris is generally familiar from other
books. But no other book is of this authority and distinction,

and no other so strongly conveys (largely by omission, of course) the sense of time regained. This, however, is to be understood as a side-effect of the principal effort, which is to celebrate the hero and his struggles. What happened in Paris was important in so far as it helped or hindered him. Being in love, knowing Pound and Sylvia Beach, going hungry, watching the fishermen, helped. Racing, though absorbing, didn't, so it had to be given up. Many things were positive hindrances: people who interrupted him as he wrote in cafés, and were foully insulted; people who upset him by being homosexual; people who in one way or another were out to con you. Some of these were well-known people, and the most obviously interesting thing about the book is that it says disagreeable things about such people.

There is a malice here, recollected in tranquillity; as in the pages on Stein, and those on members of what she called the lost generation. (Incidentally Hemingway's explanation of the expression '*la génération perdue*' is that Miss Stein got it from a garage proprietor who was reproving the help for slowness or ineptitude in repairing her Model T. This is far less convincing than John Brinnin's version, which is that she borrowed it from a hotel-keeper who argued that men got to be civilised between eighteen and twenty-five, or never, and that a generation had missed its chance of civility because of the war.) It was obviously fun to get back at Stein for the nastiness of the Toklas book, and Hemingway invents some beautiful dialogue—which he could always do, and which she, he claimed, could not—to say wicked things about her. The two chapters on Stein are written like very good stories, especially the second, called 'A Strange Enough Ending,' which has in it why he could never make friends with her again; the reason given is not, most of us would think, a good one, but it sounds good. Wyndham Lewis is disposed of in a hideous little vignette; Hemingway goes home afterwards and tells his wife, 'I met the nastiest man I've ever seen today.' 'Tatie, don't tell me about him,' she said. 'Please don't tell me about him. We're just going to have dinner.'

Ernest Walsh, who was dying of consumption, flaunted a 'marked-for-death look': 'and I thought, you con man, conning me with your con.' Of Ford Madox Ford: 'I took a drink to see if his coming had fouled it.' Scott Fitzgerald is a kind of critical case, absurd and offensive but a writer. So to him is devoted the most elaborately written section of the book, a carefully devised tragic farce about a trip to Lyon, with a scene in which Hemingway takes Fitzgerald's perfectly normal temperature with an immense bath thermometer. The food and the conversation are remembered or invented with total authenticity. From start to finish this is the work of a great writer.

This, as Hemingway himself suggests, is a work of fiction, and ought to be considered among his novels. It is an ingenious and deliberate way of revisiting the sources of a great writer's strength; and it displays that strength as very little else of his had done in thirty years.

(1964)

XVII. SAMUEL BECKETT

(i) *Waiting for Godeau*

The expression that there is nothing to express, nothing with which to express, nothing from which to express, no power to express, no desire to express, together with an obligation to express. . . .

Feeling that this is what art should be, Mr Beckett—who else?—opts, he says, for writing which deserts the plane of the feasible, 'weary of its puny exploits.' Mr Kenner[1] quotes this with some indications of agreement. More specifically, he suggests, Beckett rids himself of the problem of how to go on from Joyce by abandoning the narrative tradition with its 'idiot consistency' and fining fiction down to the point where it is clearly absurd to go on with it, except that writing is being alive and we've all been tricked into the cowardice—as Beckett called it in the Proust book—of thinking we're better suited that way.

Beckett is worth a lot of trouble, if only because of *Waiting for Godot*, and if Mr Kenner, in taking trouble, seems to absorb rather than describe the *oeuvre*, that may be said to be true of very good critics. Mr Kenner, indeed, has sent most of the great moderns spinning with the velocity of his passage, and it was not without relish that one saw he was going to give Beckett a whirl. However, the question is not whether Kenner is good at absorbing Beckett, but whether he is informative or otherwise helpful.

---

[1] *Hugh Kenner, Samuel Beckett* (London, Calder; New York, Grove).

The answer is, slowly, yes; but the cost to the reader is high enough to be worth counting.

Speaking of the trilogy (*Molloy*, *Malone Dies*, *The Unnamable*), a work with 'a fastidious stench,' Kenner says, among other things, that it is 'a compendious abstract of all the novels that have ever been written,' 'a sardonic counterpoint to the epic tradition of the West,' a progress from *sum* to *cogito*, and a happy dissolution of fiction to the point where it describes nothing but itself being written ('pure act by pure inaction,' or, if you like, 'pure activity, the Ape of pure Act'). Similarly with the plays: they reduce themselves to actors acting acting before a time-bound audience being an audience—unless it walks out, it has to be. Allowing that there are historical reasons for all this, why is it good? Why is idiot randomness any better than idiot consistency? Please explain, we ask, how the trilogy sums up all the other novels, and counterpoints the epic. Well, declares Kenner, I can tell you that if Homer had been a 20th-century Irishman living in Paris, he 'might well have written the first half of *Molloy*.'

The truth is that this critic does much more absorbing and converting than explaining. His prose is atwitch with the exertion of wit and intellect and it has a narcissistic glow. 'All Beckett's writings bring some sustained formal element to the service of some irreducible situation round which the lucid sentences defile in baffled aplomb.' This is useless. Sometimes there is a disastrous self-admiring joke: Beckett's bicycle is *maestro di color che vanno*.

However, the book does provide some information about published and unpublished work of Beckett. And Mr Beckett himself contributes a highly significant piece of information about his interest in a racing cyclist called M. Godeau, whom Kenner accordingly hails as Beckett's 'Cartesian Man in excelsis.' The book is strongest, in fact, on bicycles, the frequent occurrence of which in Beckett testifies to his interest in them as emblems of *l'homme machine*. Indeed, Beckett is obsessed with the description of movement, and the reduction of human activity to mechanical stereotypes. It is the decay of a bicycle that reduces Molloy, and the lack of one condemns the Unnamable to inert cogitation. In this Cartesian connection, Mr Kenner has usefully looked up the obscure Belgian Occasionalist

Geulincx, whom Murphy quotes. This author believed that the division between mind and body was complete, rejecting the pineal gland theory, and that a separate act of God was required for every physical movement. The textbooks, if I remember rightly, claim that Occasionalism was knocked out by Leibniz, but according to Kenner Mr Beckett has shown it to be 'aesthetically relevant' to our time. The book is also good on the counting mania suffered by so many Beckett characters, and Mr Kenner ingeniously works out a comparison between irrational numbers and the clown or *clochard* figures—shadows behind the neat rationalist rows of bourgeois numerals.

Beckett, in the trilogy especially,

takes stock of the Enlightenment, and reduces to essential terms the three centuries during which those ambitious processes of which Descartes is the symbol and progenitor accomplished the dehumanization of man.

This book is a rhapsody on that theme, with illustrations from Beckett. It is Kenner's own theme, though of course it isn't a novel one, and Beckett grew up with it; but I suspect that Kenner's view of it, which is the fashionable thing about our being trapped at the end of a technological epoch, is not really Beckett's. He is much more old-fashioned, having a more biological approach, and also more theological interest than this book indicates. He was also, as the Proust book shows, affected by Bergson: the bicycle is a Bergsonian laughter-maker, and the famous 'I can't go on. I'll go on' is the beastly plight of a thinker acknowledging his instinctive adaptation to life, his involuntary survival kit. Anyway, if the forthcoming *Comment C'est* merely illustrates the Kennerian Beckett as accurately as this book predicts, I shan't be reading it. Possibly it won't; Mr Kenner can be extremely reductive, as in his handling of *All that Fall*.

(1962)

(ii) *Beckett Country*

How, if this novel[1] were by an unknown author, would one set about the reviewer's task of giving some notion of its contents, and throwing in an appraisal? First, perhaps, by dealing in

[1] *How It Is*. Grove.

certainties: for instance, this book was written in French under the title *Comment C'est*. The translation is by the author. It is on the whole about as literal as a comparison of the titles will suggest, though one notes a lost pun (*commencez*). And since *Comment C'est* are the last words in the book, they impart to the design a circularity which is, perhaps not too unhappily, lost in English. Where the English is obscure the French in general helps little: 'the history I knew my God the natural' comes from *l'histoire que j'avais la naturelle*. Where the English looks wrong the French looks just as wrong: 'of the four three quarters of our total life only three lend themselves to communication' sounds as if the first 'three' has got in by mistake, but the French says *quatre trois quarts* and adds to the muddle by saying *deux seuls* for 'only three.' It seems unlikely that the reader loses much in clarity by using the English version. The syntax is neither English nor French, but that of some intermediate tongue in which 'ordinary language' cannot be spoken. This language goes indifferently into French or English. It eschews marks of punctuation, although the novel is divided into paragraphs of unequal length, signifying, why not, the fluttering of some moribund intellectual pulse, rather than successive stages of meaning. At its climax the story virtually disclaims its own authenticity, and this uncertain commitment to ordinary criteria of meaningfulness is also characteristic of the language in which it is told.

The meanings present in this language are not valid outside the book, being mostly the products of intensive internal references and repetitions. Phrases of small apparent significance occur again and again with some kind of cumulative effect: 'something wrong there,' 'bits and scraps,' 'quaqua,' 'when the panting stops,' etc. The speaker of these phrases looks forward keenly to the end of his task, frequently promising that we are near the end of the first, second, or third part, and rejoicing especially in the final paragraph, only to be thwarted by the Finnegan-begin-again trick mentioned above. In short, the whole book refuses to employ the ordinary referential qualities of language, and frustrates ordinary expectations as to the relation between a fiction and 'real life.' It is as if the old stream of consciousness were used in a situation where there is nothing but the stream to be conscious of.

Not very helpful, says the reader. What *is* the story? Well, it is spoken by a nameless man face down in mud, and apart from him its principal character is called Pim. Three sections describe how it was before, with and after this Pim, who is therefore a measure of time and history. Pim was long awaited, then he arrived and lay down in the mud beside the speaker and his sack full of cans; but things didn't go well, and he passed on. Where, or to whom? Before Pim, the speaker had been alone; perhaps, he thought, the 'sole elect,' moving at intervals with his sack and his can opener ten or fifteen yards through the mud. His only contact with the world 'above' is the memory of a past idyllic scene with a girl and a dog; and another of a marriage that failed with the waning of desire. After Pim he sees that he is really one of a great number, all on the same impossible muddy journey. Somehow it has been arranged that its progress is circular and endless.

With Pim, the situation was at least not solitary. Pim brought a watch and one could listen to the delicious ticking away of the seconds. Furthermore, the speaker devised an elaborate signal code by which he induced Pim to speak: as by jabbing the can opener into his rectum, beating him on the kidneys, or, to make him stop, on the head. Pim, being a man, is a kind of machine, *l'homme machine* in fact, responsive to external stimuli. Nevertheless he clenches his fists in pain, and his nails grow through his palm. The close relationship of the couple is that of tormentor and victim. When Pim abandons the speaker he leaves very little, but still something, behind him, 'with Pim all lost almost all nothing left almost nothing but it's done great blessing.' This example of dream parataxis, translated into English, means, I suppose, that the residual benefits of Pim's sojourn are small but important, perhaps only because they prove that we have lived through one more stage and are nearer the last. Later we gather that as far as the speaker is concerned we can do what we like with time—reverse it, for example—so long as we always give Pim and the Primal Scene a central place in it: 'on condition that by an effort of the imagination the still central episode of the couple be duly adjusted.'

After Pim, the world is full of tormentors and their victims, an endless chain in which each man repeatedly changes his role from one to the other. Over vast stretches of time, one torments and is tormented. The speaker moves on through this suffering inflicted and received, towards reunion with Pim. But in the end the voice we are listening to rebels, denies that all he has said is quoted from some external authority, claims that it is all a fiction ('all balls'); that there was something, yes, but no 'quaqua,' no *logos* or revelation from without, only himself, face in mud, making it up and mumbling. Then the last sentence, with its ambiguous denial of this disclaimer.

What kind of a story is this? Certainly there is a fiction; and there is a chain not only of torment but of rhythmical incantation. But the reader who wants more than a form commenting upon itself, an autistic stir of language, will be tempted to look aslant at the book, to seek allegory. I myself have already slipped into allegory in describing Pim's watch, and in hinting that the tormented relationship between the speaker and Pim stands for the incarnation, which, we are told, gives history such meaning as it may be said to have, and could be regarded as affording the type of human love-relations ever since (the love of the Word unable to speak a word speaks, under painful stimulus, when it is embodied in *l'homme machine*. Pim has nails through his palms, and is pierced by a kind of spear).

Perhaps, as the speaker felt when he denied the authenticity of 'quaqua,' the intervention of that word was all a fiction anyway. Even so, his dreams are penetrated by it. Thus there are in the book echoes of Christian figurations of experience: hints of millennialism, of the *logos* as distorted by mud. In the first part a vague 'epiphany' suggests an involuntary memory of Eden. The sack is a figure for the body, support and burden of the soul, which the Christian centuries would have had no difficulty in recognising; in the third part we have a picture of the history of the elect parallel to Milton's in the last two books of *Paradise Lost*, except that we lack the assurance of Pim's second coming in majesty. The book offers an open invitation to such allegories, even though everybody who accepts it will soon feel lost and uncertain.

In view of all this it is, I suppose, just as well that we *do* after all know something, if only a little, about Beckett. The Speaker in this book is the latest in a long line bred from his obsession with Dante's Belacqua, who could not enter purgatory until he had relived his slothful life. Beckett's dream of life is purgatorial.

or would be if salvation waited at its end; as it is, his characters are, as Mr Rooney says in *All that Fall*, 'like Dante's damned, with their faces arsy-versy.' There is a Beckett country in which we feel half at home; and we know the Beckettian *homo patiens*, sinking progressively into immobility. His role as victim and tormentor we recall from *Godot*. His relation to the past we learned from *Krapp's Last Tape*. And so on. In addition there is, to provide a physics for the Beckett world, his early book on Proust, as well as such sophisticated experiments as Mr Kenner's book. So we have some knowledge, not much, of the physical laws governing this new book; we have keys to its meanings. 'No symbol where none intended,' noted Beckett in the addenda to *Watt*; but by establishing a world of uncontrollably interrelated objects and meanings he makes this injunction impossible of fulfilment.

A few instances will serve to illustrate this. There must be a connection between Pim's watch, Pozzo's watch in *Godot*, and the passage in *Proust* on Time's 'ingenuity . . . in the science of affliction.' Time is the means by which we are punished for having been born. For Beckett as for Proust our only means of triumphing over it is the involuntary memory; in Beckett this operates infrequently and unsatisfactorily, as with Krapp's tape or the Speaker's recollection of the girl and of his marriage. We are enslaved by time; when eternity, the *nunc stans*, the *durée*, came down to save us, it apparently failed. So much for the 'succour' which, as Molloy observed, you ought to consider as a possibility before, inevitably, you reject it. Pim is one name for it. Trapped in time and space as the fallen categorise them (and what other way is there?) Beckett's figures are all, as Mr Kenner demonstrates, more or less conscious Cartesians. They are all, perhaps, Descartes himself, contemplating the world from a position prone or supine (Yeats remarked that the world changed when Descartes discovered that he could think better in bed than up).

Contemplating a world so changed, Beckett is moved to 'jettison the very matrices of fiction—narrator, setting, characters, theme, plot,' and 'devote his scrutiny (under the sign of Belacqua) to the very heart of novel writing: a man in his room writing things out of his head while every breath he draws brings death nearer.' So Mr Kenner. He is also much interested by human inventions which reflect the factitious order and inter-relatedness of the objective world to which he cannot belong; his relation to this common-sense reality is exactly that of a circus clown, who can do apparently impossible things but finds easy ones incredibly complicated. The fundamental absurdity of the subject–object situation is for him figured in clowns and *clochards*; and so is our imperfect control over space, time, and death. Beckett's humour derives entirely from this. It is a stateli-ness of speech, a clownishness of philosophical language (dealing with the complicated things and finding the easy ones too hard); in action it is the Bergsonian pratfall. This is the humour of man as machine, whether rhetorical or locomotive.

Beckett can thus be read as a philosophical fantasist: His bicycles are Cartesian symbols, his submen Prousts who have *really* contracted out, and so forth. Sunk in a sub-social, sub-psychological dream, they all merge in one's mind—Watt, Molloy, Malone, the Unnamable, the unnamed of the new book. They may sink deeper into a state of pure rejection, pure nega-tivity—indistinguishable, as Molloy noticed, from God's. But because they are all aspects of the same figure, inhabiting similar worlds, we have relevant knowledge to bring to this new book; we can live with it, perceive something of its rhythms and stresses—in short, receive it.

That, at any rate, is a way of putting it. Yet it may tell little more than a small part of the truth about how Beckett has to be read. To emphasise the formal interest can be a fashionable way of concealing the true nature of our curiosity. Beckett is a puzzle-maker, quaint and learned. We look for clues, guess at meanings. His formal sophistication may be the meat the modern burglar brings along to quiet the *avant-garde* housedog. Under it all, he is a rather old-fashioned writer, a metaphysical allegorist. Take, for example, *Watt*. There he made his hero's name the first word of a metaphysical conundrum; and Knott, whom Watt serves, is the god defined by negatives, perhaps also time itself, inexplicably regular. Watt has only oblique religious experiences. He meets a porter whose lameness causes him 'to move rapidly, in a series of aborted genuflections,' and a Mr Spiro, Catholic propagandist, who gives prizes for anagrams on the names of the Holy Family. (Out of Mr Spiro's motto, *dum spiro spero*, we get the interesting anagram *dum*: mud. Since *dum* is 'while,' here meaning one's time on earth, it isn't hard to see why the latest hero spends his time in the mud.)

Watt, however, is not good at symbols: he had 'lived, miserably it is true, among face values all his adult life . . . whatever it was Watt saw, with the first look, that was enough for Watt . . . he had experienced literally nothing, since the age of fourteen, or fifteen, of which in retrospect he was not content to say, "That is what happened then." '

To enjoy Beckett, one mustn't be a Watt. When we meet, for example, the Lynch family, we must take their heroic efforts, ruined by disease, to reach a combined age of a thousand years not as merely grotesque humour, but as a hopelessly human millennialist aspiration, an absurd plot to overcome history, bring time to an end. If we know that Beckett's names and titles often contain puns, sometimes obscene, let us also look for allegorical meanings in such names as Malone and MacMann, Godot, and even Pim.

This suggests that the delights offered by Beckett are of an old and tried variety. He has re-invented philosophical and theological allegory, and as surely as Spenser he needs the right to sound sub-rational, to conceal intention under an appearance of dreamlike fortuity, to obscure the literal sense. The only difference is that his predecessors were sure there was such a sense, and on this bitch of a planet he can no longer have such certainties. This difference does not affect the proposition that Beckett's flirtations with reality are carried on in a dialect which derives from the traditional language of learning and poetry. It is nevertheless true that the more accustomed we become to his formal ambiguity, the more outrageously he can test us with inexplicitness, with apparently closed systems of meaning. *How it is* differs from the earlier work not in its mode of operation but principally in that it can assume greater knowledge of the Beckett world. Such assumptions have often and legitimately been made by major artists, though we should not forget that this is not a certain indication of greatness. Prolonged attention given (from whatever motives) to a minor but complex author may allow him to make them. But who can be sure which is which? It is a perennial problem for critics of *avant-garde* art, and Beckett raises it in a very acute form.

(1964)

XVIII. ZEMBLANCES

The age is grown so picked that the toe of the critic comes so near the heel of the artist, he galls his kibe; Mary McCarthy's authoritative exegesis of *Pale Fire* has been available for awed inspection since September, whereas the novel itself is only now offered to the public.[1] Although it is still 'unlike any novel you have ever read,' as the publishers say, it does remind one occasionally of Miss McCarthy's article, and one especially remembers, as one obediently reads back and forth through the book, her final assertion that it is 'one of the very great works of art of this century.' This thesis has been severely blown upon by Dwight Macdonald, who thinks Miss McCarthy has been caught in a tiresome critic-trap. One doesn't read novels primarily in order to find out whose side one's on, but I am clear that Miss McCarthy, who boldly neglects all her own forcibly expressed opinions on fiction when she writes on *Pale Fire*, is largely right about detailed interpretation and largely wrong about the value of the whole work.

Pale Fire is got up as an edition of an autobiographical poem by a distinguished old sub-Frostian called Shade—on the evidence provided, a somewhat uneven performer. The man who is editing the poem, in the teeth of Shade's widow and his friends, is a refugee from Zembla called Kinbote, or, by other people, Botkin. This crazed homosexual believes that Shade had really wanted to include in his poem a full account of Zembla, and especially of the revolution which resulted in the flight of the King, who is none other than Kinbote himself. The commentary explains how this Ruritanian romance got submerged in Shade's poem, and how the assassin dispatched from Zembla to liquidate Kinbote accidentally killed Shade instead, just as he was entrusting his poem to the hands of his Zemblan friend. Hints are dropped to give us the true story: the murderer is really an escaped criminal lunatic who seeks revenge on the judge who committed him, and whose house Kinbote has rented; he shoots Shade in mistake for the judge.

This, as Miss McCarthy observes, is only the start of it. *Pale Fire* is certainly one of the most complex novels ever written. Kinbote builds up his fantasy out of stray bits of associative

[1] London, November 1962, Weidenfeld & Nicolson; New York, Putnam.

material. He projects the events of the campus on to Zembla, the fictive land, the country of semblance. He suffers, you are allowed to think, from the sort of verbal disorientation which is symptomatic of some forms of insanity (an idea used by Musil for his Clarisse). Thus he deals in all manner of occult associations, private meanings which shape his fantasy-world; and these are not merely verbal but also enter into astrology and colour symbolism. The merest hint in Shade's poem sets off a train of Zemblanisms, and what may be inverted is inverted, like a mirror-image and like Kinbote's name and sexuality. The private and mad character of his activity is suggested by his failure to perceive obvious allusions in Shade's poem—he cannot even understand the title, because his copy of *Timon of Athens* is a Zemblan translation.

There is here a fleeting resemblance to Golding's method in *Pincher Martin*; but the tone and purpose are very different. Nabokov, having researched all these occult interrelations, hands them over to poor old crazy Botkin to make a world of, but leaves enough Nabokovian traces on the text to assure us that he's there, sane and interested. And the big question isn't whether you can spot all these weird multiple associations, but why Nabokov should have wanted to make them up—he says he loathes 'symbolic' novels—and present them to his madman.

To answer it, one would need to look at Nabokov's whole output, which includes a large element of what Dwight Macdonald calls 'high-class doodling.' This, abating the pejorative implication, would indeed do to describe his whole method. His attention all goes to the formal aspects of the work; he is fascinated by the medium. To describe the relation of his fictions to reality would be an impossible assignment; and this is one of the points of *Pale Fire*. In a novel, the facts need not be true, but their interrelations must be; and the novelist's world stands in relation to common reality as Kinbote's commentary stands to Shade's poem. Both are out of focus, both deliver versions of reality different from the brute facts. Hence Kinbote's homosexuality, which is a metaphor for the artist's minority view of a bad world, of 'our cynical age of frantic heterosexualism.' If one dared risk a guess at correlative idiosyncrasies in Nabokov himself, one would have to point to his intellectual disgust with

Freudianism or, recalling that he is a member of the Russian émigré minority, his loathing of Marxism.

But the main reason why Kinbote serves Nabokov's purpose is that he is obsessed, intoxicated by his text, exactly, and with the same disinterest, as Humbert Humbert was obsessed by his girl. Nabokov's novels are usually concerned with elevated, amoral states of mind comparable no doubt to that of the author in creating them. One consequence is that they have the kind of contempt for realism demonstrated, in the degree of mania, by Kinbote. On one occasion Kinbote describes some royal Zemblan portraits in which the painter, master of *trompe-l'oeil*, has emphasised his skill by sometimes inserting pieces of wool, gold or velvet, instead of painting them. This, says Kinbote, has 'something ignoble about it,' and discloses

the basic fact that 'reality' is neither the subject nor the object of true art, which creates its own special reality having nothing to do with the average 'reality' perceived by the communal eye.

Incidentally, this trick deceives the Russian experts who tear the palace apart looking for the crown jewels. No Soviet realism for Nabokov; he is a formalist. And he repeatedly draws attention to the artifice which constitutes his reality higher than the communal 'reality.' He has always done so, and Kinbote's whole fantasy is merely a bold development of this prejudice. His Zemblan fantasies are a metaphor for the world of fiction.

Pale Fire, however, includes not only Kinbote's fantasy but a version of the communal reality as well: Shade's wife and tragic daughter, Botkin's campus enemies, the poem which is a rival, saner version of the real. Thus the author has to show us not only that Kinbote's activity is the model of his own, but that Kinbote is justly to be called mad. There ensue many delicate acts of dissociation, little authorial plots against Kinbote. For example, he is given certain mannerisms of style which reflect his sexual interests in a dismally coy light:

When stripped and shiny in the mist of the bath house, his bold virilia contrasted harshly with his girlish grace. He was a regular faunlet.

When Nabokov makes Kinbote speak like this, or otherwise betrays him, we remember Humbert slipping unwillingly into compassion when Lolita comes, defeated, to his motel bedroom.

Yet none of this affects the basic validity of the metaphor; Kinbote's obsession represents what Nabokov calls 'aesthetic bliss.'

> For me a work of fiction exists only insofar as it affords me what I shall bluntly call aesthetic bliss, that is a sense of being somehow, somewhere, connected with other states of being where art (curiosity, tenderness, kindness, ecstasy) is the norm.

This is the state of being enjoyed by Humbert and Kinbote; it sets them against the world which prefers men like machines, supports commonplace dictators like Paduk in *Bend Sinister*, or disgustingly sexless, unextravagant, mechanical men like Gradus, Kinbote's imaginary assassin, who is studied throughout the work with fascinated revulsion. Yet *Pale Fire* is, as I've said, technically more ambitious than *Lolita*, because it renders not merely isolated bliss but the communal, blissless, 'reality.' And the occult relations explored by Miss McCarthy reflect the complicated ties between reality and 'reality,' the artist's vision and the mere facts.

One instance of this is worth mentioning. Shade is a Pope scholar, and there are several allusions to *The Essay on Man*; this is not a wanton choice of Nabokov's—though he might be held to have used it wantonly—because he saw in it a relevant approach to aesthetic bliss. Shade, meditating an absurd mistake which had seemed to bring together two dreams of after-life but depended entirely on a fountain/mountain misprint in a written report, observes that such near-coincidence is in a way stronger evidence of 'correlated pattern in the game' than perfect similarity. 'All Chance, Direction which thou canst not see' is the line at the back of his mind. The game metaphor is continued; he thinks of the players,

> aloof and mute,
> Playing a game of worlds, promoting pawns
> To ivory unicorns and ebon fauns;
> Kindling a long life here, extinguishing
> A short one there; killing a Balkan king . . .
> Co-ordinating these
> Events and objects with remote events
> And vanished objects. Making ornaments
> Of accidents and possibilities.

Here Shade is remembering part of Pope's Second Epistle, and perhaps more extreme statements of an 18th-century position we know best from Johnson's assault on Jenyns: disease, madness, sorrow, may be part of some game played by higher creatures than men. And Nabokov is remembering that the novelist can, after all, amuse himself by making a man tumble over in an epilepsy, run mad, or be confounded by fantastic coincidence. His is the bliss of co-ordinating events and objects with remote events and vanished objects; he can sit, if he wants to, like the saints enjoying the torments of the damned.

Pale Fire reproduces this divine game and offers us the pleasures of process as well as of product. But it is only a kibitzer's pleasure. Nabokov's relationship with his world is very exclusive; his is the creative logos, we are, at best, angels privileged to stand by and applaud. As to those readers who are enslaved to the communal 'reality,' they can expect nothing at all. As a class, they may be identified as those who thought *Lolita* was about, not aesthetic bliss, but nympholepsy. For all such readers the author, engrossed in the sublime images he has made of his own delight, feels nothing; or, if anything, contempt.   (1962)

XIX. A HERO IN BAD FAITH : SARTRE AND THE ANTI-NOVEL

Sartre is a very big writer, an obscure and copious writer; he has powerful and variable opinions about almost everything, and it is quite certain that so long as he is in production nobody will ever be able to grasp him firmly. Even if one tries merely to find out what he means in relation to a special and limited interest, it is by no means easy. The new work pours out, altering the picture as a whole, and, by implication at least, changing even those details which are not directly under consideration.

Thus it can be said with some assurance that Sartre is a figure of importance in the theory and practice of the modern novel; but this does not mean that we can have a clear view of his opinions, as we have, for example, of Robbe-Grillet's. In an early essay he said one ought to look behind every novel for a hidden metaphysic, and it might seem useful to have, behind *Nausea*, the immensely visible *Being and Nothingness*; indeed it has often been argued that these works are very intimately related. This is about half true, perhaps, but even if it were wholly true it would be of limited interest to most readers of the new paperback *Nausea*,[1] who might reasonably want to get to know this central work without being obliged to break into so vast and harsh a freedom-fortress as the 'essay on phenomenological ontology.' Some might choose to do so with the aid of the keys, admirably simple and well-cut, provided by Mrs Warnock in what is far the most practical and humane introduction to Sartre I know.[2]

Translation lags behind, but there is a new volume of essays containing pieces from *Situations IV* and Sartre's preface to Sarraute's *Portrait of a Man Unknown*.[3] Apart from the Sarraute essay, it contains little comment on literature, but there is a good deal that ought to be taken into account whatever the angle from which one views the author. The translation (except in the Sarraute piece, which was done years ago by Maria Jolas) is slapdash, and at times worse than that, but even so the huge and alien personality blazes through. The opening piece on Tintoretto, too long, inappropriately rhapsodic, reminds us that Sartre sometimes writes 'at top speed, with rage in my heart, gaily, tactlessly.' The point is that this painter, under the shadow of Titian, exposed or reflected the corruption of his city: 'anxious and cursed, Venice produced a man riddled with angst,' a man whose art 'rent the age with slashes of fire' and proved him 'a Darwinist before the fact.' It is by most standards a very bad performance; but such judgments have to be suspended with an author like Sartre, for excess and disorder acquire significance in the total context.

The long essay on Merleau-Ponty is in some ways a similar problem. Although their friendship was evidently shot through with philosophical accords and disputes, Sartre is allusive rather than expository when he discusses their intellectual associations. What comes through very powerfully is the strange set of profiles their friendship and half-quarrels present: it is like something from one of the novels, or a fictional illustration in *Being and Nothingness*. The account of how they dealt with one another on *Les Temps Modernes* has its farcical side;

---

[1] *Nausea* (Harmondsworth, Penguin; New York, New Directions).
[2] *The Philosophy of Sartre* (London, Hutchinson; New York, Hillary).
[3] *Situations* (London, Hamish Hamilton; New York, Braziller).

and yet what comes of this essay in the end is not amazement at the improbable conversations of co-editors but a fine sense of the quality of Merleau-Ponty, of a man who could think desperately and live as one who could reasonably argue that every life and every moment are incarnations, singularities which deform yet illustrate the universal.

What is constantly surprising about Sartre is this charity, this insight into others which, the early philosophical work suggested, could not be had, but which novelists need, if only as an 'as if.' The new book reprints his vehement attack on Camus. At first the tone is almost comically mean.

> Your combination of dreary conceit and vulnerability always discouraged people from telling you unvarnished truths. The result is that you have become the victim of a dismal self-importance. . . . Sooner or later, someone would have told you this. It might just as well be me.

Twenty or so pages of this, then Sartre says he has reached the end; but he thinks of more he wants to say. He obligingly outlines his thought for Camus, who seems to have misunderstood it, and quite gratuitously embarks upon a penetrating estimate of Camus himself in the days when he was 'alive and authentic.' There follows his obituary of Camus, this 'Cartesian of the absurd'; it is rough with sorrow and love.

Friendship and its corollary, the posturing row, are simpler in the occasional writings than they were shown to be in the third section of *Being and Nothingness.* So with the long memoir of Paul Nizan, who taught the young to be angry and refused to accept the old explanations of conditions as 'natural'; between him and Sartre, as between Camus and Sartre, the old myth of friendship, as something ultimately indestructible, intervened. Yet one would look to these essays, rapid and generous as they are, for evidence that much of the original thinking of Sartre survives the obscure Marxist 'conversion' Mrs Warnock labours to define. They are prodigiously thoughtful, and the thought has its roots in the old Existentialism.

This is also true of the essay on Giacometti, which is as impressive as the Tintoretto is tawdry; it also reads like an exemplum from *Being and Nothingness.* So, too, with the introduction to Sarraute, which calls—he may have been the first to do so—

certain 'penetrating and entirely negative works' anti-novels. He admires her because her subject is inauthenticity, and because she understands, as he has understood, what he called the 'viscous.' In allowing us to face what we normally flee, she presents human reality 'in its very *existence*' and so herself, presumably, achieves a condition, or anyway a model, of authenticity. Subsequently he has attacked the formalist obsessions of the *nouveau roman*; but here he obviously admires Sarraute's tentative, exploratory rejections of all the paradigms, of what in another connection he calls 'the eidetic imagery of bad faith.'

This brilliantly concise expression, thrown away in a footnote to the piece on Merleau-Ponty, may have more value to the literary critic than anything else in the new book. Long before, Sartre had adopted the term 'eidetic reduction' from Husserl; it is part of the method of the phenomenologists. But here I take him to mean that *mauvaise foi* (a comfortable denial of the undeniable—freedom—by myths of necessity, nature, or things as they are) derives its paradigms from illusions left over from the past—as some abnormal children can 'see' the page or the object that is no longer before them. Sartre uses the phrase in a political context, as it happens, but it serves to describe in part the critical position not only of the exponents of the *nouveau roman* but also of the younger Sartre himself. He thought of some great 19th-century novelists as collaborators in Bad Faith, and held that it was as bad to diminish the liberty of a character by conventional devices of 'form' as to betray one's own 'project' by *mauvaise foi*. In this new *Situations* we find him asking whether music, because it has 'wrenched itself from its alienation and set about creating its essence while freely providing its own laws,' cannot be a model for the working class as it tries to do the same. To do so it must ignore '*a priori* limitations,' falsely said to be inherent in nature. The artist must 'break the already crystallised habits which make us see in the *present* tense those institutions and customs which are *already out of date*.' *Passéisme* is a manifestation of bad faith.

Thus, in his own peculiar dialect, Sartre, a very inclusive thinker, makes the species 'anti-novel' a component of his system. On the proper relation of the self-created forms of the modern novel to the 'eidetic' paradigms surviving from the past—or, to put the same thing in another way, on the relations between form and freedom—there is a growing literature. Miss Murdoch calls form 'an aspect of our desire for consolation'; it interferes with the profoundest task of the novelist, which is to create irreducible and opaque persons. Every concession to form is a reduction in that 'respect for contingency' which is essential to imagination, as opposed to fantasy. In short, the eidetic imagery of novelistic forms helps to protect us from the real, is the agent of bad faith. Miss McCarthy says something like this, perhaps more superficially, when she attacks 'myth' and calls 'factuality' the one distinguishing feature of the novel. Mrs Spark has not written discursively about the problems, but her latest book[1] is, among other things, a defence of eidetic form, and a rejection of the anti-novel. Robbe-Grillet is against the retention of any paradigm which may suggest that the world means something, or even that it doesn't. 'Quite simply, it *is*.' This anti-essentialist position, logically developed, calls for a gap of the kind Camus would have called 'absurd' between the autonomous structure which is the novel, and the world. The time of the novel is its own affair (as in *Marienbad*, there is no reference to any past or future, and the time of the film, however you look at it, is one and a half hours); and the only 'character' is the reader. The ambition of the new novel, he says, is to make something *ex nihilo* which will stand on its own without reference to anything outside it.

Sartre undoubtedly has his place in the development of this new radical formalism; that he rejects it seems to me not an indication that he is old-fashioned but a proof that his existentialism *is* a humanism. The most extraordinary claim Robbe-Grillet makes is that the new novel will appeal to ordinary people because it is truer than the old one to their own lives. This ignores the large element of the merely fictive we all use to get by—to console ourselves, as Miss Murdoch says. It's not really surprising that Robbe-Grillet should find fault with *Nausea*. He acquits Sartre of the charge of essentialism, but accuses him of escalating the characters of Roquentin and the Autodidact into a state of 'necessity,' so bringing back into the novel what he should have kicked out—nature and tragedy. This is saying that Sartre uses the eidetic imagery of bad faith; that he has failed to make a novel signifying nothing, and so

[1] *The Mandelbaum Gate* (London, Macmillan; New York, Knopf).

slipped, like any other *salaud*, into prefabricated formal attitudes. And it is true. When Sartre shows us a man in anguish, 'choosing what he will be,' completely and profoundly responsible, he tries to show also that this man is 'a legislator deciding for the whole of mankind.' This man is very like the eidetic image of a tragic hero. And he is explicit that to *be* rather than to exist is to resemble the hero of a novel; the comparison recurs in *Nausea*. Whether Robbe-Grillet likes it or not, the Sartrean hero is, must be, the demythologised modern equivalent of the tragic hero; the old imagery lingers.

In the earlier volumes of *Situations* Sartre himself looked into some of the problems arising from this survival. The characters must not be predetermined by plot; they must be what a truly Christian novel would make them, 'centres of indeterminacy.' He attacks Mauriac for playing God to his characters, and also for failing to reproduce the action of time; for Sartre the temporality of a novel is satisfactory when it is closest to 'real' time. When he writes of Camus, he admires *L'Etranger* for creating its own order and expunging 'necessity' from fiction; yet he denies him the title of novelist, largely because his book lacks 'continuous duration, development, and the manifest irreversibility of time.' Curiously enough, Sartre read this book, even in some ways misread it, as if it were an anti-novel *avant la lettre*; but he is quite sure for all his admiration that *L'Etranger* is not a novel; whereas *Nausea*, for all its emphasis on absurdity and viscosity, did by implication deserve to be called one.

And so it is. It is certainly an illustration of absurdity and contingency, but also illustrates the power of fiction to free us from them. Since that is a traditional task of fiction, it is not surprising that the ghosts of old novels would not be entirely exorcised. Sartre began the book as a discontinuous and episodic work; but to write '*comme les petites filles*,' as Roquentin says, is no way to achieve a cure, which this book has to be. So it develops design and structure. *Quelque chose commence pour finir*. The novelist has to avoid the errors of Roquentin, the historian who imposes an order, and of the Autodidact, who reduces the world to an alphabet; without falsifying contingency, he has to make 'adventures' and rhythms, establish the place of the 'privileged moment' in the 'irreversible flow of time.' This is to do what has been done before. 'Beware of literature,' says

Roquentin; Sartre is cautious, but remembers and echoes Proust. Roquentin comes at the end to believe that he can see the shape of his life, and that he knows how to implement the lesson he learned from the song 'Some of these days'—*il faut souffrir en mesure*. What is needed is a novel, 'beautiful and hard as steel.' *Nausea* contains the viscous and the absurd, but aspires also to this condition. Consequently it yields a little, as a fiction must, to tyrannies and consolations of inherited forms. It fakes, as good novelists fake, honestly. It is the only way for the hero-novelist to 'wash himself of the sin of existing.'

Like the *nouveau roman*, *Nausea* is a fiction that explores the forms and status of fiction; but it has a deeper tone than the new works, and this is in part because of Sartre's sense that even when nothing is beyond question 'given,' everything cannot be new. Form is, under one aspect, necessarily eidetic; it persists, like friendship. A critical devotion to both will not preclude rant or betrayal; but Sartre in his way shows this devotion, and it places him not among the *passéistes* but among the heroes.

(1965)

XX. THE LATER GOLDING

William Golding's *Lord of the Flies* has sold over a million copies in the American paperback edition alone. It has, by all accounts, succeeded *The Catcher in the Rye* as the *livre de chevet* of educated American youth. I doubt if anybody is really qualified to say why this should be so: books make their way inexplicably. This one was published in 1954, and certainly it was noticed; E. M. Forster commended it and 'everybody' talked about it, but with a sense that it was caviar rather than chowder—a book to tempt an intellectual into believing he had discovered a classic at its birth, but hardly a best seller. In the years that followed Golding did much to confirm this belief, but very little towards making himself a popular novelist. *The Inheritors* is a technically uncompromising, fiercely odd, even old-fashioned book about the overthrow of Neanderthal man, very distinguished but inconceivable as a big seller; *Pincher Martin* is as difficult as it is masterly; and *Free Fall* is complex, original, and in many ways reader-repellent. Golding's fifth and latest novel,[1] coming five years after *Free Fall*, is unsurprising

[1] *The Spire*. Harcourt, Brace and World.

in one way at least: it is fire-new, written in what, despite its novelty, we can identify as a style bearing the impress of Golding's peculiar presence; but difficult, inviting only slow and submissive readers.

And yet *Lord of the Flies* has the vast readership. One can't help guessing at the reasons. For one thing, it is a comforting book; it assures us that evil is natural to men, and not something that we have recently invented. It is absolutely free of desperately 'forward' thinking—no Zen, no diagnosis of modern civilisation, only of civilisation. Yet it is spare and diagrammatic, and lends itself to techniques of sophisticated reading now widely taught in American colleges. Ultimately it derives from, or, as the word is, displaces, a familiar myth, that of the Earthly Paradise, which it handles ironically. And as it develops the myth with intricate passion, it alludes implicitly (as Golding, I think, could never do explicitly) to Freud and to all other conceivable systematic explanations of the phenomena. One might say cautiously that the book has a kind of innocence, thinking of two things: the later novels, which are more occult; and Golding's own view, since abandoned, that there is only one true way of reading a novel, and that the author knows it best, and takes upon him the responsibility of ensuring that a good reader can read it in that way.

This is a bad doctrine, and it does not distinguish between a novel and a riddle. It cannot be maintained in respect of *Lord of the Flies*, but Golding thought it could; and oddly enough the error had beneficial results. The novel has an extreme sharpness of outline, an exactness of invention, which come from its closeness to diagram. *Lord of the Flies* (aided, no doubt by the snowball law of popular acclaim) made its way by *not* being like Kafka, or like *Death in Venice*, by *not* being psychologically occult; the plot explains its own profundities. Furthermore, it has closed form, whereas the more brilliant contemporary American novelists have reverted to open form. You live along the lines of the book and feel, in its pattern, a total explanation. It belongs, to use a distinction of Iris Murdoch's, to the crystalline rather than to the journalistic pole of fiction. The virtuosity of (say) Philip Roth, belongs near the journalistic pole; the needs of Golding involve him in experimentation of a virtuoso order, but this is a matter of structure and hardly at all of drawing—

the quick accuracy of a Roth conversation or interior. His complexities are not ways of rendering nature or society, but new shapes produced by the pressure of a theme. And there perhaps lies the principal explanation of the success of *Lord of the Flies*: it is a sharply imagined account, a new clear outline, of what one vaguely knew, and many readers are sufficiently skilled to see this outline and to be shocked by it.

And yet not everybody sees the same outlines; and Golding saw that however closed the form and limited the intention, people could not be prevented from walking round the books and validly seeing not the shape he thought he made, but others, which were there and which were good. His change of opinion was later than *Free Fall*; but even before that book there were signs that he was aware of the power of his fictions to support interpretations he himself had not foreseen. Perhaps the very contrivances of his stories persuaded him better than the remonstrances of critics; thus the best scene in *The Inheritors*— where the Neanderthal man watches his new enemies as they act out their strangeness in the clearing below him—required an imaginative feat of such intensity that its result is, self-evidently, a properly mysterious poetry and not simply a diagram of corruption as it might be observed by the different senses of such an animal.

In *Pincher Martin* there is, as it happens, something like an allegory of the situation Golding was in; for Pincher is all egotistic assertion, making plausible and familiar structures out of memories and his knowledge of his own body, indisputably, he thinks, master of his rock, defying, with growing terror, all other interpretations of his plight. But he is wrong, merely a dead man whose interpretations are fairly, for all his resistance, destroyed. In *Free Fall* there is a slightly less proprietary attitude to the theme, which consequently grows more intensely obscure. The book opens, as Golding's books always do, with an absolutely crucial thematic passage, about free will, the state preceding the free fall; but the course of Sammy Mountjoy's life is not diagrammatic, like that of the boys on the island, and the assertions of the last page (always equally crucial) are more ambiguous, less prescriptive than before. Golding has changed his attitude to his fictions. And there is also a change of manner; more than before, the force of the book is generated by the pressure of casual figures as they gain power in the turbulence of language. The later books have a linguistic density absent from *Lord of the Flies*, a quality of vision smokier, less accessible.

Although *Free Fall* disappointed me, I must say that I could not imagine a literary event more interesting to me than the publication of the next Golding novel; and here it is, a most remarkable book, as unforeseeable as one foresaw, an entire original, yet marked throughout by that peculiar presence. Golding shares with Conrad the habit of writing each new novel as if he had written no other, and certainly no book that had sold a million copies. With the other novels in our head we can of course see how it fits in the sequence: it is 'late,' it is less assertive as to its possible meaning than *Lord of the Flies*; it has the later density, indeed fierceness, of language, and the power to generate meanings internally—meanings that grow out of the fiction and are not imposed from without. Consequently its themes are occult, as in *Free Fall*.

The Spire tells the story of Jocelin, Dean of some cathedral, and his efforts to realise a vision and a vow by building on to his church a 400-foot spire. That is all. And we see the entire action not so much through the eyes as over the shoulder of Jocelin; such facts as where the money came from, and what other interested parties think about the crazy dean, we gather by using the corners of our eyes. It is sometimes, for Golding's other books, both easy and useful to know his point of departure; nobody is the worse for understanding how *Lord of the Flies* is related to Ballantyne's *The Coral Island*, or for taking note of the epigraph of *The Inheritors*, which is from H. G. Wells's *Outline of History* and congratulates *homo sapiens* on his successful campaign against the Neanderthals. Here we are not told of any similar starting point; but Mr Golding must have got up the subject of how to build a spire, and the one he has in mind is Salisbury. He makes the spire 400 feet high—Salisbury is a little over that—and the highest in England, as Jocelin wants it to be. It is surmounted by a capstone and a cross, as Salisbury spire is. It is octagonal, with a skin of diminishing thickness, and has no orthodox foundation, like Salisbury, of which it has been said that the dangers and difficulties of adding the spire were enough to frighten any man in his senses from trying it. Iron bands strengthen the structure. The four columns over which the spire was raised settled or bent in Salisbury, as in the book, and the spire at once slipped out of its true perpendicular, as here. In short, this is basically the spire at Salisbury. There was even a 12th-century bishop called Jocelin. Despite some topographical mystification, the scene is consistent with this, and especially the Hanging Stones, which must be Stonehenge. And although it is no business of ours, Mr Golding lives near Salisbury. I don't know exactly where he got the facts about the mason's craft, however[1].

In outline the story tells how the making good of the vision entails endlessly disagreeable and unforeseeable discoveries. It seemed simple enough; yet it has sordid material causes, unsuspected sexual motives; and it can be realised only in the teeth of technical obstacles which a sane man would regard as prohibitive. The cathedral being a bible in stone, the spire will be the Apocalypse; but it is also a human body and the spire its erect phallus. It all depends upon how your attention is focused. As Dean Jocelin himself observes, 'the mind touches all things with law, yet deceives itself as easily as a child.' The opening paragraph shows us Jocelin laughing, shaking his head so that a glory consumes and exalts Abraham, Isaac, and God; his ways of looking, the moods of his mind, make and unmake vision and sacrifice. At this point Jocelin controls a manageable glory. But there is the question of the foundations, the palpitating human substratum that must maintain this glorious erection. And to its splendour the church is sacrificed, defiled by pagan workmen. Obscenely superstitious, they work as if taking part in some pagan rite. When they pry up the slabs at the crossways, it is clear that there are no foundations.

Against the will of the other principal Persons, against the skilled advice of the master builder, Jocelin forces the business on; whatever the foundations of the spire—whether you take them to be mud, or the corrupt money of his aunt—he will have his four hundred feet and his cross with its Holy Nail, a diagram of prayer. Rain water in the excavations finds the corpses and makes the church foul; the master builder seduces the wife of a church servant; the spire seems founded on human filth, the earth 'a huddle of noseless men grinning upward.' The workmen

---

[1] In fact Mr Golding worked it all out himself, simply walking round the Cathedral and asking himself how *he* would have done it.

The ballet for which this music was written was based on the Blake engravings—the Old Testament in an extremely heterodox interpretation. The music is in the full voice of Vaughan Williams's already slightly archaic but fully idiomatic, mere English, pentatonic manner; it goes directly to the large statement about good and evil: Satan falling. Elihu beautiful, the sons of the morning at their sarabande. Vaughan Williams had some of the sensitive bluffness, much of the true privacy, of Golding; and he was another late starter who continually experimented but stayed out of touch with the contemporary *avant-garde* There is a squareness, a clumsiness; but in some works—in *Job* especially, and in the later music which remembers *Job*—we hear the clear strange tones of the visionary whose idiom we can learn (a saxophone for the comforters), and who speaks as directly as may be of good and evil.

Golding writes rather like that. Look at this passage, chosen quite at random:

> The evening turned green over the rim of the cup. Then the rim went black and shadows filled it silently so that before he was well aware of it, night had fallen and the faint stars come out. He saw a fire on the rim and guessed it was a haystack burning; but as he moved round the rim of the cone, he saw more and more fires round the rim of the world. Then a terrible dread fell on him, for he knew these were the fires of Midsummer Night, lighted by the devil-worshippers out on the hills. Over there, in the valley of the Hanging Stones, a vast fire shuddered brightly. All at once he cried out, not in terror but in grief. For he remembered his crew of good men, and he knew why they had knocked off work and where they were gone.

The 'cone' is the unfinished spire; we note how unashamedly the sentence passes from its rim to the easy grandeur of 'the rim of the world.' We might regret 'terrible dread,' and yet it is somehow purged by the absolute plainness of reference elsewhere, by 'knocked off work,' for instance. The last sentence might seem altogether too artless were it not that on this very page the whole strange plot is undergoing a subtle change of movement, modulating into violence.

It is a prose for violence. All Golding's books are violent; as I say, his basic figure for terror, violence, and bloody creation is childbirth. As such it is used in this book, and it breaks out of the language into the plot. This is part of a private vision; and one might hazardously conjecture that this novel, like some of its predecessors, is as much about Golding writing a novel as about anything else. But one need not believe that to agree that it is deeply personal. It gives one some idea of the nature of this writer's gift that he has written a book about an expressly phallic symbol to which Freudian glosses seem entirely irrelevant. It is remote from the mainstream, potent, severe, even forbidding. And in its way it is a marvel.

(1964)

XXI. J. D. SALINGER

(i) *One Hand Clapping*

It seems impossible to review Salinger without reviewing his audience at the same time. There are other accomplished rhetoricians in the field, but no 'serious' modern novelist has quite this rapport with a large public. The two stories *Franny* and *Zooey* are seven and five years old; they appeared accessibly in the *New Yorker*, and have been widely discussed. But when they appear as *Franny and Zooey*[1] in hard covers there is a marked excitement on both sides of the Atlantic. It doesn't seem to matter that these stories are merely samples, or—to quote the author—'early, critical entries in a narrative series I'm doing about a family of settlers in 20th-century New York, the Glasses.' It doesn't matter that other fragments of the big un-realised novel are already in print, nor that if the Glass saga ever gets written it may not contain these bits in their present form. Does it matter that *Zooey*, the longer and more ambitious of the stories, is an almost total disaster? It should, for the audience is deeply involved in it.

Salinger, if we may for a moment peer through the novelist to the *guru* underneath, is against all forms of wanting and hanker-ing; he condemns the sort of religion that is eternity-acquisitive, and the sort of humanity that is culture-acquisitive, desiring to know, for the prestige of knowing, about Homer and Blake and Zen. And Salinger. For the really queer thing about this writer is that he very carefully writes for an audience he deplores, an audience that disposes of a certain amount of smart cultural information and reacts correctly to fairly complex literary

[1] London, Heinemann; Boston, Little.

stimuli: an audience that is familiar with Creative Writing, and has a strong stiffening of people who have turned in pretty good papers on Flaubert or Faulkner. Or Salinger. Now this audience is, under one aspect, precisely what makes the world so dreadful for Salinger's Wise Children, so they have nervous breakdowns from contact with it. But under another, it is what you have to have if you play the piano or write books or act. It doesn't know, as the Wise Children do, the difference between wisdom and knowledge; you may be acting perfectly, as a saint prays, but there will still be 'unskilled laughter coming from the fifth row.' And yet even if you're 'God's actress' you can't get along without an audience. So what you do is to work through a whimsical sorites and come out calling the audience Christ, even the lout in the fifth row. Salinger can thus exercise his art with reverence, while still despising the 'culture' which makes it possible.

I do not mean to make this sound repulsive, but the truth is that the position could not be maintained if the audience were either stupid or holy: it has to be smart, and the novelist counts heavily on that. The art which has so much to say against culture-acquisitiveness really depends on it, and a lot of Salingerian legerdemain is devoted to concealing this fact. The epigraph of *For Esme with Love and Squalor* is a Zen koan: 'We know the sound of two hands clapping. But what is the sound of one hand clapping?' A brutal, occidental answer might be: Salinger without a culture-acquisitive audience. The mythical Fat Lady—the Glasses invent her as an excuse for giving good performances to stupid audiences, but really despise her ('very thick legs, very veiny. . . . She had cancer, *too*')—has to provide the other hand.

The Irish-Jewish Glass family consists of nice ex-vaudeville parents and seven fantastic children, two of whom, as in 'We Are Seven,' are dead. These children all appeared at one time or another on a radio-show called 'It's a Wise Child'—based on the Quiz Kids of history. They all know a lot, especially about the importance of unknowing, and when they grow up they are still in this respect entitled to be called Wise Children (another reason, sympathetically suggested by Leslie Fiedler in his superb *Partisan Review* notice of this book, is that Salinger really thinks they're a lot of little bastards. This is a good example of the way Salinger attracts benevolent interpretations). Wisdom, Yeats remarked, is a property of the dead, a something incompatible with life; and the Glasses find it so. Seymour, the venerated eldest brother, committed suicide in the ravishingly written story, 'A Perfect Day for Bananafish.' Another brother is dead, another a Jesuit; a sister is married, and Buddy, the next best counsellor to Seymour, inaccessible. That leaves Franny and Zooey, with Franny in a religious crisis.

Franny has her breaking down at lunch with an oafishly cultured Ivy League date, and it is irreproachably written. *Zooey* shows her back home in the big New York apartment, an amusingly furnished womb, a cosy place for a breakdown. Mother Bessie is in attendance, and there are 'hot and cold running ghosts,' especially Seymour, whose private telephone is still listed, and whose room is unchanged. But housepainters stand outside the door waiting for Franny to move out; and Zooey, in his anxiety, can only talk the author's customary desperate whimsy.

Franny's crisis is big and worrying, but pretty typical, one feels, of the Glass children; it has to do with the phoneyness of the world they grow up into, full of boyfriends discussing football, Flaubert, life. She has become obsessed with 'the Jesus prayer'—a formula by which you pray incessantly. This seems wise, but it drives her to the edge of breakdown. She wants to talk to Seymour, but Seymour is dead (Holden Caulfield had similar trouble). Buddy is away. Bessie, her mother, offers homely advice and chicken soup. It is up to Zooey to save her from the psychiatrists who might make her want to live in the world she now rejects; sweating with love, he does so, Franny accepts his advice. It is sort of religious, and also involves acting in the world as it is. The religion Salinger has to sell to his culture-acquisitive audience; the need for action he has to sell to himself. This explains the method of the book.

Signs that there *is* a method are characteristically minimised; there is a lot of carefully planned improvisation. Essential information about the book is wrapped round it in a blurb or given with an air of inevitable clumsiness in a footnote (footnotes are called an 'aesthetic evil'). Buddy Glass, the narrator, takes a deal of space to explain why the book is so randomly shaped. Zooey, we hear, dislikes his brother's handling of the narrative, and, according to Buddy, further complains that the plot hinges on mysticism . . . which . . . can only expedite, move up, the day and hour of my professional undoing. People are already shaking their heads over me, and any immediate further professional use of the word 'God,' except as a familiar, healthy American expletive, will be taken . . . as the worst kind of name-dropping and a sure sign that I'm going straight to the dogs.

In case we don't find this sufficiently disarming, we are encouraged to believe that Zooey, in voicing these forbidden thoughts, is merely providing another example of the off-beat loving which goes on in the Glass family. The fact that it is Zooey who is voicing them is meant to prevent us from doing so. The same sort of endearing duplicity is involved in Buddy's apology for the endless talking that goes on in the book: that's the way it *was*, you can't change the Glasses. Buddy also has tricks that allow him to speak frankly of Zooey's incredible beauty, or rather the 'authentic *esprit*' of his face: a bit embarrassing, but that's the way it is. He is even capable of a parenthesis stating that 'all this data is, I think, to some degree relevant.'

The author knows the public knows he isn't clumsy; but just in case anybody thinks he's really slipped into awkward simplicity there is the television script Zooey is reading, a piece that 'stinks of courage and integrity.' 'It's down-to-earth, it's simple, it's untrue.' This is to prevent anybody using such words of *Zooey*; yet, all this legerdemain apart, they apply. So let us use such words; when the fog of technique and comparative religion clears away, *Zooey* is simple (it says, with Carlyle, 'Do the work that lies nearest to thee') and untrue.

It should in justice be said that he succeeds in all sorts of ways: with Bessie Glass, in the protracted, funny, yet economical bathroom scene that takes up half the book; with Zooey's droll, teasing ways. But not with Bessie as the priestess of the Fat Lady's altar, not with Zooey as the book of the dead. Buddy's enormous, apparently amorphous letter, which Zooey reads through as a preparation, saved Zooey years before, and provides the pattern for the saving of Franny: neat, and in some Salingerian sense true. But the treasured wisdom of Seymour about 'unlearning the differences, the illusory differences, between boys and girls, animals and stones, day and night' had to be mediated to Buddy by a little girl in a supermarket who says her boyfriends are called Bobby and Dorothy; a similar angel passes before Zooey's eyes as he works on Franny. The missions of these girls (and of the one in 'Bananafish') may be to play tiny Iphigenia to adolescent Orestes—as Fiedler observes; but their message is death or nirvana, and for Buddy and Zooey to interpret it as a call to action in 'this goddam phenomenal world' seems false both to Salinger and the audience.

This is really the crux. Franny has got this Jesus prayer wrong: Zooey has to straighten her out. First he tries to show her she's wrong about Jesus, who was extremely tough and intelligent, a cobra not a bunny, as she seems to think. This fails; when he succeeds (under terrific emotional pressure) he does it by using Seymour's telephone; first pretending to be Buddy then not quite pretending (even Salinger couldn't quite try that) to be Seymour. What he says on the phone will keep the explicators happy for ages, since it turns on a pun: Zooey is an actor; Franny could be. Von Hügel called prayer an 'ever-increasing predominance of Action over activity,' and Zooey has a similar notion in mind, perhaps (not that I understand Von Hügel's remark). Franny is well-informed on religion, and he doesn't have to spell it out. She must *act*. It seems that acting is Franny's karma; she must be God's actress, and that will be her Jesus prayer. If it seems strange to be saying a Jesus prayer to a lot of louts in a theatre, she is to remember that they're all Christ. Franny, restored, happy and self-controlled, drops into a calm sleep.

It is to make us accept this conclusion that Salinger has worked so deviously. And, as one of his admiring audience, I find it hard to believe he could be selling anything so simple and untrue. The wise child would certainly have discounted this effort of Zooey's as a last desperate attempt to save her from the professional headshrinker. Salinger has at last overestimated his rhetorical control over us. When Bessie's chicken soup turns out to be eucharistic, like the colonel's hash in Mary McCarthy's diatribe against Creative Writing courses, we feel let down. When Zooey's exhausting effort to save Franny's life and wisdom comes down to a trouper's advice to go out there and wow them, we know that Salinger's exhausting effort to satisfy us and himself has failed. He cannot, for all his skill, make it appear that a good performance as Pegeen Mike in *The Playboy* is an adequate substitute for being dead.

The author of *Zooey*, a work designed with extraordinary care and even a kind of passion, is certainly a master of sorts. Perhaps he's 'grown too fond of Seymour, perhaps he's been oversubtle about his audience. For whatever reason, he has slipped badly, and *Zooey* doesn't work. The Fat Lady, obstinately unholy, doesn't move a muscle; the artist's single hand silently beats the air.

(1962)

(ii) *The Glass Menagerie*

In this book[1] a couple of koans, first exhibited in the *New Yorker* in 1955 and 1959, are trapped between hard covers. The first takes the form of an anecdote about Seymour's wedding day, the second is a discursive study of Seymour's sanctity—a summary which will serve only if you underline the word 'discursive' with almost hysterical profuseness. The whole thing is dedicated to the amateur reader, to show that the author is sick of being read by people who may seem clever but are so ignorant of Zen that if they took up archery they would assume their job was to aim at the target. The second story contains several careful allusions to the peculiar and terrible relationship obtaining between this author and his readers. It is admitted that Seymour personally laid it down that the amenities of exposition ought to be respected, but argued that in this case they can't be, because of immediate needs of Buddy, the narrator. These cause certain essential modifications which unskilled readers may treat as marks of authorial self-indulgence, or as signs that Buddy is cleverly pushing St. Seymour out of the limelight. Buddy suggests early on that awkward customers should cut their losses and leave right away.

'I'm told,' says Buddy, 'that I have many surface charms as a writer.' We may have been over that before, but certainly a gesture of compliment is in order for 'Raise High,' a funny-sad piece with something of the period atmosphere of 'For Esmé.' Seymour fails to turn up for his wedding, abandoning Muriel, chosen for her dullness or because she was like old Charlotte, a childhood sweetheart whom Seymour once hit with a brick because he loved her. Buddy has to entertain hot and angry

[1] *Raise High the Roof Beam, Carpenters* and *Seymour An Introduction* (London, Heinemann; Boston, Little, Brown).

friends of the bride. There are cunning dips into the vast lake of Glassiana which lies beneath the Salinger surface. If I dare to say what I dislike about the story I shall give myself away at once as fatally un-hip to Seymour. For I am not moved by his soothing the 10-month-old Franny by reading her a Taoist tale, and in fact am no longer surprised that she turned out badly and fell for Zooey's bogus Zen trickery in the last book. When Seymour's journal erupts onto the page I expect and get something more than tiresome, such as the bit about his being so holy and sensitive that if he touches a thing he loves for too long—Zooey's hair or Charlotte's dress—he develops stigmata on his hands. When Buddy tells the truth about Charlotte's scars he chooses as sole audience a sympathetic funny old deaf-mute—pure Seymour this, like Zooey's bogus telephone call, and characteristic of that chic Western Zen which, Buddy assures us, the real thing will survive.

All the same, you could put this story in a book with good Salinger-Glass, such as 'A Perfect Day for Bananafish,' without doing much harm. 'Seymour' is, on the other hand, close enough to mere rubbish for someone who enjoys exaggeration to call it that. Here art destroys art, or rather disorder goes through an elaborate and skilful process and comes out as disorder. Seymour is the key to Glass, and it is presumably important for us to see him plain. He is presented as a sort of American Prince Myshkin, a saintly fool whom Buddy will, in an interminable monologue, describe and expound. Because of Buddy's 'extremely pressing personal needs' the monologue eschews orderly narrative, using anecdote for purely panegyric purposes and dwelling, with a calculated air of fortuity, on the situation of Buddy himself as he writes.

Still, we do add to our knowledge of Seymour; and if you already have a fairly deep impression of his beauty, his intellect and his charity, this new onslaught of his identity may make you want, like Keats in a similar situation, to leave the room. Seymour is, frankly, 'the artist and Sick Man.' Starting life as a Wise Child on the radio, he grows up into a Seer, 'the heavenly fool . . . dazzled to death by his own scruples, the blinding shapes and colours of his own sacred human conscience.' He is a top American poet; Salinger gets round the obvious creative-writing problem this creates (for poets must be harder to do than saints) by merely paraphrasing a couple of poems and describing their form: double haiku, 34 syllables, basically iambic. The poems aren't autobiographical, or don't, at any rate, refer to Seymour's most recent incarnation, but they are related to his vaudeville ancestry—'highly literate vaudeville,' a kind of Zennish balancing act. When Seymour's athletic skills are dis-cussed it is once more the oriental aspect that is stressed, as when he wins at marbles by not aiming. His face, and his love for Buddy, are very fully described. It is part of Salinger's own technique of indirection to blur the line that divides the per-sonality of Seymour from that of Buddy (and, incidentally, the line between Buddy and Salinger). Buddy is also something of a happy fool, as well as being very clever and inclined to treat the reader as the Fat Lady. He dwells on his resemblance to his brother and then blames himself for doing so, attributing the error to his egotism, the one thing he has that Seymour lacked.

Having found 'Seymour' very tedious at first reading I ought to add that I had a second try and found it somewhat less insufferable. If you read the book as primarily about a crisis of Buddy's, parallel to that of Franny in the last book, and resolved in much the same way (Buddy goes off with joy to face his audi-ence of college girls), you might be able to stand the rich flavour of Seymour, or even convince yourself that Seymour isn't a straight character at all because Salinger is working with irony. But in the end I don't think this will hold up. The ironies do nothing to dispel the incense cloud round Seymour. There is a genuine sense of the sheer difficulty Buddy has in getting what he has to say past large psychological blocks, but the disorder that results tells us nothing about Seymour and nothing interesting about Buddy. In short, 'Seymour' is a bigger frost than 'Zooey.' The question as to why Salinger should devote his skill to tying himself up into knots is still intriguing, but such topics have small staying power, and it may shortly be superseded by the question as to what possessed so many people to take him so seriously.

(1963)

XXII. MURIEL SPARK

(i) To *The Girls of Slender Means*

Muriel Spark—as Derek Stanford rather quaintly observes in
his new book about her[1]—is in her prime; like her own Miss
Brodie she has a set, and to it should belong anybody who takes
an interest in the ways fiction can body forth the shape of
things unknown. This remarkable virtuoso being in her prime,
new books are happily frequent, and the latest, called *The Girls
of Slender Means*,[2] is, like nearly all the others, in some ways the
best. They are all pretty alarming, and the reasons why they are
also funny are very complicated. Some literate people dislike
them, though not, so far as I know, for decent reasons. It's true
that there is an unfashionable element of pure game in these
books—they are about novels as well as being novels—but this is
simply part of their perfectly serious way of life. It won't do to
call them bagatelles. And there is another rather moral objection, quietly voiced by Mr Stanford in a footnote, to the effect
that Mrs Spark lacks charity. This also misses the point, since the
concept, cleared of cant, may be entertained in precisely the
gratingly unsentimental way in which this pure-languaged
writer understands it.

There is certainly a remoteness, a lack of ordinary compassion, in her dealings with characters, but this is part of the
premise of her fiction; if we feel sorry in the wrong way, it's
because our emotions are as messy and imprecise as life, part of
the muddle she is sorting out. In her story 'The Portobello
Road' one of the characters says of a murdered girl: 'She
was at Confession only the day before she died—wasn't she
lucky?' And she is described as 'speaking from that Catholic
point of view which takes some getting used to.' The Spark point
of view is like that, not only because she is an unremittingly
Catholic novelist committed to immutable truths, but because

[1] *Muriel Spark*. Centaur Press. It wouldn't be true charity to call this a good
book, since it is sometimes sloppily handled and, in the biographical part, a shade
embarrassing. But Mr Stanford makes many profitable observations, and is
interesting on the verse, which her publisher ought to reprint. [He has now done
so, 1967.]

[2] London, Macmillan; New York, Knopf.

she is uncommonly interested in the shapes assumed by these truths as perceived in the tumult of random events and felt upon insensitive fallen flesh. The question for the reader is not at all whether he accepts the truths, but whether the patterns are made good and recognised. Reading them, like writing them, is a work of the imagination, fallen or not. What establishes their validity is not the 'sharp reminders of eternity' mentioned in the blurb, but imaginative cohesion, a rightness of the shapes, a truth sensed in the fictions.

The easiest way into this kind of fiction, which shows the world as bearing obscure figurations of meaning like a novel, is by way of *The Comforters*,[1] the first of the series. Here is a novel which looks into the question of what kind of truth can be told in a novel. It creates a quite powerful sense—still not absent from later and less openly experimental stories—that to make fictions is in a way a presumptuous thing to do, because the novelist is, unlike God, free at the expense of his creatures. Of course the characters fight back: Caroline, the heroine—who as a Catholic convert knows about absolute truth and is also expert in theory of the novel—does her best to resist manipulation by the mind of the unseen novelist who is putting her into a story and trying to shape her life. So she tries to spoil the plot by an exercise of free will: 'I intend to stand aside and see if the novel has any real form apart from this artificial plot. I happen to be a Christian.' And later, when the writer tries to make her lie low in hospital and let her get on with other parts of her pretty complicated plot, Caroline forces her way back into the book by saying that she's being left out only because the writer can't cope with a description of the hospital ward. There follows a deliberately perfunctory description of the ward. The voices Caroline hears recounting or prophesying her actions are novelistic: they are one voice differentiated into many, always speaking in the past tense. (Later Mrs Spark is often, as a novelist, devious about tenses.) The novelist arbitrarily arranges fantastic and pointless coincidences. Mrs Hogg, standing for a singularly odious piety, vanishes when not in the story, having no other life.

The tone of *The Comforters* is civilised and often frivolous, but it is naggingly about something serious, and about the difficulties of saying such things in terms of a convention so absurd and

[1] Harmondsworth, Penguin; Philadelphia, Lippincott.

arbitrary as a novel. The plot is deliberately complicated, since the question asked is, how can such an organised muddle of improbabilities, further disordered by the presumptuous claims of the writer on space and time, say anything true or interesting? One of the answers, if one may abstract it, is that even among the falsities of a novel, as among the shapelessnesses of ordinary life, truth figures; and it does so because the imagination, in so far as it is good, is bound by categories which stand in a relation to absolute truth. This shows up in a certain repeated atavism in Spark plots—the assumption must be that the ancient patterns have a more certain relation with the truth. Thus Caroline deals with her demon while crossing water; but this is only an early instance of a device very important to Mrs Spark. And it doesn't detract from the frivolous pleasures of flux.

None of the other books is so obviously an inquiry into the way fictions work, but by now it's plain that Mrs Spark will not relinquish the investigation. In this, as in other ways, she remains a poet, for poets have always bothered more than novelists about the exact nature of their chosen mode. A Sparkian aphorism, 'There is more of everything than poetry,' is quoted with some show of disagreement by Mr Stanford, but it seems very pregnant, and an accurate if queer account of her novels. Of these *Memento Mori* (there is more of everything than holy dying) seems the best known. Certainly it has a superb morbid accuracy, a poetic concentration on a narrow society of people and ideas. The ancient characters are all different, united only by the common summons of death, as in the *danses macabres*; and the most notable of them is not the evil Mrs Pettigrew but the revitalised Charmian, a novelist within the novel, still giving 'to those disjointed happenings a shape,' and well aware that this shape is a deception, like all fiction. 'In life,' she says, 'everything is different. Everything is in the providence of God.' This is the simple point; the scientist's notes perish in a fire, like the dross they are (Mrs Spark often burns a building for parabolic purposes). He knows how death comes, but it is Jean Taylor who knows what to do about it, its right place among the four last things. *Memento Mori* may be slightly overloaded with incident; at this stage Mrs Spark wants swirling activity as well as subtle dialogue and occult figuration.

The Ballad of Peckham Rye is nearer to fable and shorter. It

has so many heavy hints about the diabolic nature of Dougal
Douglas that it could be made to look like a more fictional
Screwtape Letters, but it is really a subtle book. The typing
ghost of *The Comforters* now roams arbitrarily about interfer-
ing in everybody's life. The devil as father of lies is the patron of
novelists; Dougal is writing a highly fictional biography of an
old woman, and he records in his notebook lists of useful if low
novelist's commonplaces, useful blunters of truth and sharp
perception. Like a novelist, he seduces people into wanton or
even self-destructive acts: the bridegroom who says 'I won't,'
the head of the typing pool who is murdered. Again there is an
intense concentration on a small society, again there are tell-tale
atavisms (Dougal's dread of water, the cysts on his head).
There are also chill Edinburgh high spirits; the novelist herself
wantons with the story of the tunnel and the dead nuns.

The last of the heavily plotted books (so far) was *The Bachelors*; but the world has the same arbitrary limitation, a world of
bachelors, their friends and mistresses. Just as, in *The Comforters*, we are asked to consider the analogy between the
writing of a novel and a temporary loss of sanity, we are here
made to see an affinity between novel-writing and mediumship
(fraudulent and authentic in indeterminable degrees, but fundamentally alien to the truth) and between mediumship and the
disease of epilepsy. Mediums, like novelists, speak in a variety
of voices, depend on stock responses in their audiences; yet they
are no more their own masters than epileptics, who suffer (as all
stories do) from atavism in the central nervous system. Yet, like
writers, they are sometimes thought very wise. *The Bachelors* is
a comic performance, although it is, as the hero notices, 'all
demonology and to do with creatures of the air.' Its comedy
arises from the corruptions it deals with; and these imply a
primal innocence, which later became Mrs Spark's central
topic.

Thus *The Prime of Miss Jean Brodie* treats of the loss of
innocence. It may well be the best written of these cunningly
written books; there is a fusion of tone and material. There is a
characteristic Spark voice, slightly pedantic, produced in
Scotland's good schools. In *The Comforters* she can write that
Father Jerome 'had used to send the lay brother to her'—a usage
probably not to be found in other living novelists. This faint

pedantry suits Miss Brodie, and the book should ideally be read aloud by a lady who has preserved the Edinburgh accent in all its soft severity. The tone is now more important than the plot: ordinary expectations are flouted by skipping to and fro in time from the 'Thirties and the schoolgirls to the present time of their maturity.

The unpredictable and often absurd acts and assertions of Miss Brodie are precisely what amuses us; but they also have unpredictable consequences (one girl burnt in the fire, being Miss Brodie's notion of dross; another, taught to transfigure the commonplace, herself uncomfortably transfigured). Miss Brodie fancies herself one of the secular elect, a modern justified sinner; and she assumes a novelist's, or God's, power over character. But her life assumes penitential patterns familiar to the instructed, and repeated with pain by the treacherous Sandy. Hindsight is liberally provided from the outset; but the dominant image is of the justified Miss Brodie presiding calmly over a lost innocence.

The new book is rather on the pattern of *Miss Brodie*; it is about a group of young ladies living in a genteel hostel near the Albert Memorial, during the months between the end of the war in Europe and the end of the whole thing. As in *Brodie*, the history of the time is touched in, neatly and with full relevance. The girls are poor though not in want, like the English generally at the time; they are beautiful in poverty, slender (some of them) in means and figure alike. They have a Schiaparelli dress, held virtually in common, and have dealings with an anarchist poet, Nicholas Farringdon, who sleeps with the most beautiful of them, Selina. We know all along about Nicholas's later martyrdom, but the focus is on the days just before the hostel is destroyed by an old bomb and a fire.

The arrangements are such that slender means and bodies become figures of beautiful poverty; but it is Selina's slenderness that enables her to destroy the image of paradise by a breach, as it were, of the rule of the order, so providing Nicholas with the vision of evil which leads him to the Church, and in the end to martyrdom. While they exist, 'the graceful attributes of poverty' are enhanced by Nicholas's anarchism, and by the poems intoned by the elocutionist Joanna. These are relevant because paradisal, or sometimes quite fortuitously, as with Drinkwater's

'Moonlit Apples' or Shelley's 'West Wind'; most relevant to the crisis is 'The Wreck of the Deutschland,' and the Anglican liturgy proper to the day of the disaster.

It may seem that the parable element bulks rather large, that the novel is itself trying to get through the eye of a needle. But Mrs Spark uses all her power 'to love and animate the letter.' The commonplace may show the operation of these figures, and others, but it is still represented with an arbitrary novelistic richness; and if 'charity' is a word to be reserved for the future of Nicholas, it might still be said that the society of girls is handled with cool tenderness.

Such novels assume the reader's sympathetic participation in muddle, they assume a reality unaware that it conceals patterns of truth. But when an imagination (*naturaliter christiana*) makes fictions it imposes patterns, and the patterns are figures of the truth. The relations of time and eternity are asserted by juxtaposing poetry and mess, by solemn puns about poverty. None of it would matter to the pagan were it not for the admirable power with which all the elements are fused into shapes of self-evident truth—the power one looks for in poems. Mrs Spark, in her prime, is a poet-novelist of formidable power.

(1963)

(ii) The Novel as Jerusalem: Muriel Spark's *Mandelbaum Gate*

People—novelists even—have been heard to say of Muriel Spark that she is gifted and elegant, but a fantasist, a trifler. This at any rate allows one to see why the old topic of the death of the novel is still dusted off from time to time. Mrs Spark is a novelist; she is not an antinovelist or a philosophical novelist, a realist or a neorealist, but a pure novelist. She is evidently not of the opinion that the possibilities of the form are exhausted, since she is continually finding new ones. Her novels quite deliberately raise difficult questions about the status of fiction, but she has not been driven to violence in her attempts to answer them; she does not cut her books up or fold them in or try to make them random. If there is to be randomness, she wants to be in charge of it. If the characters have to be free, then their freedom will have to be consistent with contexts not of their own devising, as in life. If the reader thinks that the shapes and patterns, the delicate internal relationships, of a well-written novel give the lie to life and suggest impossible consolations then he must content himself with some other thing, with whatever unconsoling fiction he can find. Mrs Spark is even somewhat arrogant about the extent of the novelist's power: knowing the end of the story, she deliberately gives it away, and in a narrative which could have regular climactic moments she fudges them, simply because the design of her world, like God's, has more interesting aspects than mere chronological progress and the satisfaction of naïve expectations in the reader. Yet all the elements of this world come from the traditional novel.

The suggestion is, in Mrs Spark's novels, that a genuine relation exists between the forms of fiction and the forms of the world, between the novelist's creation and God's. At the outset of her career she wrote a novel called *The Comforters*, which is quite deliberately an experiment designed to discover whether this relation does obtain, whether the novelist, pushing people and things around and giving 'disjointed happenings a shape,' is in any way like Providence. This quotation is actually from *Memento Mori*; Mrs Spark's later novels are all very different from *The Comforters*, but all are in a sense novels about the novel, inquiries into the relation between fictions and truth. You may treat her last two books, *The Prime of Miss Jean Brodie* and *The Girls of Slender Means*, both very brief and exquisitely formed, as beautiful jokes; they have a constantly varying formal wit, an arbitrariness of incident under the control of the writer's presumptuous providence, that warrant the description. But like the wit of the 17th-century preacher, they are jokes for God's sake, fictions which have to do with the truth.

'I don't claim that my novels are truth,' she once said in an interview.[1] 'I claim that they are fiction, out of which a kind of truth emerges. And I keep in mind that what I am writing is fiction, because I am interested in truth—absolute truth. . . . There is a metaphorical truth and moral truth, and what they call anagogical . . . and there is absolute truth, in which I believe things which are difficult to believe, but I believe them because they are absolute.' This absolute truth is, of course, the teaching

[1] Broadcast by the B.B.C. and condensed in my article 'The House of Fiction,' *Partisan Review*, Spring, 1963.

of the Roman Catholic Church. The lies of fiction can partake of this truth, perhaps give it a useful, though imperfect human application. It is, perhaps, inconceivable that the creator of fiction can—insofar as he looks at what he has done and sees that it is good—make shapes and depths utterly dissimilar from those of God. In a sense, this makes his work a daring kind of game. He lies like truth. He simulates the plots of God, even when he plays at being arbitrary and contingent. The tragic aspect of this is the subject of another Catholic novelist, Graham Greene, in *The End of the Affair*; Mrs Spark is more concerned with the comedy of the situation. The novelist, presumptuous, arbitrary, scheming, and faking, lying like the fiend, makes things like worlds, plots absurdly like God's.

The interest of this for nonbelievers is that even they must make worlds like plots. Even if they reject the Absolute as itself a fiction, they are by nature structure-makers and impose this human need on history, on nature, on poems and novels. They seek and accept images of order. They need not be alienated from a novel because it represents a world designed to possess formal relationships, rhythms, and certainties under the wild muddle we see at first glance. In other words, they are as well equipped as a Catholic to understand the power and beauty of Mrs Spark's most ambitious creation game, her new novel, *The Mandelbaum Gate*.

Mrs Spark here tells a story, and a good one; she is a novelist all through, extremely inventive, at ease with complex plots. But she presents the story in discontinuous bits, blurring the climaxes, giving away the surprises. Why? Because in reality this occurs, and it occurs without making any difference to the certainties of the world and its design. She sets the story in Jerusalem because Jerusalem, as the medieval map-makers knew, is the centre of this world, the core and paradigm of God's plot. Jerusalem brings the two plot-makers together. The book is a confrontation, or rather a concord of plots. God's plot is Jerusalem itself, the ancient *données* divided by the Mandelbaum Gate. To recognise them is to know something of the ways of God to men; they lie timeless and unchanged under the extraordinary contingencies of modern Jerusalem. This is the plot the novelist confronts, with which she seeks concord. How does she set about such a task? By taking as a central figure Miss Barbara

Vaughan, who is half Jewish, an English Catholic convert, and setting her down in Jerusalem on a pilgrimage to the holy places, which are divided by the Mandelbaum Gate. She is on the Jewish side of the gate; the Arabs will let her pass if convinced that she is a bona fide Christian, but they do not recognise half-Jews any more than they recognise Israel. The story is of the adventures of Barbara on her pilgrimage, and also about her love affair and how it prospered when her lover succeeded in having his first marriage annulled at Rome. It is also about smuggling and spying and smart Arab operators and British consular officials. It is a complicated story. To explain how it is made to match Jerusalem, I shall have to speak in some detail at least about the two opening chapters.

First we meet Freddy Hamilton from the British Consulate, upper-class, talented, agreeable in his fifties, and a bit wet. He is given to composing *vers de société* in archaic verse forms, and is walking back through the Mandelbaum Gate making up a bread-and-butter letter to his weekend hostess on the Jordan side. It is to be a rondeau. He bumps into a Jewish child, then into a Jewish-looking Arab in European dress. He meets Miss Vaughan and hears her chidden by an old Jew for a dress which, though it seems modest enough in the heat of the day, offends the sensibility of two thousand years. Proceeding, he carries on with his thank-you verses as he passes a school where the children are chanting in Hebrew. He reflects on the Greek meters, 'pitting culture against culture.' At his hotel he calls for a drink, and the Israeli waiter reminds him of a line from Horace. He remembers Miss Vaughan, and the small embarrassment when she told him she was half a Jew; but in spite of that they had contrived to be comfortably English together. Miss Vaughan had complained, as the English will, of un-English activities among the natives. Her guide was interested in modern cement factories and had been reluctant to take her to the top of Mount Tabor, 'probable scene of the Transfiguration.' Then Miss Vaughan turns up, speaking of her dangerous trip to Jordan to see the other holy places, and of her archaeologist fiancé, who is seeking the annulment in Rome which she, not he, regards as indispensable to their union. Freddy does not know much about Miss Vaughan; she looks spinsterish to him. Later

In this Jerusalem, as in the real one, there must be variety, confusion, conflict, not only between Semites but between everybody. Indigenous characters soon begin to pour into the story—Orthodox Jews, Orthodox Catholics from Lebanon, Arab operators. The muezzin wakes you on the Israeli side; to touch the Wailing Wall you have to go by the gate to the Arab side. People in England, only remotely concerned, are drawn to Jerusalem, encountered in the polyglot confusion of the holy places. Barbara, Jew turned Catholic, visits the shrines disguised as an Arab. She buys from a Lebanese Christian merchant a chain with the Christian fish symbol but also with Turkish charms to counteract it.

The adventures of Barbara in Jordan, and Freddy's liberated behaviour as, in flight from his mother, he accompanies her, are narrated in discontinuous but amusing fits. The Ramdez family, all charming, all making a good living out of refugees, spying, smuggling, the peccadilloes of English and American government officials, move into the centre, as much a part of Jerusalem as the Zionists, the Scots Presbyterians, the priests and nuns. Farce works for Mrs Spark as heavier irony for other writers; and underneath the story, with its farcical, anarchic, naturalistic incidents and encounters, are the holy places. To recognise them, even in this fugue, is what makes Barbara 'all of a piece,' though a 'gentile Jewess, a private-judging Catholic.' The heart of it all is the memory, the anamnesis, of these places: Nazareth, 'where it really began'; Cana and the first miracle, for 'everything begins with that'; Capharnaum, where 'the spiritual liberation of the human race had begun'; the birthplace of Mary Magdalen. In Jerusalem, observing the 'actual Gethsemane passively laid out on the Mount of Olives,' she feels the relation of this Jerusalem to that other of poetry and hymm, 'my sweete home, Hierusalem.' The pilgrimage may well be without emotion; it is essentially a simple act of recognition.

The quality of the book's imagination is suggested by the inclusion of the Eichmann trial among these objects of Christian recognition; if one had to cite a single example to show Mrs Spark's deepening power, this would serve. All Barbara hears of the trial is a dull day when Eichmann is being interrogated by his own counsel. She sees it, however, as 'the desperate heart' of the whole process: the dead mechanical tick of the discourse, words and statements divorced from all reality and all pity; and she thinks of the French anti-novel, the discourse dead, the subject living. Barbara here decides, as it were, in passing, that she has to see the holy places on the Jordan side. They are basic to *her* kind of meaning, as to Mrs Spark's. It is a meaning you may find in a novel, not in an anti-novel. The Eichmann passage is characteristic of Mrs Spark's sensibility, and of her desperate confidence in the novel. So that we may see how this confidence is based, she includes (as Camus and Iris Murdoch have included) a sermon, about the point of the holy places and their involvement with fraud and false emotion. She is telling us that her novel too gets its meaning from truths which can be misunderstood, and that it is an analogue of Jerusalem; but she is also saying that we need to see it as Jerusalem-shaped without forgetting that it contains, like the city, a good deal that may seem hard to relate to that model.

To emphasise this, the quality of observed life, she brings into play the sharp ear and the key-cold charity known from her earlier books. The dialogue is exemplary, Forsterian in its command of dialect. If she describes a cellar in Acre where the Crusader wall is still a foundation, she makes it a real cellar, not a symbol. People act credibly, are funny, make love, or fight like people in the real Jerusalem. To write such a book, one needs to be very inward with the novel as a metaphor for the world. Mrs Spark is precisely that; the book is, in an age of rather clumsy argument about fiction, a demonstration that great things can be done when a strong imagination determines to take up many aspects of the 'kind of truth' that fictions provide and bind them up into one volume.

(1965)

XXIII. BERNARD MALAMUD

Bernard Malamud, having like many American writers to buy time in academies, has written only three books since the appearance in 1950 of his volume of stories, *The Magic Barrel*.[1] They are *The Natural*, his first novel, which came out in 1952,

[1] New York, Farrar, Straus.

The Assistant, published five years later, and *A New Life*, which now reaches England.[1] The early stories were well received here, but the novels, which many Americans rate very highly, are not well known, and the new one provides an opportunity for English reviewers to consider them all.

These books have been slow to take because Malamud is in some ways a writer of alien sensibility. The pressure behind his work, in fact, is a powerful Jewish–American fantasy, a ghetto-dream coloured by a New World environment and qualified by an ironical self-criticism which controls, without quite drying up, the wetness of its self-indulgence. Diligently his characters make their own prisons in hopeless shops and mean rooms, and then inhabit them with ancient resignation. The reader has to decide how far the irony moderates his easy stock response. This is indeed a central difficulty of Malamud's work, and clearly it is more testing for the foreigner. You have to know whether the occasional corruptness of style and invention is there because a dream is out of control or as a justifiable complexity of tone.

In the broadest terms Malamud's method is to conduct his characters through a more or less plausible series of events to a climax by which they are frozen into ritual attitudes, and to allow this tableau to close the work. In a story called 'The Mourners,' a landlord tries to evict an agonised tenant but only reduces him to an hysterical act of mourning; the story ends with the landlord tearing a sheet off the bed, wrapping it around him, and joining in. In 'The Lady of the Lake,' Henry Levin has a dreamlike affair with a girl he believes to be the daughter of a rich and ancient Italian family; in its course he casually denies he is a Jew, and in the end loses her because of this, since she is really the caretaker's daughter, has a Buchenwald brand on her breast, and will marry no one but a Jew. The real point of the story is that 'Freeman'—as Levin calls himself, supposing it to be possible to be un-Jewish—represents not a special but a universal self-deception, though his being a Jew gives him access to a language of ritual gesture:

He groped for her breasts, to clutch, kiss or suckle them; but she had stepped among the statues, and when he vainly sought her in the

---

[1] Eyre & Spottiswoode. A fourth novel, *The Fixer*, appeared in 1966, and there has been a further collection of stories called *Idiots First*.

veiled mist that had risen from the lake, still calling her name, Freeman embraced only moonlit stone.

In the title-story 'The Magic Barrel,' what seems to be a folk-tale about a marriage-broker—the kind of thing you might read in, say, Isaac Singer—takes a very odd turn, and has a ritual ending which seems to me comic; but an American Jewish friend finds it macabre.

Such is the ambiguity inherent in this use of ritual poses; again and again there is a contrast between some climactic tableau and the struggling day-to-day life of the characters, between deep emotions and English distorted by Yiddish idiom. The difference is comic or pathetic or both, and sometimes one wonders if Malamud ever means to be funny at all. But this doubt is dispelled by examples of sheer intelligent farce, like the theological debate between Negro Jews in 'Angel Levine.'

These highly accomplished early works make available the theme of the imprisoned Jew; subsequently it can be shown that he is only a classic case of what everybody suffers from. Time and again Malamud returns to the small shop, the family whose tiny stake in the city is steadily reduced by supermarkets and slick competitors. Enterprise or education seem to offer a way of escape from one's hole-in-the-wall; but the physical prison is only an external symbol of the real thing, which is the Jewish capacity to suffer, to achieve a sort of dignity in suffering, as a substitute for success and freedom. And this leads on to more general statements of the same theme. You may think that bricks and mortar are depriving you of Nature and so of Life. You rush at Nature and seize her breasts; but she soon has you back in prison. It is, in the end, the fact of being alive that shuts you off from Life.

Malamud repeatedly has his people make love for the first time in a field or a forest, often by a lake: good natural sex, but a dubious boon, and Nature soon has you back in a guilty bed, staring worriedly at the ceiling. The alfresco sex is the dream of an adolescent in his hole-in-the-wall; when he wakes up he's still there behind the counter. This device is paralleled by a very personal stylistic habit, a blend of urban sex-slang with very careful and respectful natural description; deliberately and indeed ludicrously the two are fused in, for example, the description of a girl undressing in a mean bathroom: 'her ass was like a flower.'

The pressure of this urban myth of natural freedom, and its ironic qualification, are easily spotted in Malamud's strange first novel, *The Natural*, which is all baseball. It's hard to imagine any English analogue to this one. Imagine a serious novel ending with a gripping match to decide the county cricket championship. Literary cricket is entirely a matter of Georgian pastoral. This book takes baseball without whimsy and whole; not only the players but the financiers and gamblers, the crackpot fans, the heroic myths, the insane statistics. (Last summer people were asking was it *right* for a ballplayer to break Babe Ruth's venerable home-run record.) Here the game does the work of Jewishness in the stories; its mythology is set down uncritically, inflated indeed, to stand for the urban dream. The great player is a power like one of nature's.

In one season the hero, a veteran of 34, rises to the top. As a boy genius, a natural, he had been maimed by a maniacal girl who picked up top athletes and shot them with silver bullets. Years later, recovered, he has his one season, breaks hundreds of records, makes the dream true. 'Knock the cover off it,' orders the manager. He does so, his bat (carved by his own hand out of virgin wood) gleaming in the sun, its impact producing a sudden thunderstorm. For this kind of thing Malamud uses a grotesque, bombastic prose, a deliberate impurity of style: 'The third ball slithered at the batter like a meteor, the flame swallowing itself. He lifted the club to crush it into a universe of sparks. . . .' Roy, the hero, falls under the spell of a bad girl, Memo (morality names), and dreams of silver bullets. After a losing spell he meets a lifesaving natural woman, makes love to her in a field after a swim, and regains his form. But she turns out to be a young grandmother, as you might expect of Dame Nature, and at a game he lays her low with a foul ball. After a bout of heroic overeating he falls ill, takes a bribe so as to get Memo, and is finished as a player.

The baseball fantasy serves a sophisticated allegory[1]; so does the prose. Even when Roy dreams of his disaster the language is ironical: 'cut down in the very flower of his youth, lying in a red pool of his own blood.' This is not the bad fine writing Malamud

[1] Exegetes have shown that *The Natural* closely follows Arthurian legend.

produces when he is self-indulgent, but an example of that occurs on the same page, when Roy finds himself in bed with Memo, thinking he is having a fine dreamy rural love affair, but actually sleeping with the old evil. The point of *The Natural* is precisely that Nature *does* betray the heart that loves her—the fact of life Malamud hates most.

The Assistant, most achieved of the novels takes us back to the ailing Jew in his collapsing business trapped in his shop and a lightning conductor for the trouble of a whole neighbourhood. Trade was never worse but the holdupniks rob his till and break his head rather than those of the prosperous liquor dealer across the street. The life of the shop, the Yiddish English, the ghetto patience, are perfectly done. But there is much more to it; Malamud is a big, ambitious writer. *The Assistant* is, for the most part, the story of how the Bobers, against their will, acquired an assistant, a down-and-out Italian who insinuates himself into their lives though disliking Jews; he cannot resist the quality of their misery and patience. The first ritual climax of the book comes when the assistant has wormed his way not only into the shop but, very slowly, into the favour of Bober's daughter. She is about ready to sleep with him when a criminal associate of his tries to rape her in a park; the assistant saves her, but, caught up in the sexual excitement, rapes her himself. 'Afterwards, she cried, "Dog—uncircumcised dog!" ' A great deal depends on the success of this strange sentence, for the rest of the book deals with the man's attempt to recover his position (Malamud seems to like the situation of a man courting a girl he has already had) and so prepare his complete surrender to the Jewish thing, marked by his circumcision on the last page. I think the trick works. Malamud does it by rhetoric, and by a sort of impurity of tone in the build-up to Helen's cry; for a moment this makes you lose touch with the existential situation, and you take the cry abstractly, as part of some ritual pattern, which it is.

Malamud depends heavily on this power to modulate from personalities into abstractions, from life to ritual. What he is doing has a clear sociological basis in the etiolated survival of one culture within another, of old-world Jewishness in America; the literary problem is whether the sentimentality this situation generates escapes from the story and infects the teller. The answer is probably that it does so far less often than might be feared.

A New Life is much bigger and looser. A New Yorker called Levin gets a job in a fifth-rate college in the Far West. He has had a rough life; at 30 he wants to leave it behind, enjoy teaching, come to terms with Nature. The college is terrible, and we hear a lot about it, its courses and its politics; an election, for the chairmanship of the department, is one of the points to which the whole story moves, through ambushes of intrigue, concealed and stolen documents, tale-telling etc. But there the resemblance to Snow ends. Levin is prone to absurd behaviour—a farcical attempt on a waitress, lecturing with his fly open—but there the resemblance to Amis ends. There is so much of this, such careful recording of professorial idiosyncrasy and faculty parties, and in particular so detailed a record of one married couple, the Gilleys, that it looks for a while as if Malamud had rid himself of his obsessive plot and decided to give personalities their simple value. There is even, at first, no emphasis whatever on Levin's Jewishness.

But this is a trick, like the careful non-committal record of trees, flowers, rainfall. Levin is the urban Jew who has made it out into Nature, 'that marvellous invention.' But the traps are set; first the waitress, in a barn, among cows, until a rival comes and steals their clothes. Then, as a further warning, a colleague who, like Memo, has a fibroma in a breast; and finally Pauline Gilley, a real Nature figure, married to a hopeless, seedless husband whose main interests are various rapes on nature with gun, rod and club. She is clumsy and untidy in her house; when Levin meets her in a forest (which turns out later to be college property) they make love at once. But soon she is visiting him secretly in his lodgings amid increasing difficulties; he is not on Gilley's side in the election campaign, he is jealous of his predecessor, another liberal from the East, with whom Pauline had also slept. He suffers a presumably psychosomatic affliction, a 'fiery pain in the ass at emission.' Malamud puts an enormous amount into the chronicle of these grandeurs and miseries, and skilfully conducts the politics and the lovemaking to a simultaneous crisis.

Yet it is at the very end that his real power shows. He has spent a lot of trouble on Gilley, so that character is ripe for a superb scene with Levin when he knows his wife is leaving him. Gilley is now the bachelor, Levin the married man, his Jewishness leaking through into the text as his burden increases. Gilley tells him what he is taking on, information not to be had simply by sleeping with Pauline. What he is really explaining is the Nature that drives men back to their holes-in-the-wall, into a necessary Jewish patience. She is congenitally discontented, given to nervous depression, domestically inefficient, irregular in her menstrual cycle. Then there are the adopted children—delightful, but there is the eczema, the bronchitis . . . Gilley, from his strong position, gives Pauline custody of the children on condition that Levin gives up college teaching. As he prepares for a life of patience, Levin discovers that Pauline had selected his application from the pile because his photograph reminded her of a Jewish boy she had once known. 'So I was chosen,' he says; they drive off, snapped by Gilley's Leica, with the pregnant Pauline carrying her ointment-smeared baby. Levin gets the Nature he went West for.

A New Life carries its irony hidden in the title, and—mature, craftsmanlike book as it is—carries its myth deep, gives way less easily than the others to the big ritual gesture. But its power comes from the same source, and its failures too. Levin himself is the most serious of them; his necessary past is not fully authenticated, his farcical aspect does not belong. Yet the conception works; unlike his namesake in the early story, he reaches the breasts of his beloved, but they are still signed with the mark of prison. All in all, the book has, under its carefully presented plot and character, the old obsessive, ritual theme.

(1962)

XXIV. BELLOW'S *Herzog*

There is one famous compliment to a novelist that nobody is ever going to offer Saul Bellow, and that is to say that his books are the product of a sensibility so fine that no idea could violate it. It seems doubtful whether any interesting writer, even James, really fits that formula; in any case, if you think that is the condition the art should aspire to, Bellow is not your man. Yet for many people he is the man. In America, where more and more the hypotheses of literary historians jostle works of literature, Bellow has already been snugly fitted into neat intelligible patterns. He is the big novelist who emerged at the precise conjunction of race, milieu and moment—when, as Leslie Fiedler puts it, 'the Jews for the first time move into the centre of American culture' as the group best-equipped to act as an urban, Europe-centred élite. Augie March is Huck Finn Chicago-Jewish-style, still, in Mr Fiedler's dialect, in search of a primal innocence, but above all an urban Jew, with the appropriate worries, failures and aspirations. Or, according to Norman Podhoretz, Bellow in 1953 came through with *Augie March* at just the right moment to encapsulate and typify the new revisionist liberalism, moving away from the Left at the same conscientious pace as *Partisan Review*.

Aside even from these professionally large and resonant explanations, much has been written about Bellow, and this is not surprising. When all the reservations have been made he is so good that anybody can see it with half an eye; only severe doctrinal adhesion prevents the recognition that he is a far more interesting writer than Mailer.[1] One remarkable thing about him is that along the way he has conjured out of the air new talents, powers he apparently did not have, even *in posse*, when he started in the 'Forties. With this bonus he is more gifted than the gifted young, including the handsomely endowed Philip Roth. Furthermore, he is, for all the glitter of ideas, accessible, easier to get to than John Hawkes, further out in the open, less constricted, than Malamud. Thus he made everybody flock to read him without sacrificing intellectual seriousness, and without growing plump enough to be caught in the meshes of the critic's hypotheses.

Bellow's career has some curious aspects. He has never lacked support. *Dangling Man* brought him respect, nearly 20 years ago, not only in America but here. Rereading it now, one finds it a little rigid, worthy but off-putting, a book one does not wish longer. I suppose that at the time, in a different and on the whole duller literary epoch, the intelligence with which the wretched but hard-thinking hero was placed, his eloquent and intellectually respectable introspection, were what won perceptive praise. Now the diagrams of alienation seem too square, the prose somewhat

---

[1] I should now say that *An American Dream* has caused me to modify this view.

inelastic; it is hard to find in it the vivacity and inventive power one associates with Bellow. Perhaps it might be said that the austerity of the book gives it a kind of fidelity to its moment. Anyway, *The Victim*, though it had some of this rigour, and some of this period quality, was more various and flexible. But the big change, the *détente*, came only in the early 'Fifties, with *The Adventures of Augie March*.

It would be easy to run through the roll-call of this book's deficiencies, but the point is that Bellow had found his new form. Perhaps it struck him that the tragic stance of classic alienation, and even the existence of intellectuals, looked funny in this new world. They became a source of gags, and the hero turned picaro. Simultaneously with this new circumstance, Bellow became profusely inventive, exhibited a sense of the true comedy of intellect, which is painful as well as funny. There was some lamenting about what he gave up—the effects which arise from a firm management of structure, for example; it seemed that he thought these appropriate only to the short novel, and this guess was apparently confirmed when he next wrote a very good novella, *Seize the Day*, and went on to another inventive sprawl in *Henderson the Rain King*.

At least one ingredient is common to all the novels: the hero is, in Alfred Kazin's phrase, 'burdened by a speculative quest.' They all have the same humble need (however little this humility comes through in their conduct) to sort out human destiny by sorting out their own. In a world of chaotic particulars, where the only speculations which draw any support are bogus, vulgarised or corrupt, the speculative quest turns into a sequence of extravagantly funny or pathetic gestures, and the happiest ending that can be hoped for is that of *Seize the Day*, when Tommy Wilhelm, a middle-aged flop, winds up weeping at the funeral of somebody he doesn't know.

The great merit, and at the same time the great difficulty, of such writing is that it does try to get into fiction the farcical excitements of thinking as distinct from behaving. To do this straight seems almost impossible, or, if you think it works in *La Nausée*, unrepeatable. Bellow gets round the problem in the same way every time. The speculative interest is never put straight in. In *Seize the Day* the wise sayings come from the fraudulent Tamkin; in *Henderson* fantasy bears the freight of speculation. The new book[1] is full of furious thinking, and Herzog, the hero, does most of it, but not 'straight.' The first sentence of the book says: 'If I am out of my mind, it's all right with me.'

Herzog is in the line of the fat novels, but has more structure than the others. The hero is a very well-read Chicago Jew on the point of a breakdown. Most of his thinking is done in letters, the kind of letter you might frenetically compose, if you had enough in your head, in the early stages of a sleepless night. 'Dear Herr Nietzsche, May I ask you a question from the floor?' 'Dear Doktor Professor Heidegger, I should like to know what you mean by the expression "the fall into the quotidian." When did this fall occur? Where were we standing when it happened?' 'Dear General Eisenhower . . .' The letters, in a sense, do the work of Tamkin. As a way out of the difficulty, which was to show an intellectual operating in the world, they seem to me to have the exceptional merit of turning the technical trick and then, because sparingly used and full of wit, to become delightful in themselves.

Herzog is an authority on everything from Romantic theology to fish-scales, but all this equipment is of interest only as useful in the speculative quest. After all his adventures he may wind up where we find him at the start of the book, in his weird derelict Vermont country house in a state of peaceful choicelessness. But the main business of the novel is Herzog, under stress, trying to sort out Herzog. He can in various ways tell us all about himself: a genuine old Jewish type that digs emotion, but grown at this moment—his second marriage ludicrously broken—narcissistic, masochistic, anachronistic. His friends a sort of traitors, a bunch of real grotesques (one of them gives the kiss of life to a monkey dying of tuberculosis), seem to be engaged in 'a collective project' to destroy his vanity and push him 'down in the mire of post-Renaissance, post-humanistic, post-Cartesian dissolution, next door to the Void.'

Out of the goings-on that ensue there begins to emerge an interesting design. Herzog, forced into sacrifice anyway, sees that what he has to sacrifice himself to is the truth, and we watch him both consciously trying to do this and unconsciously doing it. Under the pressure of his 'reality instructors' he moves

[1] *Herzog* (London, Weidenfeld & Nicolson; New York, Viking).

hastily about, colliding with the world from which he is dissociated; in the subway he writes letters about negative entropy, and emerges to observe 'an escaped balloon fleeing like a sperm, black and quick into the orange dust of the west. . . .' (This is not only powerful and versatile, it concretely presents the dissociation between things as they are and Herzog's speculations.) He is on the way to see a splendidly undemanding sexpot, whom he enjoys with the same comic metaphysical detachment from sense. The truth about sacrifice can't be got to by that route, nor by fast useless journeys, made by Herzog with 'all the dead and mad' in his company or custody, nor by surveying 'the story of my life—how I rose from humble origins to complete disaster.' When the answers eventually come, they come both from without and within.

The long climactic passage of this novel, which is about Herzog's trip to Chicago to see his daughter, is the first piece in which Bellow has improved on *Seize the Day*, a book it somewhat resembles. It has many layers, and a diagram would be misleading, especially if it sounded conventional or banal; but Herzog pays an important visit to an old, still Yiddish aunt, and carries off a gun he had once seen ineffectively flourished by his father. By this agency he gets his chance to come, though imperfectly, to terms with indignity and suffering, and that is a step in the necessary direction. As he had informed General Eisenhower in a particularly abstruse letter, the forces that make us human are history, memory, and a knowledge of death. A day in a New York courtroom had taught him more—for example about how high he stood in the scale of affluent misery; and he feels this more keenly when in a prison cell himself, knowing that this is not the place for him to do time; he belongs to the privileged classes who do it on the street. Finally, as in *Seize the Day*, the decisive message comes from the wisdom of a crank: you can't live until you know death; practise lying in a coffin, know it while you still live; then live. So, as far as it can be done in a self-hating civilisation, in an emotional language corrupted by all the fraudulent modern talk of crisis, apocalypse, desperation, Herzog touches bottom and finds health.

Bellow must be sick of hearing about his deficiencies, especially about his failure to invent women. There isn't a conventionally well-written woman in *Herzog*, though the hero's second wife is convincing as the inhabitant of a bad dream, a figure of fun who then bursts nightmarishly into the police station to press Herzog down to the bottom. The other girls, Herzog's mistresses, are about as real as Smollett's, but little more is needed. This is a slightly caricatured world, male, Jewish, comic and pathetic, temporarily crazy too, so that the men friends are no less grotesque than the wife, and the remnants of Herzog's childhood are endearing emblems rather than original experiences profoundly evoked. This is the world refracted through the ageing Bellow hero: bricks and mortar, cab-drivers, what might be seen from the corner of an abstracted eye, are idiomatic, accurate; dialogue also can have accuracy as well as comic energy. But the nearer the foreground, the nearer the main interest, they come, the more distorted the characters tend to look.

Still, it is plausibly the view from Herzog's disciplinary coffin. So although the book has clear limitations, they are a long way off. And why should we be surprised that Americans make much of such powers of invention and intellect, such comic energy, so genuine a speculative quest? Wouldn't we?

(1965)

XXV. RAMMEL

'Rammel' is a word that recurs frequently in Mr Sillitoe's books. It isn't in the Concise Oxford, nor yet in the Shorter, but it makes a decent showing in the OED itself, which says that the primary meaning is branches, twigs, bits of old wood, but gives examples of its use in the Midlands and specifically Nottingham as a word for old rubbish of all sorts. One way of understanding why it is so often on the tip of Mr Sillitoe's pen is to carry out upon it the operation which Kenneth Burke calls 'joycing': *ram* and *mel*, strength and sweetness, violence with a sexual note that the taste of honey reinforces, and the whole thing against a background of urban and industrial waste. *Rammel*, in short, means Saturday Night and Sunday Morning.

A deep and studious interest in the constituents of rammel is one of the determinants of this author's talent. True, his first book was the thing itself; but even in *The Key of the Door* it is lovingly catalogued, and the violence it promotes channelled into the peculiar tough sweetness of the sexual descriptions. Even the Forces, for all their bull, present an orderly paradigm of the industrial arrangements that excrete rammel. 'If it moves, screw it; if you can't screw it steal it; if you can't steal it set fire to it', is a rammelly ethos. Mr Sillitoe's heroes are moving out of Nottingham, but this is the mark set upon them—tough talking, drinking, screwing, stealing, insubordination. What they acquire in the world is a respect for books and thought; in this way they learn to despise rammel, to estimate the degree to which the poor who live in it are cheated and deprived. So they move out of the world that cheated them into jungle or desert, not so much in order to help the Malayan Communists or the FLN as to find themselves in a world purged of rammel.

These preoccupations impose a pattern on Mr Sillitoe's novels. Their base is *Saturday Night and Sunday Morning* with its back-to-backs, factories and pubs. Their climaxes are fights with rivals and husbands, and they end in action on behalf of the militant proletariat as a means to personal salvation. This is, at any rate, the goal towards which he has been moving, and the paradigm appears in almost ideal clarity in *The Death of William Posters*.[1] The language in which it is presented has an appropriate blend of rammel and bookishness. The hero, ageing a little from book to book, is potent, belligerent, a drinker (double rums with pints), victimised but independent. The difference is that he is, on the first page, on his way out of Nottingham.

Frank Dawley has sold his car, parted with his wife, and set forth. Only the flashbacks are set in Nottingham. The first section is about an affair with a district nurse in Lincolnshire—urban man in an icy pastoral environment, labouring, reading, meeting a primitive artist. The second part is set in London—an affair with an LSE girl, wife of a surveyor. Each part ends with a violent encounter: Frank beats up the first husband, is knocked down by the other's car. The third and final section shows Frank on the move again, taking his girl with him, all the way to Tangier, where he leaves her, pregnant, and goes off to run guns to the FLN in the desert. In *The Key of the Door* we are always being brought back to Nottingham; we have to feel it and the jungle all at the same time. Here the burden of rammel is borne by the characterisation and more especially by the prose.

[1] *The Death of William Posters* (London, W. H. Allen; New York, Knopf).

Sillitoe's style is one of habitual violence, a deliberate reflection of the hated, cheated prole, crossed by a certain awkward artifice, which is correlative with the hero's self-education. It is clear that the maintenance of this stylistic attitude presents him with enormous problems. There is evidence of slackness, fatigue; there is the practical difficulty of making fights violent when everything else is violent. So the language becomes loosely ecstatic, as in talk of

a hand cracking on flesh, and the purple spark-fanged floor on the sway and loose burst at Keith like a piece of ice over the eye-face, an engulfing polar cap.

Or a fist is described as 'bursting, a whale-head driving across the light, packed with flintheads and darkness.' A violent hyperbole afflicts the homely prose of the working-man hero: 'The sky eats into my brain here,' he notes. It is a thought one doubts ever got thought. Mere description blossoms with a rash of irrelevant conceits: 'The island lay like a death-mask, the tip of its black chin flashing a lighted pimple in dubious welcome to the ship.' When a man has a hangover he leaves his body and travels 'among star-sparks of half life on his way back into his eyes and brain, toes and stone-cold bollocks.' For a conceited orgasm, try: 'Flames from all her limbs leapt to the middle of her as if to greet the guest that slid so ceremoniously in.'

This is the prose of a writer dangerously stretched; and for that reason and others it occasionally reminds one of the Lawrence of *Lady Chatterley*. In one passage Sillitoe achieves the unnecessary feat of parodying a chat between Mellors and Connie. The LSE graduate is in bed with Frank, and he lectures her on love and work:

In my ideal society all advertisements would be ripped off the streets, and instead there'd be well-placed neon signs in red saying: 'Work! Work! Work!' Maybe now and again there'd be a little one going on and off saying: 'Fuck! Fuck! Fuck!'

With Frank's 'broad-shouldered nakedness looming in the half-light,' Myra is healed by darkness: 'In spite of the black passion of his desires, her body seemed to belong to her again. . . .' With these blunt lectures and coitional therapy we're not far from the gamekeeper's hut and the old magic carrying out its 'desperate healing of the interrupted bloodflow.'

It seems that lust and rage, dancing attendance on a novelist's rhetoric, can have the effect of parching it. And in his concern for rhetorical effect, he can be negligent of structure. *Key of the Door* was messy, the new book is obvious and untidy. In the first part, the Lincolnshire affair, paragraphs about Frank's early life are dropped into the narrative, and especially into the dialogue, and they do a lot of harm. Sartre, who is exceptionally uneasy about fictional temporality, used to argue that novels are at their strongest in dialogue, because the time of dialogue is so closely analogous to that of the reader, so that he is in less danger of 'jumping out of the book.' There is something in this; Sillitoe's reminiscences are a great drag on the dialogue in this novel, and the reader may have some sympathy with Sartre, who would be in and out of it like the lady in bed at old fairgrounds.

It's impossible to guess how much damage all this does to a writer like Sillitoe, a writer ambitious enough to write not what Frank calls 'shit-novels' but the sort that 'prises open previously unknown regions within yourself.' He mentions Conrad, Melville, Stendhal; but Conrad stands not only for an occasional hysterical inflation but for intense concentration on form. It seems characteristic that the best writing in Sillitoe's last two novels comes at the time of his heroes' self-expression in action, and in a context of guerrilla warfare. Give him a small society of men, their ankles tied together with string, lying in ambush for the imperialist French, and he will release his hero and his style at one stroke. Even so, these advantages can be thrown away by a rhetorical over-explicitness, as in this book. 'Something in him was going to be reconstituted. . . . His life had to be filled from the fountains of his own desert. . . .'

This book is certainly, by any standards the author would accept, a failure. The first—the Country—section has excellent passages registering the cold, the hero's adaptation to country ways, the fantasy of life in the cottage of the primitive painter (his masterpiece is 'Christ the Lincolnshire Poacher'). The second section—London—has a not unsubtle contrast between Frank's integrity and the endangered gift of the painter when taken up by smooth metropolitan artmen; there is also some point in making the second girl's husband nice (he loves the country and goes on three-day drunks) so that Frank doesn't have to beat him up, as he did the adman husband of the nurse.

But the final—Desert—section is the best-written; the style is released with the man.

The mythical figure of Bill Posters is certainly an agreeable invention. He is the figure who at all times and everywhere 'will be prosecuted.' He represents the indestructible cunning and evasiveness by which a man survives among the rammel; admirable in some ways, his is a way of life that has to be destroyed on the way to self-fulfilment. The myth is well, if predictably, handled, and it will cause little surprise that Frank in a revery associates him with his friend's picture of Christ. Breaking free from Bill Posters, Frank attunes himself first to a Mellors-like independence (sturdily antinomian, indifferent to work as the bosses understand it, educated) and then to the sort of anguish Bill Posters, preoccupied with his incessant tricks and escapes, has no time to feel. The conversation between him and the wild and wily painter on the subject of art and pessimism, and the rejection of art in favour of action, is beneficial to the novel; but mostly Frank preaches without resistance. His hatred of the telly, the ads, the London crowd scurrying for comfort into the tube at rush hour, have imaginative vivacity; but both he and Albert the painter sink into lay figures, flatly and feebly rendered from the outside. Albert is 42 but could be seen as 'little more than a man of 30 who had already suffered the fires of life's iniquity.' Frank is labelled 'a strong character' with 'a rich mineral coal lump' of a brain. Nothing much about him really matters except the fantasy that he chucked up everything and, at the end of some nut-strewn road, killed Bill Posters.

Curious that this English dream should appear at the same moment as Mailer's *American Dream*. Mailer's is metropolitan and by comparison distinctly upper-class, but it is certainly violent, and has to do with changing the patterns of social and individual life. But that it *is* a dream is a *donnée* of Mailer's book; and for all its absurdity, its intellectual irresponsibility, its dangerously ambiguous presentation of pathological data, it shows what a difference it makes to have a richer and more relaxed rhetoric, a more natural control of the emblematic situation (in Mailer's book, the high balcony) and of the imagery necessary to writing of this kind. Avoiding the indiscriminate sensationalism of Sillitoe, Mailer, at the risk of absurdity, makes smell the king of the senses. I'd rather be found to share Sillitoe's view of the world than Mailer's magical nonsense about cancer, orgasm and the moon; but in the unjust world of the novel it is Mailer who sounds right. They both send their violent fornicators into the violent world; what makes Mailer's much more pretentious hero work is a kind of cheating: an irony, as in the characterisation of the police, which is totally absent from the English writer.

It does seem unfair. Reviewers have quoted pages of rammel from Mailer. Sillitoe feels strongly that newspapers are termites devouring civilisation, and this kind of observation is made in Mailer's book only by square professors of psychology. It's just that he can write novels—look at the dialogue, proceeding as it does from situations preposterous in the last degree, but racing forward, creating its own reality. Look at the saving salute to sanity from dementia in the last paragraph. It seems the first truth about novels is still that they have to be made, and as novels, not as curtains of violent-coloured words draped over plot-props. It may be something wrong in the nature of things that allows Mailer's novel to be so much better than Sillitoe's, but it seems to be so, and there's a moral in that.

(1965)

EPILOGUE

XXVI. DANTE

The 700th anniversary of Dante's birth has come and gone without giving rise to much dancing in the streets, or formal eulogy in the reviews; and yet, if centenaries are important at all, this one was worthier of celebration than the 400th of Shakespeare, amply honoured in 1964. We should have been reading and talking about books whether Shakespeare had lived or not—differently, no doubt, in some ways, but still reading and talking about books, belonging to the club that does so. But Dante founded the club, and if you belong to it you cannot leave him to the Italianist, or simply be grateful that he proved useful to Shelley or Eliot. A parallel text of the *Commedia* will convince you that he was a great poet; but even that isn't enough. One needs, somehow, to reach an understanding of the fact that what most of us think of as literature—modern as opposed to ancient literature—and also the reading public of which one is a member, are in large measure Dante's invention. He ought therefore to have been praised by layman as well as by scholar; and the scholar should have tried to explain why.

A number of celebratory books did appear in English. Thomas Bergin's[1] is an introductory study by a Yale professor, and its tone, despite the long encomium in *Time*, is the tone of the graduate school. It sets out with more patience than grace to sketch the political, ecclesiastical, linguistic and literary backgrounds, and studies each of the major works in turn—most interestingly, as far as I can judge, the *Convivio*, which is treated as a sort of digestive exercise for the *Commedia*, and the work in which the famous vernacular manner, 'robust and severe,' was beaten out.

The English contributions come from Oxford and Cambridge,

[1] *An Approach to Dante* (London, Bodley Head; New York, Grossman).

and each is a collection of papers. The Oxford Dante Society is august and exclusive, and these papers[1] aren't intended for the profane; in fact this book is as much a celebration of the Society as of Dante. Yet there is one paper, no less learned than the others, which speaks to the condition of outsiders in our larger, less exclusive club: this is Cecil Grayson's '*Nobilior est vulgaris*: Latin and Vernacular in Dante's Thought.' Dante spent much thought on the topic of nobility; he held that in men it was not something integral that you inherited, but an innate quality that flourished or did not, according to how you fostered it. About language he felt in a similar way: the vernacular—in his case, a variety of Italian—can and ought to have a nobility greater than that of Latin. The argument is complicated by the difficulty of determining what the vernacular is, and what may be its relation to Latin; but it can be said that before he wrote the *Commedia* Dante had felt the possibility of a European culture—to be defined politically as well as linguistically—continuous with that of Rome and yet consistent with political and linguistic nationality. Such a culture survives not in the immutability of the old empire and the old language, but in the changingness of the new.

All manner of difficulties surround Dante's exposition of these and related matters. Nevertheless it seems clear enough that some such modern attitude helped to determine his choice of a language for the *Commedia*, so that he seems to have predicted the conditions under which the literature of Europe (which is, for most of us, quite simply 'literature') could be established. If we are to have our essential great literature we must have it coloured by our nationality and our language, and vulgar languages are, unlike *grammatica* (a language of artifice, occasionally synonymous with Latin), subject to change.

These topics are raised also in the much more humane, much more vernacular Cambridge collection of lectures.[2] It is the recognition of mutability in our cultural elements that predisposes us towards the historical in scholarship, and the Cambridge volume opens appropriately with a notable essay by Natalino Sapegno on the modern reaction from Croce's antihistorical appraisal. To the poetry of a *grammatica* the most suitable critical method would be, no doubt, rhetoric; to the

[1] *Centenary Essays on Dante*. Oxford.
[2] *The Mind of Dante*. Edited by U. Limentani. Cambridge.

poetry of the vernacular, the illustrious vulgar, history is essential. No poet, perhaps, has ever been more conscious of transition than Dante; and an essay in this volume, by Kenelm Foster, extends the significance of this to matters of doctrine. Dante assumed that by speaking about the particular historical crisis he knew—in detail ranging from the merely municipal to the imperial—he could speak about everything important; and it is part of his achievement that we, in reading him, may make the same assumption.

Not only scholars, but laymen also, belong to the *popolo santo*, the continuity of the imperial people. Of course the *popolo santo* is a myth, as Professor Limentani says; so is the Monarch, and this was clear by Dante's own day. Yet it is a myth we need; and Dante himself was not at all a vague idealist. What he wanted, it seems, was an internationalism compounded of nationalisms, an approach, based on the illustrious vernacular, to some 'universal human civility'; and so far as it is to be had he prefigured it. He knew, as we do, that the illustrious vulgar is as near as we shall get to a lost 'language of grace.' And he provided the great example: we are always having to remind ourselves of the need to emulate that robustness and severity, that transparency.

More than anything else, in fact, it is this doctrine of a vulgar language capable of an imperial civility and grace—a doctrine enforced by marvellous instances—that binds us, after an interval of 700 years, to Dante. It was he who elevated the vernacular to the dignity of *grammatica*; and he did it not so much by writing the *De Vulgari Eloquentia* as by writing the *Commedia*. To Dante, the illustrious vulgar was an Italian language; but we can borrow the expression for all the languages of Europe which have experienced the translation to civility or to grace: all the languages which, changing in time and in space, accommodate that transfigured natural speech by which, in the modern world, the work of the more artful, less mutable Latin must be done.

It is precisely because the invention of the illustrious vulgar, and of the modern reading public, is our greatest debt to Dante, that of all the books to appear in 1965 the most profound and important is an old one, now translated into English: Auerbach's study of the birth of literary language and a literary public.[1]

---

[1] Erich Auerbach, *Literary Language and its Public in Late Latin Antiquity and in the Middle Ages* (London, Routledge; New York, Pantheon).

Erich Auerbach died in 1957, and his fame outside the academies is largely posthumous; his celebrated book *Mimesis* did not appear in English until 1953, and has steadily grown in influence. Of this work, subtitled 'The Representation of Reality in Western Literature,' one may say with some envy that no living Englishman could possibly have attempted it. The peers of Auerbach are Curtius, and perhaps, for all their political differences, Lukacs. The opening chapter of *Mimesis* contrasts Homeric with Old Testament methods of ordering and representing reality—the first all foreground, the second at once mysterious and historical, absolute yet dark and incomplete, calling for constant reinterpretation, not merely fact but also *figura*, and the root of centuries of European representation of the world and its history. Auerbach goes on to study in a similar way texts by a great diversity of authors—Petronius, Ammianus Marcellinus, the *Chanson de Roland*, Dante, Cervantes (a brilliant central essay), Stendhal, and so on. Behind the method employed in *Mimesis* is a conviction that Christianity rendered absurd the classical levels of style and, in the language of its scriptures, provided a new basis for human representations of reality.

The present book is in one sense a vast supplement to *Mimesis*, and it explains in detail what this new basis consists of. On a long philological view it might be said that Christianity, which in matter and language identifies the sublime with the humble, made the high and middle styles mere functions of the low style. Hence the long tradition of *sermo humilis*; educated pagans despised the style of the scriptures, the Latin of the Vulgate, but the Holy Ghost managed with the humble style and even with vulgarisms; and from Augustine it was seen to have the possibility of profounder sublimities than the Latin of the schools. Classical revivalists will sort out the common words and restore grand ones; but an equally strong impulse in our tradition is to upset such revivals, and restore the humble word. Fanciful etymologies for *humilis* ('of the earth' etc.) suggest that somebody should have brought in *sermo humilis* at the *Lady Chatterley* trial: Lawrence was trying to restore it.

The existence of a reading public is a necessary condition of literature; and Auerbach's book is an attempt to describe its formation. It is the audience of the high vernacular, and it came to being after 500 years during which Europe had no literature because it had no language for it. A new Latin might, says Auerbach, have developed; but this was prevented by the success of the Carolingian classical revival. So the sublime was confined to religion, and literature was the preserve of the church schools. And this state of affairs continued until love provided the topic of the secular sublime, and the vernacular assumed the power and authority of Latin. This was, largely, Dante's work; at a moment and in a place peculiarly favourable to the operation, he created not only great modern literature but a public for himself and his successors—a public as indispensable to literature as its language, cultivated but not learned, a public of many languages but one common European spirit.

Auerbach's view of Europe is long, and he says it could be had only now, when we are near the end of the story and can see the nature of an epoch or a great work in relation to the tradition of 3,000 years. We may question the need for this eschatological justification of the author's immense synoptic inquiries, but this will not affect the argument that Dante represents a great crisis in the development of Europe and its literary public, or the validity of Auerbach's *Hochsprache*—the many-tongued vernacular, nobler than Latin, which has been the medium for all fruitful collaboration between writer and literary public. *Mimesis* neglected the period 600–1100 (when there was virtually no literature because there was no such language, except in England) and it also omitted a very Dantesque strain in Auerbach's thinking, a kind of linguistic imperialism which, as the European tradition draws to an end, sees the power of Virgil's Rome translated to the Florence of Dante, and thence to other vernacular Romes, much as the imperial power became German or French.

I do not know whether, given the necessary learning, one would accept all the implications of this book and of *Mimesis*. They raise the question as to where historiography ends and apocalyptic begins. But I suppose one may be uncommitted on some of the sublimer issues and yet still accept what Auerbach says of Dante as the creator of the literary language and the literary public which made possible the great vernacular literature. It is a literature of change, if only in the currents of resistance to what Auerbach thinks of as its Christian 'figural' basis, and it may not always be easy to see its languages as aspiring to an ideal *Hochsprache*; but when we need, as we sometimes do, to think about literature as a whole—as having, like the *imperium* itself, a perpetuity defying change—we may also think of Dante as, of this literature, the principal patron.

(1966)

FRANK KERMODE was born on the Isle of Man in 1919. He received his B.A. from Liverpool University and was elected Fellow of the Royal Society of Literature in 1958. He is now a Lord Northcliffe Professor of Modern English Literature and head of the literature program at the University College in London.

Mr. Kermode's critical essays have appeared in such journals as *The New American Review, Encounter, The New Statesman, The New York Review of Books, The Atlantic Monthly, The Kenyon Review,* and *The Sewanee Review.*

He is the author of *Romantic Image* (available in Vintage Books), *Wallace Stevens, Puzzles and Epiphanies,* and *The Sense of an Ending;* he is also the editor of *The Living Milton.*

Mr. Kermode lives in London with his wife and their two children.